SKILL AND THE
ENGLISH WORKING CLASS,
1870–1914

CROOM HELM SOCIAL HISTORY SERIES

General Editors
PROFESSOR J.F.C. HARRISON and STEPHEN YEO
University of Sussex

Skill and the English Working Class, 1870-1914

Charles More

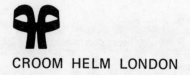

CROOM HELM LONDON

© 1980 Charles More
Croom Helm Ltd, 2-10 St John's Road London SW11

British Library Cataloguing in Publication Data
More, Charles
  Skill and the English Working Class, 1870-1914 – (Croom Helm social
  history series).
  1. Skilled labour – Great Britain – History – 20th
  century
  I. Title
  331.7'94   HD8390

ISBN 0-7099-0327-8

Printed and bound in Great Britain by
Biddles Ltd, Guildford and King's Lynn

CONTENTS

TABLES

PREFACE

The history of the institutional structures of work — of wages, hours, bargaining organisations and so on — is now at a mature stage. The history of work itself is in its infancy. This book is an exercise in this infant discipline. It is a study of skill, an aspect of work which is often commented upon but rarely analysed.

In Victorian and Edwardian Britain, skilled workers were sufficiently distinguished from the unskilled for the description of the former as an aristocracy of labour to be commonplace. Although there are several recent studies of skilled workers in this period, which are discussed in the last chapter of this book, they skirt round one of the most crucial questions surrounding the labour aristocracy: how did the skilled workers which comprised it acquire their skill?

If we wish to answer this question, we are faced with a problem, for there are two sorts of answer to it, and the one we are given will depend, more or less, on whether the respondent is an economist or a sociologist. Most economists would reply that skill is acquired by training, and that membership of the labour aristocracy therefore depended on the amount of training a worker has received. Whether or not he was able to obtain training in the first place might depend, of course, on socially determined factors such as his family's income: but the training itself would confer real, and perhaps even measureable, skill. Many sociologists, on the other hand, would answer that skill itself is a social artefact, produced by restrictions on the entry of workers to certain trades, or by other means the common aim of which is to artificially delimit the tasks of different workers. In this analysis, skill is not necessary to the efficient functioning of industry but is 'socially constructed'.

The main task of this book is to use historical evidence to assess the validity of each of these two explanations, but the first chapter is, of necessity, theoretical in nature. I hope this will not put the reader off, but the intention is to make the later stages of the book clearer, and not to introduce theory for the sake of it. The last chapter returns to the subject with which we began, the aristocracy of labour, and relates the findings of the book to this concept.

A number of people have given me help in connection with the investigation on which this book is based, and some of this help is acknowledged in footnotes at the appropriate place. I would, however, like to extend more general thanks to the following.

First of all to David Lee, the influence of whose work is apparent at several points in the book, but whose approach to the problems it is concerned with has influenced me more generally; he is not responsible, however, for my naïve excursions into sociological analysis. Also to Stephen Wood; John Harrison and Stephen Yeo, the editors; the ubiquitous Michael Gee; and Mrs Joyce Maxwell. I would like to acknowledge an intellectual debt to the contents of an unpublished paper by Bryn Jones. And I must thank the Social Science Research Council for the grant which made my research possible.

Most of all I would like to thank Dudley Baines, whose frequent criticisms were always justified, and whose occasional praise was probably not.

ABBREVIATIONS USED IN THE TEXT AND NOTES

PP	Parliamentary Papers
Mun.	Ministry of Munitions records, in the Public Records Office
Bev.	Beveridge Collection in the British Library of Political and Economic Science
EcHR	*Economic History Review*
ASE	Amalgamated Society of Engineers
PRO	Public Records Office
SRO	Scottish Records Office

Part I

SKILL: THEORY AND FACTS

1   THE CONCEPT OF SKILL

Skill

Anyone who has attempted a task usually carried out by a craftsman will know that manual work demands certain qualities which we do not all possess. One of these qualities is manual facility, which can be defined in psychological terms as the ability to perform quickly and effectively complex actions which necessitate the co-ordination of perceptual and motor activity. This ability is sometimes referred to as dexterity, but since the latter word is often used to mean innate abilities, rather than learned ones, it seems best not to use it here; industrial psychologists, on the other hand, call this manual facility skill, but since it is doubtful whether it is all that is meant in common parlance by skill I propose to call it manual skill. In common parlance skill is, I think, usually taken to mean the alliance of manual skill with knowledge. Thus when we speak of a carpenter's skill we are referring to the combination of his manual skill, in sawing, planing and so on, with his knowledge of different sorts of wood, different types of joint and so on. So the two useful qualities of workers, or at least the two pertinent to us, are manual skill and knowledge, and the two together are usually thought of as constituting skill.[1]

If skill is defined as simply the possession of some quantity, however small, of the two useful qualities of manual skill and knowledge, then all workers possess skill. This, however, is not the whole of the story, for something a little different is meant when we label someone a 'skilled' worker. We usually mean by this that he possesses a considerable quantity of one or the other, or both, of these qualities: as H. Renold put it, skill can be defined as, 'Any combination, useful to industry, of mental and physical qualities which require considerable training to acquire';[2] and this would probably be acceptable to most people as a useful working definition. The amount of training required to reach the level at which a worker can be called skilled might be estimated by reference to some traditional course of induction which the worker has to undergo, such as an apprenticeship; or it might be measured more scientifically.

When sociologists cast doubt on the reality of skill, they are not necessarily casting doubt on the reality, or usefulness to industry, of mental or physical qualities which might be possessed by workers. What they are doing is questioning either the reality of particular qualities which certain workers believe themselves to possess, or which other people believe them to possess; or, while accepting the reality of these qualities, they are questioning their actual usefulnesss to industry.

It will be clear from this that the theory of the social construction of skill is not a simple one. In order to prevent it becoming even more confused, it would be wise to start by clarifying our terminology: in the ensuing discussion, I will use the term 'genuine skill' to mean some combination of manual skill and knowledge, not necessarily very considerable, which is useful to industry; and the term 'socially constructed skill' to mean the attribution to workers of labels denoting them as skilled, semi-skilled, or unskilled, together with the differentiation of wages and status which usually accompanies such labelling. It will be clear from this that I do not consider that the labelling of workers as skilled can be considered in isolation from the labelling of workers as semi or unskilled. Why this is so will become apparent as the discussion proceeds. It is also important to note that when using the term 'genuine skill', I am referring to the possession of some qualities useful to industry, but the amount is not specified and might be small. Figures 1.1 and 1.2 provide a starting point for our discussion.

Figure 1.1 shows a situation in which technology is given: that is, the machines which a firm uses, and the tasks which are performed, are not alterable by management to any major degree, although management or workers might have the power to impose minor variations. Given this basic fact, there are two different routes to skill: the path on the left-hand side leads to genuine skill, required because of the complexity of the machines or tasks in question, and that is an end of the matter. (The skill needed might be quite limited in scope, of course). The other path leads, via perhaps a strong union which upholds high wages among certain groups of workers, to a differentiation of workers into grades, some of which are better paid and are regarded as more skilled; management may, or may not, play a collusive part in this process — for instance it might accept the situation if it thought that it would gain through giving workers a channel to promotion, however artificial. If management is neutral, or opposes the situation but cannot alter it due to the strength of the union or some other factor, it might be able either to pay other groups of workers less and thus keep up its profits margins, or pass on the cost to the consumer; otherwise it would have to accept a diminution of profit margins. There might finally be a situation in which management, for reasons of

Figure 1.1

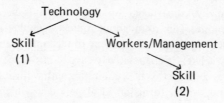

Figure 1.2

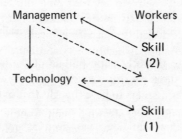

Skill (1) = genuine skill
Skill (2) = socially constructed skill

its own which will be discussed later, artificially differentiates grades of labour without any help from the workers.

Figure 1.2 shows a situation where technology is not given. This could be the case where it is possible to use different machines to make the same product, and/or it is possible to alter the tasks performed. Here, then, the initiative starts with workers or management. Again for some extrinsic reason, such as the existence of a strong union, or custom, workers succeed in differentiating grades of labour, and thus socially constructing skill. This process is shown by the arrow leading from workers to skill (2). This affects management, as shown by the arrow leading from skill to management, because it puts up costs, but since technology is not given they can react more positively than in Figure 1.1. Their reaction to this social construction of skill − which means, *inter alia*, the differentiation of wages − is to alter the technology, so that the value of the product of the groups earning higher wages is itself higher, or in economic terms so that marginal productivity approaches as closely as possible to wages. This might be done by extracting more effort from the workforce, a solution which is not considered in Figure 2.2 because it is not relevant to skill. The other way would be to adopt an alternative technology in which the skill socially constructed by the workers is used and therefore becomes genuine. This roundabout route to genuine skill is shown by the arrows leading from management to technology and on to skill (1). This strategy is likely to be relatively easy to introduce because workers often try to construct skill by limiting entry through, for instance, apprenticeship, which forms an ideal period in which the worker can acquire some genuine skill. There is one other possible route to skill of both kinds, shown by the dotted lines in Figure 1.2. In this management predetermines the degree of skill it wishes its workforce to possess, and then designs or accepts an appropriate technology. Whether or not the skill required is genuine or socially constructed is not formally relevant.

We can now relate this schematic outline of the means of socially constructing skill to the ideas of the various theorists who have written about the subject. Marx seems to have thought that modern systems of production, which he called machinofacture, were technologically determined, that is the technology was given; at any rate, he did not suggest alternative models.[3] Continuation of the division of labour, which had been characteristic of the previous period of manufacture, was however not technically necessary but was insisted upon by capitalists: 'Instead of the hierarchy of specialised work, which was characteristic of the manufacturing division of labour, we find that in the automatic factory there is a tendency towards the equalisation or levelling down of the work which the assistants of the machinery have to perform'; but although machinery 'makes an end, technically speaking, of the old system of the division of labour, that system . . . is subsequently remoulded systematically, and established in a yet more hideous form as a means for the exploitation of labour power'.[4]

If we want to fit Marx's account of the division of labour in machinofacture to one of the paths towards skill, whether genuine or socially constructed, shown in Figures 1.1 and 1.2, we must first try to resolve one particular ambiguity in the concept of social construction. If there are two possible methods of carrying on work, and management chooses the more economically rational, does this constitute social construction (or destruction) of skill? A Marxist answer would almost certainly be in the affirmative, as it would be argued that what was most rational to the capitalist would not necessarily be so to the worker. An answer using the assumptions of neoclassical economic theory would probably be in the negative, as it would be argued that the use of the word social implies that non-economic criteria are taken into account, and neoclassical theory would assume that the lowest-cost option would, in general, be the only economically rational one.

Our conclusion, then, is that the ambiguity remains unresolved and will remain so unless we can decide between Marxist and non-Marxist economic assumptions. This conclusion is pertinent to Marx's account of machinofacture because although Marx by his emotive language implies that there was something non-rational about the capitalists' insistence on the continued division of labour, his other comment suggests that, in strictly economic terms, it was rational, because the 'expenses of the workers' reproduction [are] considerably lessened'.[5] What Marx can only mean by this is that operating a machine requires some training, and consequently it is cheaper for the worker to be trained to work one machine only. Rather than decide between two competing economic theories, it seems best simply to comment that the skill, albeit of an attenuated kind, possessed by Marx's machine-workers could be regarded as genuine, and arrived at as outlined on the left-hand path of Figure 1.1; or it could be regarded as 'socially destroyed' – attenuated precisely because capitalists preferred to make workers serve one machine rather than become expert on a number, and therefore arrived at as outlined on the right-hand path of Figure 1.1. In spite of this ambiguous conclusion, however, we should re-emphasise that in certain essential points Marx was a technological determinist as regards skill: as we have seen he regarded the technology of manu-facture as given, and the basic tasks as essentially the same although capable of subdivision; and as we shall see, he regarded certain tasks as not susceptible to social construction or destruction at all.

So far, then, we have not found a clear-cut type of social con-struction, but the work of H.A. Turner provides us with two types. Turner is in the mainstream of an important current of ideas among British writers on industrial relations, which focuses particularly on the arrogation to themselves of 'skill' by certain groups in the British workforce: the views of these observers are summarised by David Lee, who says, 'Those who follow this line of analysis . . . may even doubt whether [craftsmen] have undergone training in conjunction with apprenticeship so much as a period of ritual servitude designed to reinforce exclusive unionism.'[6] In actual fact, although this summary accurately described Turner's ideas on some kinds of work, his full typology of social construction is more complex.

On the one hand, Turner's description of the spinners' tactics is a classic example of social construction of the straightforward kind shown on the right-hand path of Figure 1.1. In late-nineteenth-century England the male cotton-spinners had for various reasons such as their early organisation in strong unions secured for themselves a level of wages usually associated with workers who had served a long apprenticeship, even though the actual work of the spinners did not take long to learn. These wages were not achieved at the expense of the owners so much as at that of the spinners' senior assistants, known as 'big piecers', who did much the same work as the spinners, but earned far less. As in Marx's model, the technology of the industry was given: it is true that management made use of the spinners' successful attempt to differentiate themselves from the piecers by giving the former supervisory functions over the latter, and this slightly altered the allocation of tasks; but the essential features of the work were the same in Lancashire and in Glasgow, where gangs of women with no pretensions to any high degree of skill were supervised by overlookers.[7]

On the other hand, Turner postulates that other groups of workers will socially construct skill by the route shown in Figure 1.2, and this will lead eventually to the acquisition by them of genuine skill. Thus in the building and engineering industries,

> The sharp demarcation between skilled and unskilled workers . . . is largely a product of the traditional apprenticeship system, by reference to which those who may perform 'skilled' tasks are distinguished from those who may not;

but,

> Granted such a restriction of entry as apprenticeship . . . workers who have passed through the gate will naturally try to keep it narrow by increasing the tasks that new entrants must master, and by specifying these tasks as monopolies of the properly admitted. While employers who are confronted with such a restriction naturally insist, since they cannot engage labour for 'skilled' jobs as they please, that the workers they *may* employ be as competent as possible.[8]

Although Turner does not pursue this line of reasoning, it is arguable that the need to use skilled workers would allow management to economise on the use of expensive machinery by maximising the input of skill, or in economic terms that there would be a shift along the production function in the direction of lower capital intensity. This could be achieved because in engineering, in contrast to cotton-spinning, it is possible to make the same product either on one general purpose machine operated by a skilled worker, or on a series of special purpose machines operated by less skilled workers. If management is not allowed to employ the less skilled workers, for instance because of union rules forcing it to man all machines with time-served workers, then it will be sensible for it to adopt the first alternative, since special purpose machines are expensive and cannot be switched about to different types of production.[9]

One final type of skill construction is that described by H. Braverman. In this, management is concerned with removing control of the labour process from the workers, in whom, up to the nineteenth century, resided a 'body of traditional knowledge' which might be greater than that of the employer.[10] Braverman sees the Scientific Management movement of F.W. Taylor as essentially devoted to changing this state of affairs: 'Taylor was not primarily concerned with the advance of technology ... His concern was with the control of labour at any given level of technology.'[11] The same comments apply to Braverman's views as to Marx's. If the most economically rational course (in capitalist terms) is not regarded as an example of social construction or destruction, then Scientific Management as Braverman describes it is not a social but an economic technique, because like Marx's capitalists, Braverman's capitalists are concerned with reducing the value of labour power, and hence costs, as well as with more general notions of subjugating the workers.[12] Once more, then, we are faced with making a choice which depends upon our underlying assumptions about economics. If we do not accept Marxist economics, then Braverman's capitalists were pursuing a rational course in deskilling their workforce, and followed the path shown on the left-hand side of Figure 1.1 (the skill resulting from their policy was of course very limited). If we do accept Marxist economics, then Braverman's capitalists were following a rather more complex strategy than Marx's: in spite of his remarks about Taylor's lack of concern for the advance of technology, Braverman makes it clear that he regarded Scientific Management as capable of completely reformulating the tasks performed at work, which must come within the ambit of technology; thus he described in detail how Taylor carefully measured the work of an engineering shop with the intention of splitting up the labour process and removing the major decisions from the workers.[13] In Marxist terms, therefore, the route to deskilling which Braverman postulates starts from management which makes the decision to deskill the workers, to the workers who are deskilled (and possibly divided into artificial grades as well), with the technology itself merely being a means of achieving management's purpose. This route is shown by the dotted line in Figure 1.2. Braverman's model differs from Marx's in that the latter sees technology as given, the former does not; and it differs from Turner's in that the latter sees the workers as initiating the process of social construction, with management's intervention leading to the need for genuine skill, while Braverman sees management as initiating the strategy, with the workers – rather surprisingly for a Marxist – not playing a part.

Discretion

So far we have discussed skill as defined either by the attributes of manual skill and knowledge, or as 'socially' defined. We should, however, consider another aspect of work which can be subsumed under the heading of skill, that is the possession by the worker of the opportunity to plan his work. The amount of opportunity he has to do this might be referred to as the 'discretion content' of work, and the degree to which the worker possesses or lacks discretion can be related to the idea of the division of labour.

The idea of the division of labour can itself be divided into a number of different types: 'separation of hand and brain', for instance, could refer to the separate direction and control of an enterprise by a capitalist, or it could refer to the removal of all but an insignificant degree of thought from work; while the actual phrase 'the division of labour' could also mean the progressive splitting of work into tasks which required less and less training. Division of tasks into smaller component parts could, however, proceed without necessarily affecting the amount of training and thought needed, for example in the medical profession where specialisation leads if anything to an intensification of skill.

Marx was of course concerned intimately with the vesting of control of enterprises in the hands of capitalists; but it would seem that in referring to the division of labour in manufacture and machinofacture he was primarily concerned with the second development, the separation of conception from execution in the labour process, and both he and Braverman saw this, together with the progressive differentiation of work, predominating over the last kind of division mentioned above, which if anything heightens skill.[14] Thus Marx described manufacture, that is the stage at which work is subdivided but not mechanised, as revolutionising the earlier methods of simple co-operation, and cutting at the roots of individual labour power; furthermore, 'It transforms the worker into a cripple, a monster, by forcing him to develop some highly specialised dexterity at the cost of a world of productive impulses and faculties.'[15] This occurs, of course, before the even greater indignities forced upon the worker by machinofacture: in manufacture, the worker uses a tool, and 'the movements of the instrument of labour proceed from the worker'; in machinofacture even this control is denied him, and 'the movements of the worker are subordinate to those of the machine'.[16] Braverman develops this idea, stressing in particular the separation of conception and execution: 'the separation of hand and brain is the most decisive single step in the division of labour taken by the capitalist mode of production'.[17] Both Marx and Braverman, of course, also see sub-division of work and the separation of hand and brain as leading to a decline in the actual amount of training needed, as it is this which cheapens the value of labour power to the capitalist; but it is the loss of the worker's control over the labour process which fills them with the most indignation.

The separation of conception from execution is logically distinct from a reduction in training times, although as we have seen Marx and Braverman both consider that under capitalism there is a general tendency towards the latter as well as the former. The non-identity of the two can be clarified by considering Jaques's discretion content theory of work: discretion is low where routines are prescribed — get such and such records out each Friday, use British standards in drawing etc.; and high where the prescription is imprecise — use the best method in the circumstances, keep a satisfactory standard of finish etc.[18] But work where routines are prescribed might none the less take time to learn — indeed the very necessity to learn some routines will enforce some learning time, unless the routines are very simple. Work with, in Jaques's terms, high discretion content, is in effect work where conception and execution remains integrated, and vice versa. We could therefore add discretion to the two components of skill we have already identified, viz. knowledge and manual skill.

Alan Fox considers that there is considerable validity in Jaques's contention that the discretion content of work is open to empirical measurement. If this is the case, then Marx and Braverman's belief that conception and execution have become increasingly separated should be susceptible to empirical testing; and Fox locates the period when such testings might prove particularly fruitful in the late nine-teenth and early twentieth centuries. In Fox's view, 'Broad brush generalisations' about the effects of the Industrial Revolution on the division of labour, and the amount of discretion exercised in work roles, fail to recognise that 'in all phases of the Industrial Revolution many new skills and occupational groups have been created as well as old ones destroyed'. But he suggests that the last decade of the nineteenth century saw the emergence on a noticeable scale of, 'a quickening pace of rationalisation, mechanisation, measurement and "speed-up" which is particularly significant for the concept of the low-trust syndrome' (by which he means a relationship of suspicion and hostility between management and employees which he sees as not an inevitable, but a frequent, result of the extension of low-discretion work).[19]

Clearly we are faced with an important decision as to the direction our study of skill in the late nineteenth and early twentieth centuries should take. We can consider either the manual skill and knowledge requirements of jobs, or we can consider their discretion content, that is, in Marxian terms, the degree to which conception was inte-grated with execution; or we can consider both. Although the separation of conception from execution is in many ways at the heart of the Marxian analysis of work, and in spite of Fox's suggestion that ours was a period when the decision content of much work was drained away from it, this thesis will largely be concerned with assessing the knowledge and manual skill content of jobs.

There are a number of reasons for limiting our enquiry. Although Fox suggests that it might be possible to measure the discretion content of work in the past, Jaques's description of the measurement technique indicates that it would be extremely difficult to use it historically, for it involves the questioning of individual managers and supervisors in order to find out how often they check the work of those under them.[20] Even if, however, a technique could be developed which was applicable to the written record, there would be considerable problems in integrating it with our more straightforward study of learning times. It would seem to be a task for a separate enquiry.

On the more positive side, a study of skill in the more limited terms in which we have defined it is by no means valueless. First of all, it is a visible method for investigating the social construction of skill, a concept which is definable independently of the discretion content, or lack of it, in work. Second, it enables us to examine the ideas of Marx insofar as they relate to the type of work in nineteenth-century industrial society — that is, his concept of machinofacture, his suggestion that the bulk of the workforce would become machine-tenders and so on; and it also enables us to examine the ideas of Marx and Braverman insofar as they suggest that, along with the separation of conception from execution, there was also a reduction in the actual training time needed for most jobs. Third, it enables us to assemble a body of evidence on the subject of skill, which may be of use to other investigators.

Having said this, it remains true that it is impossible to write about skill without saying something about the discretion content of work. In Chapter 9 in particular, where changes in skill levels are considered, this subject comes under discussion; and it is suggested there that Fox's contention that the late nineteenth and early twentieth centuries were crucial periods for the extension of low-discretion work is problematic. But with the exception of parts of Chapter 9, and at one or two other points, we will be using the word 'skill' to mean, as I think it is commonly taken to mean, the possession by workers of useful qualities, as defined at the beginning of this chapter.

Summary

As we stated at the beginning, no one would disagree that there are some useful qualities possessed by some workers and not by others. Marx and Braverman would argue that these useful qualities were so attenuated that, for the most part, they did not deserve the name of skill. Marx, however, did accept that some workers possessed a higher degree of skill, which was dependent on technology rather than social construction: in factories it was necessary to have

> a staff of persons, few in number, whose business it is to look after the machinery as a whole, and to keep it in good repair: engineers, mechanics of various kinds, joiners etc. These comprise a superior class of workmen, some of them scientifically trained, and some of them skilled craftsmen; they are distinct from the class of factory operatives . . . *this division of labour is purely technical.*[21]

Turner, on the other hand, would seem to view most of the useful qualities possessed by workers as ultimately the result of social construction. In spinning, the useful qualities or skills are very limited, and the label skilled became attached to the spinners only through the mediation of the politics of the workplace. In apprenticed trades, the skills are genuine and perhaps considerable, but the possession of a variety of skills by apprenticed workers is not in fact necessary to the efficient functioning of the industry.

Marxist commentators, and others, would also stress the significance of 'discretion' in work. Although this concept is important, it is difficult both to investigate it empirically and to integrate an investigation of it with the rest of our study, and as a result it will not be treated systematically, although it will be considered from time to time.

Notes

1.   W.D. Seymour, *Industrial Skills* (1967), esp. Chs. 1 and 2, and p. 85 for the distinction between manual skills (which Seymour calls skill) and knowledge.
2.   H. Renold, 'The Nature and Present Position of Skill in Industry', *Economic Journal*, vol. 38 (1928), p. 593.
3.   K. Marx, *Capital* (Everyman edn), vol. 1, pp. 448-51.
4.   Ibid., p. 450.
5.   Ibid.
6.   D.J. Lee, 'Deskilling, The Labour Market and Recruitment to Skilled Trades in Britain', unpublished conference paper, p. 4. I am indebted to David Lee for permission to refer to this paper.
7.   H.A. Turner, *Trade Union Growth, Structure and Policy* (1962), pp. 108-14, 128, 139-44.
8.   Ibid., p. 111.
9.   It is possible to spin cotton by a completely different method, known as ring spinning, from that referred to in the text, which is known as mule spinning. But both processes need only limited skill, whereas different methods in engineering need widely differing amounts of skill.
10.   H. Braverman, *Labor and Monopoly Capital* (New York, 1974), p. 109.
11.   Ibid., p. 110.
12.   Ibid., p. 121.
13.   Ibid., pp. 110-12.
14.   Tucker suggests that to Marx even the separation of production and consumption implicit in a capitalist mode of production was included in the concept of division of labour; R.C. Tucker, *Philosophy and Myth in Karl Marx* (Cambridge, 1961), pp. 185ff. We are concerned here only with the division of labour within production.
15.   Marx, *Capital*, vol. 1, p. 381.
16.   Ibid., p. 451.
17.   Braverman, *Labour and Monopoly Capital*, p. 126.
18.   See the discussion in Alan Fox, *Beyond Contract: Work, Power and Trust Relations* (1974), pp. 16-18.
19.   Ibid., p. 191.
20.   E. Jaques, *Equitable Payment*, 2nd edn (1970), pp. 101ff.
21.   Marx, *Capital*, vol. 1, p. 448 (my emphasis).

SKILL IN THE ENGINEERING INDUSTRY

Introduction

Before we turn to study the means by which skill was acquired, we should establish that we have a subject worth investigating: for the idea that skill is socially constructed, and the idea that work has become deskilled, are not new and have not only been applied to modern work. Before tackling the subject of the acquisition of skill, therefore, we should assess these views about the existence of skill, especially as they concern our period. It is true that, even if we conclude that the views in question are incorrect, we have not solved our problem, because in Turner's more elaborate model of social construction, as portrayed in Figure 1.2, workers can possess genuine skill, which nevertheless ultimately results from a process of social construction. But it would seem to be a necessary preliminary to the investigation of Turner's theory to establish that, at least, workers did possess genuine skill, which was used. For another critic of the role of apprenticeship in delimiting 'skill', Liepmann, has put forward a viewpoint diametrically opposed to Turner's, at least in regard to one industry: in the case of printing, she argued, training for hand-composing was insisted upon for apprentices even though by the 1950s, when she made her study, it was unnecessary for many of them because they would be unlikely ever to use the technique.[1] Following this line of reasoning suggests that to study the acquisition of skill does not tell us that the skill is or was necessary for efficient production.

Our study of the necessity of skill will be limited to one industry, engineering. There seems no reason, however, to believe that the findings for this industry are atypical, and therefore no reason to believe that the conclusions cannot be taken as applicable to other sections of British industry. The reason for choosing the engineering industry is as follows. As already noted, engineering is an industry in which the product can usually be made in two ways: produced on general purpose machines by skilled workers, or on special purpose machines by less skilled workers, with a few skilled men to set up and maintain these machines. This is, of course, a very simplified account of the two alternative methods of production, but it has some merits as a descriptive model. When the First World War started, as much as 60 per cent of the engineering workforce were classed as skilled men.[2] During the war, a policy of 'dilution' was instituted. The effect of this was to transfer much of the greatly enhanced work of engineering factories to boys, women and less skilled men. On the face of it, this is *prima facie* evidence that skill *had* been socially constructed in the past, and that, whether or not workers possessed skill, they did not actually use it. It is in this way that the evidence has been interpreted before.[3] The problem of dilution, therefore, warrants a closer study.

Dilution

Dilution of labour, as the *History of the Ministry of Munitions* recognised, was not new: 'It was, in fact, merely an application of the venerable principle of the division of labour': but during the war 'its rapid development, owing to the circumstances of the War . . . [has] made it the key to the history of labour in the period under review'.[4]

The first point of interest about dilution is that in the early stages of the programme the employers were as hostile to it as the men. H. Wolfe, who had been controller of the Labour Regulation Department, wrote,

the obstacles in the way of dilution were by no means confined to the workers' side. The employers not unnaturally feared that the wholesale introduction of semi-skilled and unskilled labour upon work previously done by the skilled would seriously dislocate manufacture, and might in the long run rather reduce than increase output.[5]

This statement is borne out by material in the Ministry of Munitions archives. In a memorandum on the difficulties of dilution, written in August 1916, the hostility of the men, and the lukewarm attitude of some trade unions, were mentioned, but the first point noted was that 'the labour supply Dept. has invariably to face the opposition of the employers . . . there are, of course, outstanding exceptions . . . but for the most part our experience is of strenuous opposition . . .', and it was noted that large employers were worse than small. Reluctance to lose skilled workmen was again the reason given for this attitude.[6]

It is true that J. Paterson, the Chief Labour Officer in the West of

Scotland, had stated earlier that it was not employers, but the men and unions, which were the problem, but this was not the view of two of the Ministry Commissioners responsible for instituting dilution on the Clyde.[7] I.H. Mitchell wrote to Llewellyn Smith at the Ministry that the men at Lang's, one of the centres of opposition to dilution, 'are not intelligent and are selfishly opposed to any innovations in their trade, but this section does not by any means represent a large body of the men generally'.[8] Lyndon Macassey found that the attitude of the men was by no means uniformly hostile, but differed in different shops; he also found that in many cases the attitude of employers, fearful of losing their skilled labour, was as obstructive as that of the men.[9]

Obviously employers had no doubt about the reality of the skill exercised by their 'skilled' workers. In spite of this, enormous increases in production were achieved after many of these workers had left to go to other factories, or on to night shifts.[10] Were the employers wrong in their assessment of their workers' ability, and can the import of a mass of new workers, men and women, be taken to show that the genuine skill content of the craftsman's work had substantially declined?[11]

There is little evidence that this was the case. Every commentator agrees that for the most part women who entered engineering either worked automatic machines, or took only a portion of the skilled man's work. A vast extension in the use of automatic machinery was possible because 'munitions work for the most part consisted of the production of articles of which very large quantities were required identical in shape, weight and quality. Hence standardised repetition work or mass production took the place of the varied and variable output, characteristic of so much British manufacture before the War.'[12] This enlarged scale of production made possible a much greater specialisation of the labour force: 'In order to render the bulk of the women's work productive rapidly, it was no good attempting to teach a woman a trade but only that part of it which she was going to be employed on.'[13] And this in turn necessitated a simplification of the method of working, which mass production made feasible. 'For the bulk of the available unskilled labour . . . every sort of stop, jig and appliance must be introduced – the job had, in short, to be made fool proof.'[14] We shall see later what effect this had on the cost of production, but it clearly represented a major departure from the conditions under which much of the British engineering trade had been carried on before the First World War.

It was certainly true that in some areas women, without any help from special jigs or appliances, took over some or all of the work which skilled men were doing. That they were able to do this was the cause of the endless arguments over Circular L2, which provided that a woman on skilled work should be paid a skilled man's time rate, less 10 per cent for the extra cost of supervising and setting up; the ASE claimed that women doing a skilled man's work should have this rate, while various other groups overtly or covertly opposed them.[15] The questions we must ask are to what degree women or unskilled men took over skilled men's work; and whether, when this happened, they did all the skilled men's work or only part of it.

A memorandum prepared by the Intelligence and Statistics section of the Ministry of Munitions from the details of registered changes in working conditions shows that 9 per cent of the 14,491 changes were of women replacing skilled men, and less than 4 per cent of semi or unskilled men replacing skilled. The majority of the changes, 61 per cent, were of women replacing semi and unskilled men, boys, and apprentices.[16] This still does not tell us, however, how often the women and unskilled men engaged in skilled work did all the work a skilled man had been doing, and how often only a part.

In 1916 the Ministry considered that there were no clear cases where a woman was doing all the work customarily done by a fully skilled tradesmen, although their stance may have been influenced by the continuing argument over the implications of Circular L2, leading them to misrepresent the skill element in women's work.[17] There seems little doubt, however, that in most cases the women were only doing rough or preliminary work, or work that had been highly subdivided: 'in certain shops women who have been on the machines for a long time gradually got to setting up their work and tools, but in general one may say that in skilled work the woman does not do the whole job'.[18]

An analysis of some of the actual dilution schemes carried out by Macassey on the Clyde also suggests that complete substitution of women for skilled men was only rarely effected, and when it was it might involve cost penalties. Thus at G. and J. Weir 108 women and unskilled men replaced 108 fitters, turners and apprentices — a probable cost-saving unless the (unspecified) proportion of the latter was very high — but the work involved was scraping, rough turning and boring — the less exact part of the whole job. On the other hand at Beardmore's a large variety of skilled operations were undertaken in their entirety by semi and unskilled labour, both male and female;

but in this case to replace 88 fitters, turners and machinemen no less than 600 other workers were required. This was admittedly exceptional; in the schemes which were actually working as Macassey wrote, the number of replacements was 1,333, and of semi-skilled, skilled and other workers released was 740, about five-sixths of the discrepancy being accounted for by the Beardmore figures. In the schemes proposed for the next wave of dilution, the number of replacements was 888, and of released workers 853, although by that time it was becoming more difficult to release fully skilled men, as almost half the releases were semi and unskilled workers, or apprentices. It must also be borne in mind that Macassey did not state the number of skilled men who were required as supervisors.[19]

So far the specific evidence we have adduced comes from the Clyde, although the comments about women's work cited earlier did not particularly refer to this area. Exactly the same picture comes from London, where Deborah Thom found from her interviews with women dilutees at Woolwich Arsenal during the war that 'They performed the jobs that had been in the past everywhere, except at the Arsenal, women's work: that is, the filling of shell, cartridges and bullets and the assembly of cartridges and fuses. They never entered the highly skilled non-repetition processes that took place in the Royal Gun Factory and the Gun Carriage Department, where they only formed 4% of the workforce, mostly as general labourers . . . There was not one of the women I spoke to who could set her own machine. Though they could correct minor errors, of feeding for example, they had to wait for a tool-setter if anything went wrong.'[20]

It is clear, therefore, that while the Ministry's argument that women never did all the work of a skilled man may have been exaggerated, it cannot have been very far from the truth; and even upgrading of semi-skilled men to skilled status seems to have been quite rare, amounting to only 4 per cent of total changes. The reason why women and less skilled men were able to enter engineering factories was not because the skill content of engineering work had declined so much that women were able to do craftsmen's jobs, but because the whole method of production was revolutionised by the demand for huge quantities of standard items like shells, or because the exigencies of war production were such that higher output was necessary whatever the cost.

Technology and the Scale of Production

In the first case, the production of vast quantities of standard items made it economic to use special purpose machines, with 'every sort of stop, jig and appliance', because the initial investment in such machines and appliances, and the expensive setting-up they required, could be amortised over long runs of production. The massive reductions in the cost of shells during the war could be attributed to investment in this type of production, which was a classic example of the use of the skill-minimising method of manufacturing an engineering product outlined earlier in the chapter: it would have been possible to produce the shells using skilled men, but hopelessly uneconomic.[21]

The cases where women directly replaced men on part of the work the latter had been accustomed to performing do seem to imply, however, that the skill content of the work must have been low. But as suggested in our model of engineering production, there are usually two ways of manufacturing a product: it is technically feasible to produce almost anything using a high proportion of less skilled labour, or a low proportion: where goods are mass produced, the former is also the cheapest method; where they are produced in small quanitities, this is far less likely. In the latter case subdivision can be positively uneconomic, either because to set up a special purpose machine for a less skilled worker to produce a few items might take a craftsman almost as long as he would take to produce them himself, or because the less skilled workers, even if they could work the machines without lengthy setting-up, would be frequently unemployed due to their lack of all-round skill. Therefore it was not necessarily uneconomic for a skilled worker to carry out a task requiring only limited skill. The *bulk* of the craftsman's work could probably have been done by less skilled workers: the craftsman's skill lay precisely in the fact that he could undertake a variety of work.[22]

The implications of this for the cost of production were stated very clearly by H. Jackson, a director of Barr and Stroud, a Glasgow firm of optical instrument manufacturers: 'A skilled man gets and deserves a high rate because of his particular skill. His training enables him to do a large variety of work . . . The job on which he is engaged may be of a very simple character . . . The difference in rate is not founded upon this simple job, but upon the capability of the skilled man for doing any other job which he may be asked to undertake.' The result of employing less skilled workers was that 'it has been no infrequent occurrence to find women employed in our works sitting reading or sewing because they were not adaptable'.[23] And the dilution schemes of Macassey on the Clyde show clearly that the higher the proportion of a skilled man's work undertaken by less skilled workers, the higher the cost was.

It might therefore be asked why women were substituted for skilled men, even when it was uneconomic. The answer is that in a war, cost must be looked at in the widest sense: if the war is lost, any economy resulting from a reduction in costs will be irrelevant.[24] G.D.H. Cole, a close observer of dilution, pointed out that 'The process of dilution . . . was often carried through with very little regard for relative costs of production. The test of a new method lay rather in its capacity to produce a higher output.'[25] Given that the supply of unskilled female labour was more or less unlimited, the chief constraint was the supply of skilled men to supervise the women, set up their machines and so on. Any method, therefore, of releasing skilled men, even ones which on cost criteria were uneconomic, had to be used. It would be quite wrong to think that skilled workers were displaced in order to fight. Skill was at a premium, and as Lloyd George said, 'no amount of dilution . . . will dispense with the services of the highly skilled man. Our difficulty has been and still is that a great deal of work for the Army and Navy has been stopped because we have not got enough highly skilled men.'[26]

Failure to understand the true implications of dilution can be attributed partly to the more excitable contemporary commentators on the subject. As Cole described this phenomenon, 'During the war it was repeatedly prophesied that the era of mass production had begun, and that the old lines of division between skilled and less skilled workers would never be re-restablished.'[27] Some industrial unionists seem to have taken this view, while it was eagerly accepted by Sidney Webb.[28] The truth of the matter was that the Restoration of Pre-War Practices guarantees, embodied by law in the Munitions of War Acts in 1915 and 1916, were fulfilled by the Restoration of Pre-War Practices Act of 1919, and it was generally accepted that there was little fuss in carrying the provisions out. As the Webbs themselves admitted after the war,

> The great bulk of the 'dilutees', including substantially all the women, received their discharge on the cessation of their jobs of 'repetition work' on munitions of war, the employers preferring, in face of the immediate demand, to avoid trouble, to revert to the old methods and to get back to their former staffs, rather than engage in the hazardous enterprise of re-organising their factory methods.[29]

The force of law given to the restoration of pre-war practices, the immediate pressure of demand, and the desire to avoid labour trouble, were no doubt all factors in the withering away of dilution; but the main reason was simply that the methods of production in force during the war were not appropriate to much of the peacetime output. As Cole pointed out, the wartime commentators 'were wrong in supposing that a wholly abnormal stimulation such as that which a number of industrialists experienced during the War would retain its force when the abnormal influence was withdrawn'.[30] When that influence was withdrawn, the technological constraints imposed by the 'varied and variable output, characteristic of much British manufacture before the War', and for that matter after it, made the employment of high proportions of skilled labour a matter of necessity rather than trade union influence.[31]

The Machine Question

There remains one problem to resolve in our interpretation of the evidence: if the skilled man had nothing to fear from the competition of less skilled workers, why was the ASE so anxious to keep women off skilled work, by enforcing high rates on it through their own peculiar interpretation of Circular L2? And why, taking a more general view, was there so much anxiety in the ASE before the war about the 'machine question', anxiety which has been interpreted by various historians as justified by the nature of the new technology.[32]

The ASE's position during the war had, no doubt, a defensive element about it. In view of the predictions made by observers like the Webbs, however wrong they were, there must have been some pressure on the ASE leaders to limit employment opportunities for women; while the evidence of the dilution commissioners shows that there was a measure of shop-floor opposition to such employment as well, often no doubt based more on prejudice than on any real threat the women posed. But the ASE's position was also offensive: by limiting the employment of women as much as possible, they further expanded the employment opportunities for skilled men, who were already in great demand. Opinion in the Government was extremely hostile to the ASE at times, for this reason: in December 1915 a memo from Llewellyn Smith accused them of using blackmailing tactics, while at a conference that month Asquith told the leaders directly that he was not accustomed to threats. Addison summoned up their position with the remark, 'I dare bet my last half-crown that the Amalgamated

Society of Engineers will be, both during the war and after the war, in an infinitely stronger position than they have ever been before.'[33]

Before considering the position of the ASE before the war, it might be helpful to have a brief description of the innovations in machinery and methods, which were increasingly adopted from the 1890s on. The development of the lathe, which is the basis for all turning work, minimised the necessity for the turner to work with hand tools — something he was already doing less and less by the beginning of the period; while increasingly the planning office computed the speed of cutting and the depth of the cut — the speed and feed. The turret and the capstan were introduced, new types of lathe which could be fitted with stops to automatically engage and disengage the tools: the resulting automatic and semi-automatic machines could be operated by semi or even skilled workers, although their setting-up was often very complex and required skilled men.[34] Other important innovations were the milling machine, although this was a substitute for the lathe to only a limited extent, and the grinding machine, which made the achievement of great accuracy important, thus lessening the need for such accuracy on the part of both turners and fitters. Many machines, however, such as planers, borers, slotters, shapers, drillers, pressers and stampers, had changed little from the late nineteenth century, requiring only semi-skilled or, in the case of the two latter, unskilled labour.[35]

The detailed effect of these developments on the skill needed by engineering workers is discussed in Chapter 9; we are concerned here with whether the evidence suggests that the ASE was 'constructing' skill on a large scale in the face of possible deskilling tendencies in these developments. The policy put forward by some sections of the ASE was to 'capture' new machines for the skilled man, but it is important to put this policy in perspective. It was in no way an attempt to secure work on the simpler special purpose machines, except in the case of certain types of boring machines. Most of the simpler machines had existed for many years, and the ASE rate books recognised lower rates for them.[36] On the other hand, the grinding machine needed a high degree of skill, and there was no question of social construction here either.[37] 'Capturing the machine', therefore, did not mean that craftsmen actually worked specialised machines requiring little skill, except to an insignificant degree. What it meant in effect was that fitters and turners maintained their level of wages relative to other groups of workers, even though the work they were engaged on was relatively less skilled than before, and could have been performed by workers paid at rather lower rates.

This analysis is borne out of Weekes's study of the ASE's policy, or lack of it, on the question of capturing the machine in the 1890s and 1900s. George Barnes, the General Secretary from 1896-1908, supported a 'rate for the job' policy, in which new machines were to be rated for wage purposes at the same level as the old machine they replaced; ASE members continued to advocate a policy of indiscriminate 'capture'; but in practice skilled men sometimes refused to work automatic machines, on the grounds that the work was too uninteresting or degrading.[38] The contradictory attitudes Weekes uncovered suggest that there could be no concerned effort to socially construct skill on a large scale. It was rather a question of propping up a relatively declining position in the skill league.[39]

We will leave further analysis of changes in the skill required in engineering to Chapter 9. The purpose of the present chapter has been served by demonstrating that there was by 1914 still a demand for large numbers of workers who possessed genuine and considerable skill. This shows that a simple 'social construction' model, as outlined in Figure 1.1, cannot be applied to skilled engineering workers during our period; their skill was used, unlike that of the printers whom Liepmann commented on. But we have still not tested Turner's more sophisticiated model, which is outlined in Figure 1.2. This is in no way incompatible with the suggestion that workers *did* require genuine and considerable skill. On the contrary, its prediction is that workers in apprenticed industries would be genuinely skilled, and therefore our findings so far support, rather than rebut, Turner's suggestion.

Notes

1. K. Liepmann, *Apprenticeship* (1960), pp. 101-2.

2. Figures given by the Engineering Employers Federation after the war; cited in J.B. Jefferys, *The Story of the Engineers* (1946), p. 207. The 1906 Wage Census suggests a somewhat lower total – nearer 50 per cent; see Chapter 9, Table 9.1.

3. Dr Hinton has suggested that engineering workers were engaged in a long rearguard action before the war against dilution, in which to some extent they succeeded. The overwhelming demand for dilution during the war exposed the socially constructed nature of the craftsman's skill, as the employers were able to import in a short space of time 'a mass of new workers, men and women, on to jobs previously the preserve of skilled craftsmen', thus revealing 'the degree to which the genuine skill content of the craftsmen's work had declined'. J. Hinton, *The First Shop Steward's Movement* (1973), pp. 58-62.

4. *History of the Ministry of Munitions, 1920-24*, vol. IV, pt 4, p. 74.

5. H. Wolfe, *Labour Supply and Regulation* (Oxford 1923), p. 161.

6. Memo attributed to Sir Stephenson Kent, Mun. 5/70/324/20. (Mun. refers to the Ministry of Munitions records in the Public Records Office.)

7. Mun. 5/73/324/15/2.

8. Bev., pt. III, item 44, p. 356. (Bev. refers to the Beveridge Collection in the British Library of Political and Economic Science.)

9. Mun. 5/73/324/15/6.

10. Skilled men were not released in order to fight. See this chapter, below.

11. Hinton, *First Shop Steward's Movement*, p. 62.

12. *History of Munitions*, vol. IV, pt. 4, p. 74.

13. *Dilution of Labour Bulletin* (March 1918), p. 85. The Bulletin is in Mun. 5/73.

14. Ibid., p. 85.

15. See Hinton, *First Shop Steward's Movement*, pp. 66-70 for a discussion of the effect of L2. Among the opponents of the ASE's interpretation were the Clyde shop stewards, and the government. In the event certain deductions were made from women's wages, and they were not paid war bonuses. Committee on Women in Industry, PP 1919, XXXI, Appx I, p. 3, evidence of H. Wolfe.

16. Mun. 5/91/344/6.

17. G.D.H. Cole, *Trades Unionism and Munitions* (Oxford, 1923), p. 111.

18. Committee on Women, p. 82. Evidence of Mr Baillie, Director Technical Section, Labour Supply Department. See also evidence of Mr. Wood, Appx 1, p. 52. Further evidence to the same effect, from close personal observation, is provided by A.W. Kirkaldy (ed.), *Labour, Finance, and the War* (1916); see, e.g., pp. 107-8.

19. Mun. 5/73/324/15/9; written March 1916.

20. D. Thom 'Women at the Woolwich Arsenal, 1915-19', *Oral History*, vol. 6, no. 2 (Autumn 1978), pp. 59 and 63.

21. *History of Munitions*, vol. II, pt 2, pp. 42-4.

22. Thus Hinton's statement that 'By 1914 a substantial proportion of the work performed by craftsmen, at the craft rate, required little of their skill' does *not* necessarily mean, as he implies, that their skill was socially constructed; Hinton, *First Shop Steward's Movement*, p. 61.

23. Committee on Women, Appx 1, pp. 65-6.

24. It did not matter to individual firms what their costs were, as they were usually producing on cost-plus contracts.

25. Cole, *Trades Unionism*, p. 215.

26. Lloyd George to the ASE, Feb. 1916; Mun. 5/70/324/6. There is further testimony in Bev. III, 17, p. 116, and Bev. III, 22, p. 151.

27. Cole, *Trades Unionism*, p. 213.

28. See, e.g., Hinton, *First Shop Steward's Movement*, p. 129; S. Webb, *The Restoration of Trade Union Conditions* (1916).

29. S. and B. Webb, *The History of Trade Unions* (1920 edn) p. 642, n.2. The proportion of skilled engineering workers was estimated by Engineering Employers Federation at 50 per cent in 1921, compared with 60 per cent in 1914; Jefferys, *The Engineers*, p. 207. Considering the growth of sections of the industry organised on mass production lines, such as motor-vehicles, this figure strongly suggests that there was little change in the position in the older sections.

30. Cole, *Trades Unionism*, p. 214.

31. *History of Munitions*, vol. IV, pt. 4, p. 74. The continuing fall in the proportion of skilled workers, to 40 per cent in 1926 and 32 per cent in 1933, can be largely attributed to the continuation of the tendency for sections of the industry which used a high proportion of semi-skilled labour to grow rapidly, while the older sections stagnated or even declined; figures from Jeffreys, *The Engineers*, p. 207, and M.L. Yates, *Wages and Conditions in British Engineering*

(1937), p. 31. D.J. Lee, 'Deskilling, the Labour Market, and Recruitment to Skilled Trades', unpublished conference paper, p. 11, points out that between 1914 and 1933 output in general engineering remained, at best, static, while output in motor-vehicle, motor-cycle, aircraft and electrical engineering all grew by over 60 per cent; except for aircraft, all these sectors used a high proportion of semi-skilled workers.

32. See Jefferys, *The Engineers*, pp. 142-3; A.L. Levine, *Industrial Retardation in Great Britain* (1967), pp. 86-91.

33. Mun. 5/70/324/2/1; Mun. 5/70/324/2/3; Addison's remark was made at a conference with the ASE in Dec. 1916. At that time Addison, who had played a key role in the Ministry of Munitions from the beginning, was Parliamentary Secretary to it.

34. This passage is based on J.W.F. Rowe, *Wages in Practice and Theory* (1928), p. 264.

35. Ibid., pp. 90-2, 100.

36. Ibid., pp. 108 and 266. Some specimen figures from the ASE rate books are given below (wages per week).

		Planers	Slotters	Borers	Turners
1897	Manchester	32s	30s	30s	34-36s
	Newcastle	29s	29s	29s	33s 6d
1908	Manchester	33s	33s	33s	36-38s
	Newcastle	30s 6d	30s 6d	35s	35s

37. Rowe, *Wages*, p. 108.

38. B.C.M. Weekes, 'The Amalgamated Society of Engineers, 1880-1914', Ph D thesis, Warwick, 1970, pp. 81-90.

39. Rowe, *Wages*, p. 109. For a more detailed discussion of this issue, see Chapter 9. For some evidence on the question of the promotion of semi-skilled engineering workers to skilled status, before the First World War, see Chapter 6.

Part II

THE ACQUISITION OF SKILL

3 APPRENTICESHIP: AN HISTORICAL INTRODUCTION

Introduction

Our task in Part II is to study the acquisition of skill, with a view to collecting evidence to test the various theories concerning skill which were outlined earlier. We will start by looking at the history of apprenticeship up to the period under consideration, because, as will be shown, there are a number of different meanings attached to this word and we must be clear exactly what we mean by it. While apprenticeship was not the only means of acquiring skill in the late nineteenth and early twentieth centuries, it was the single most important, and therefore deserves the extra attention we are giving it.

If we followed the interpretation of apprenticeship put forward by some commentators around the beginning of this century, we would not be able to write about it at all, because according to them it did not exist. Thus to Olive Dunlop, writing in 1912, apprenticeship in its true form had virtually come to an end by 1800.[1] Since there were large numbers of young workers in 1912 who were called apprentices, we are clearly faced with a problem of definition. In the ensuing discussion of apprenticeship as it developed between 1800 and our period, it will be taken to be an unproblematic institution, and no consideration will be given as to whether its function was to provide a genuine training or socially construct skill; this question will be left to Chapter 7. It will be assumed, however, that one or the other of these was its normal function, and where it seems to have failed to do either an explanation will be provided.

Apprenticeship in the Nineteenth Century

True apprenticeship, as Dunlop called it, or old-style apprenticeship as we might call it, was the system of apprenticeship in which indentures were drawn up, binding servant to master and vice versa; in which the master personally taught the apprentice; took responsibility for the latter's moral welfare; and gave him board and lodgings.[2] In many industries, such as textiles, it had broken down by the eighteenth

century; it received its formal burial with the repeal of the apprenticeship clauses of the Status of Apprentices in 1814; and 1800, Dunlop
thought, marks the end of any significant influence it had on the
generality of trades.[3] Since there is, as she said, very little evidence
for the survival of such apprenticeship far into the nineteenth century,
we need not discuss it further, but can turn to the sort of apprenticeship which did survive.[4] This will be done by first distinguishing types
of apprenticeship, an analysis which for the sake of convenience will
be divided into two, with 1850 forming an approximate boundary line;
and then discussing the questions of decline and growth.

We might start with apprenticeship in high-class trades, which
Dunlop considered nearest the old type.[5] Obviously what trades were
or were not high class is a matter of opinion, and trades like shoemaking and tailoring might be divided into high and low class branches,
the latter using unapprenticed labour. The sort of trades which would
be usually accepted as high class were trades like hatting, flint glass
making, cabinet-making, carriage-building, and the latter's country
equivalent, the wheelwright's trade.

It will be helpful, however, to go further than Dunlop and divide
these trades into two types. There were those that remained organised
in an artisan-type fashion, that is the units of production were on such
a small scale that the master could still personally teach the apprentice.
Not only could it be argued that such teaching was the essence of the
old-style relationship, but some support to the concept of a separate
'artisan apprenticeship' is given by the fact that in many Continental
countries, at least until recently, such apprenticeships were recognised
as distinct, and separately legislated for.[6] My evidence for the survival
of such apprenticeships in Britain comes from the later part of the
century and will be discussed in a short while, but it seems reasonable
to conclude that if they existed then, they also existed in the first half
of the century.

Although artisan-type organisation remained important, capitalist
organisation, in which the master had withdrawn from the workshop
and become purely a businessman, was probably more common in
large centres, and particularly in London. The existence of trade
unions predicates the existence of this sort of organisation, and unions
in many high-class trades date from the eighteenth century.[7] In such
trades, apprentices were taught by the journeymen, and there was
usually also strict limitation on apprentice numbers. There is an extensive discussion of this sort of skilled work in Thompson's *The Making
of the English Working Class*, and his opinion is that in the early

nineteenth century it was flourishing.[8] In this type of apprenticeship, and also in artisan-type apprenticeship, the apprentice usually lived out and received some wages. But it is important to note that his wages were below those that could be received by workers of similar ages in other occupations.

The next sort of apprenticeship, to be considered very briefly, is what we might call exploitive apprenticeship. This is apprenticeship which failed either to teach a worthwhile skill or to limit the labour market. It may be tentatively suggested that this existed for two reasons. On the one hand, it continued in deskilled industries like textiles or pottery for the convenience of employers, who could make a profit out of the children by paying them low wages. On the other hand, parish or pauper apprentices were bound, frequently from an early age, to any workman, skilled or unskilled, who was willing to have them. Two influences acted to reduce exploitive apprenticeship. Where it was voluntary, children soon learnt to risk legal action and go where they could earn wages which reflected their productivity, since they acquired the necessary skill, such as it was, very quickly. Evidence to the Royal Commission on Children's Employment of 1843 suggests that this was happening in textiles and pottery.[9] Where apprentices had been bound by the parish, changes in the law encouraged the money hitherto spent on this to be spent instead on education: the children went out into the world older, better educated, and no longer in need of the guardianship supposedly provided by apprenticing them.[10] Since the 1840s saw important changes in this direction, it can be concluded that by the mid-nineteenth century exploitive apprenticeship was in decline.

Finally we might mention two areas where apprenticeship was a jumble of all the types we have described: these were the West Midlands and Sheffield. Exploitive apprenticeship existed cheek by jowl with trades where a lengthy training was genuinely needed; to complicate matters further the apprentice was often bound to the workman, who might at one moment be working for a master, and at another be working by himself as a 'little master'. Probably the system had never been strong in the West Midlands, and insofar as it existed at all had mainly been of the exploitive kind, at least in the manufacturing heart of the area. In Sheffield, it broke down progressively from the mid-century on.[11]

In the second half of the century, what I will call new-style apprenticeship was associated in particular with five growing industries: engineering, iron-shipbuilding, building, woodworking and printing.

Since Chapter 5 is devoted largely to a consideration of this type of apprenticeship, comment at this point will be brief: but as a preliminary observation we might note that, as can be seen from the inclusion of the latter three industries, new-style apprenticeship did not mark a radical break with past practice, but in these industries was merely a continuation of the sort of apprenticeship which was common in high-class trades; in particular, the two types share the important characteristic that the master did not himself work in the shop, yard or factory, and the teaching was done by the journeyman.

High-class trades, apart from those included in the above list, undoubtedly declined. According to Mayhew, this decline, taking the form of a growth of low-class branches at the expense of high-class, was endemic in London trades by 1850, especially in tailoring and shoemaking, but also in woodworking.[12] Certainly by the late nineteenth century, Booth's survey and other sources can point to only a few high-class occupations, like hatting, where apprenticeship with all its rules fully enforced was in full swing.[13] In specific areas where apprenticeship had once been common, such as Coventry, the second half of the nineteenth century likewise saw a sharp decline.[14]

There is, on the other hand, considerable evidence that apprenticeship in trades organised on an artisan, rather than capitalist, basis was much more persistent. In Stourbridge, a medium-sized town on the fringe of the Black Country, small employers continued to take indentured apprentices up to the 1880s, and in lesser numbers until the First World War. The school from which these apprentices came went to some trouble to ascertain the moral character of the employers, to minimise the risk of exploitation.[15] There is also evidence of the survival of artisan apprenticeship in the 'Family Life and Work' survey, which is described in detail in Chapter 4. Thirteen of the respondents, mainly from country districts and small towns, joined very small firms, often belonging to relations; it is not always clear whether they were formally apprenticed, although some were, but obviously there was plenty of opportunity for personal teaching by the master, and in several cases the master was the only other worker. The respondents who came into this category were a wheelwright from Kent; two joiners, from Chipping Norton and Berwick, and another from Corstorphine near Edinburgh, who perpetuated the old style of apprenticeship by staying with his master when his parents left the district before his apprenticeship had ended; two blacksmiths, from Cornwall and North Wales; a watchmaker, a plumber, two shoemakers, a saddler, a thatcher and a miller.

It is not difficult to explain why very small workshops were so durable. There was a growing demand for repair work, both because consumers had more goods to repair – this gave handicraft watchmakers and shoemakers, for instance, a continuing market – and because in the country increasing capital intensity of the farm meant more work for the blacksmith and wheelwright. The vast increase in the number of horses and carriages, especially in the middle years of the century, must also have been a factor.[16] We should not, in spite of this, attach much significance to the fact that 9 per cent of the Family Life and Work respondents in our category were artisan-type workers, because of the limited size of the sample, but there undoubtedly were large numbers of such workers. The Censuses from 1891 show how important small workshops were by distinguishing workers on their own account, and also employers; sharp fluctuations in, for instance, the number of blacksmiths and tailors in each category suggest that many 'own account' workers joined the ranks of the employers from time to time. We do not, of course, have any idea of the proportion of journeymen in any trade who actually worked in artisan type shops, although in trades with a particularly low ratio of employees to employers, such as watchmakers, saddlers and tailors, it must have been considerable.

We should finally distinguish one other important type of apprenticeship, known as premium apprenticeship. Sums of money, called premiums, had once been commonly paid at the start of apprenticeships; whether their function was to repay the master for his trouble, or limit entry, does not concern us here. The evidence for their continued payment when entering apprenticeships to manual work will be discussed in Chapter 5, but it may be summarised by saying that they were unimportant by the end of the nineteenth century. Hence 'premium apprenticeship' became distinguished as a special type of apprenticeship, where the premium was substantial – often £50 or £100 – and where in return the apprentice was given an education which was expected to fit him for a management role. The premiums were not dissimilar to the payments for entry to professions such as the law and chartered accountancy. The apprentice was taken through all the departments of a factory, instead of, as in a typical engineering apprenticeship, being confined to one; and he probably would receive some commercial education as well. Since it is not my intention to deal with management training, I will exclude consideration of premium apprentices in the main text; they are briefly discussed further in Chapter 5, Appendix 2.

Table 3.1: Artisan-type Workers (England Only)[17]

Number of employers

	1891	1901		1911	Figures in
Blacksmiths	12,137	7,275	(16:1)	8,553	brackets after 1901
Cycle and motor	691	1,796	(14:1)	3,095	show ratio
Wheelwrights	3,959	2,893	(7:1)	2,791	of em-
Watchmakers	3,535	1,925	(6:1)	1,511	ployees to
Plumbers	6,092	5,970	(9:1)	6,463	employers
Carpenters and joiners	11,924	8,804	(28:1)	9,591	
Saddlers	3,860	3,081	(6:1)	2,909	
Tailors	16,352	12,782	(7:1)	14,814	
Boot and shoe	17,740	8,999	(14:1)	9,905	
Electricians				1,256	
Total	76,290	53,525		60,888	(excludes electricians)

'Own account' workers

Blacksmiths	8,136	10,490	7,688
Cycle and motor	298	2,224	3,040
Wheelwrights	3,177	3,767	3,012
Watchmakers	5,727	6,364	5,154
Plumbers	3,203	4,777	5,186
Carpenters etc.	16,105	16,905	16,073
Saddlers	2,485	3,298	2,978
Tailors	13,659	15,562	11,676
Boot and shoe	38,190	38,925	31,280
Electricians			927
Total	90,980	101,682	86,087 (excludes electricians)
Employers *and* own account workers	167,270	155,207	146,975

Contemporary Views of Apprenticeship

Before turning to a consideration of apprenticeship in our period we should examine the opinions about it held by influential observers. For it was not just Dunlop who saw it as a thing of the past. Other commentators such as R.A. Bray and R.H. Tawney, who wrote on children's work, and J.A. Hobson, perceived apprenticeship as being virtually dead.[18] If this was the case, there would seem no reason to discuss it further. It will be useful, therefore, to distinguish types of decline, in order that we may see how apprenticeship's decline in certain areas and among certain types of work influenced these writers' perception of its condition.

The first distinction is influenced by an analysis in a paper by David Lee. He points out that when discussing changes in skill levels in the twentieth century, we must distinguish between the deskilling of individual jobs and industrial changes which led to the number of jobs in certain industries or occupations declining either relatively or absolutely, but not to the nature of the jobs themselves changing.[19] If we look at the nineteenth century, the first phenomenon is on the face of it the one most apparent: occupations like papermaking in the early part of the century, and shoemaking in the later part, change from hand to machine trades, and even if the skill involved was not less, it was certainly different and acquired in a different way. But a closer examination suggests that in reality we should treat the hand and machine branches of these trades as separate; as the Webbs pointed out, the hand branches survived and remained quite well paid.[20] It might well be fruitful to extend this analysis to occupations like cabinet-making, that is furniture-making; instead of seeing the growth of the cut-price branch as a degradation of the general standard, as Mayhew did, we should perhaps see it as an entirely new industry, catering for a different market. And by the time of Booth's survey, much of the cheaper cabinet-making trade seems to have become reskilled and quite respectable, perhaps as a result of the enhanced purchasing power of poorer consumers.[21] What David Lee calls the industry effect on changes in the relative importance of apprenticed and non-apprenticed trades was possibly more significant than degradation of work in the trades themselves; most handicraft trades declined gradually, and were replaced by occupations which, although they might bear the same name, were in reality completely different. Even where the decline was more concentrated, the same might apply. The fall in the number of ribbon weavers in Coventry, for instance, was not the result of technological changes, but of a decline in demand arising from a complex of circumstances: the organisation of production actually regressed technologically, so that there was no deskilling through technological change of the actual jobs the weavers did.[22]

None of this means that apprenticeship in many smaller trades and crafts did not decline, only that its decline was probably slower and perhaps less harrowing than is sometimes suggested.[23] In some cases, however, the decline itself was illusory. The first type of illusory decline arises out of the special circumstances of London, both in its type of employment, and as a locus of sociological investigation. In the 1890s, Booth thought that apprenticeship in the building trades was dying out; those who had been apprenticed were mainly of the older generation.[24] Then in the *New Survey of London*, in the early 1930s, we are told that 'the skill of the London building craftsmen, taken as a whole, is less than it was before the war . . . One symptom (if not the main cause) of the decay of craftsmanship is the almost complete disappearance of apprenticeship in the London area.[25] At both times, therefore, the existence of apprenticeship in the past, but not in the present, was observed. The explanation of this apparent contradiction is that for a long time, certainly as far back as Mayhew, many London building workers were recruited from outside London;[26] no doubt the continuous expansion of the metropolis had something to do with this, but the main reason was probably the pressure of work and the high overheads in London, which made employers reluctant to devote time and space to young workers who were not fully productive.[27] After Mayhew, the phenomenon was noted by the Booth survey itself, although it failed to draw the obvious conclusion that this was the explanation for the relatively small number of young apprenticed workers in London; while a government report on training of 1925, only a short while before the *New Survey of London*, found that over the whole country the ratio of building craftsmen to trainees, many of whom were apprenticed, was 3.6:1, whereas in London it was 7.1:1.[28]

The second type of illusory decline was purely a result of confusion over terminology, although it perhaps lies at the bottom of some of the comments about apprenticeship which were made in the late nineteenth and early twentieth centuries. There was what seems to have been a long-term decline in indentured apprenticeship in favour of simple written or verbal contracts.[29] In fact industries and simple written contracts had the same legal status; while the comments of various investigators make it clear that in practice even verbal contracts were regarded as just as binding.[30] One important practical reason why this was so will be mentioned later.

A genuine decline in apprenticeship in many trades, and the perception of decline which was in fact illusory, must have been one influence on writers like Tawney, Bray and Hobson, while there undoubtedly existed a real problem in the number of dead-end, or as they were then called blind-alley, jobs. Thus Bray found that about 40 per cent of London elementary school leavers first entered transport occupations, as van-boys or suchlike, although only about 10 per cent of adult workers were in such occupations.[31] As was pointed out at the time, such statistics could be misleading, because many quite reputable trades recruited from youths or young men, and thus

provided a way out of blind-alley jobs;[32] but none the less the problem
of those who had been permanently casualised remained. It is not,
however, our problem here: what is of more interest to us is the
assertion by some of these writers that apprenticeship itself, where it
survived, had become debased.

At this point, as a preliminary to our detailed discussion of it, it
will be helpful to summarise the external features of new-style apprenticeship in the late nineteenth century. Boys entered firms at between
fourteen and sixteen, and served usually between four and seven years,
earning progressively increasing wages which were still well below the
adult rate, and usually also below the wage earnable in non-apprenticed
occupations; the apprentices might be indentured, or merely have a
contract, verbal or written, that the employer would teach them the
trade, and the firms were of varying sizes but except in artisan-type
production were distinguished by the separation of the owner, and
in large firms the manager, from the workshop. These were the external
characteristics of apprenticeship; writers such as those cited above, and
others such as George Howell, painted a different picture of the reality
behind it, but the most complete view was supplied by the Webbs,
although it differed only in its elaboration and not in its theme.[33]
According to the Webbs, the real feature of apprenticeship in most
trades were as follows: the absence of any safeguard, following the
Repeal of the Statute of Apprentices, as to whether an employer had
any knowledge of the trade he engaged the apprentice to learn;
instruction, such as it was, given by the journeymen, who if on piecework did not want to be bothered with apprentices at all, and if on
daywork saw no object in encouraging future rivals in the labour
market; and a lack of any systematic method in this instruction. As
the Webbs saw it, the employer could not utilise apprentice labour
remuneratively, and rather than take premiums preferred to 'divide
his processes into men's work and boys' work, and to keep each grade
permanently to its allotted routine'; they gave as an instance of the
result of this 'the scores of apprentices in a modern shipyard' who 'are
necessarily left mainly to learn their business for themselves, by
watching workmen who are indifferent or even unfriendly to their
progress.'[34]

The Webbs' model of apprenticeship is extremely pessimistic.
Arguably, however, there might be a rationale for the institution in
terms of the theory of social construction: in other words, apprenticeship might not necessarily have taught a skill, but it might have been
the 'ritual servitude' which it is seen as by some modern commentators.

While the Webbs, however, admitted that this might be the case in certain instances, such as the Boilermakers, they did not admit it as a general rule; on the contrary, they explicitly stated that unions like the Compositors and Engineers had completely failed to enforce their entry regulations.[35]

At this point we should consider the implications of the Webbs' view. On the one hand, we have the problem of explaining how it was that groups like the engineering workers acquired the skill which we have seen that they possessed, when allegedly the employers divided their processes 'into men's work and boys' work', and kept each group permanently to its allotted routine. On the other hand, we have the problem of explaining how there were about 100,000 apprentices in engineering alone in any one year in the 1900s, when according to the Webbs there was *neither* an educational *nor* a trade union/restrictionist underpinning to the institution. The Webbs' view contrasts interestingly with Turner's, to whose model the effectiveness of apprenticeship as an entry limitation is crucial, and who would also argue that it must have had at least some value as a method of training.

Notes

1. O.J. Dunlop, *English Apprenticeship and Child Labour* (1912), pp. 224-36.
2. Ibid., p. 161.
3. Ibid., pp. 224 and 236. See also T.K. Derry, 'The Repeal of the Apprenticeship Clauses of the Statute of Apprentices', *EcHR*, vol. III (1931-2), pp. 67-87.
4. There is sporadic evidence of the survival of living-in apprenticeships, that is where board and lodging were given. Thus the Royal Commission on the Employment of Children found that Eyre and Spottiswoode, the printers, took such apprentices; PP 1843, XIV, p. 815. Rubin Burman, a cooper's apprentice, was clothed and fed by Truman's Brewery in London, but not paid, from 1848-55; K. Kilby, *The Cooper and His Trade* (1971), p. 166. The paucity of the evidence suggests that this sort of apprenticeship was not common by the nineteenth century.
5. Dunlop, *English Apprenticeship*, pp. 230-1.
6. G. Williams, *Apprenticeship in Europe* (1963), see, e.g., pp. 19, 81-2.
7. See H. Pelling, *A History of British Trade Unionism* (1963), Ch. 2.
8. E.P. Thompson, *The Making of the English Working Class* (Pelican edn 1968), pp. 260-2.
9. Royal Commission on Children, p. 219 (pottery), p. 1,156 (hosiery). Any written contract had the force of law, even if it was not a signed indenture. See below, note 30.
10. Of particular importance was an Act in 1844 which both abolished the compulsory obligation of ratepayers to receive parish apprentices, and also gave permission for some of the poor rate to be spent on schools. See P. Keane, 'Evolution of Technical Education in Nineteenth Century England', unpublished Ph D thesis, University of Bath, 1970, pp. 136ff.

11. S. Pollard, *History of Labour in Sheffield* (1959), pp. 54-9, 70, 137; G.C. Allen, *The Economic History of Birmingham and the Black Country* (1929), pt 1, Ch. 7, p. 26; Royal Commission on Children, pp. 738-9, and PP 1843, XV, pp. 192, 570, 605.

12. E.P. Thompson and E. Yeo, *The Unknown Mayhew* (1971), pp. 182, 251, 325, 335 and 345.

13. Charles Booth *et al.*, *Life and Labour of the People of London*, 2nd series, *Industry* (5 vols., 1903), vol. V, pp. 126-7.

14. Up to the 1850s apprenticeship in Coventry, mainly to the ribbon and watchmaking trades, kept pace with the growth of population; J. Prest, *The Industrial Revolution in Coventry* (1960), p. 87. By the 1860s, however, the number of ribbon-weaving apprentices declined sharply with the decline in trade, and eventually the watch trade declined too; information from Mr N. Tiratsoo, in an Institute of Historical Research seminar, 12 Jan. 1979, and see ibid., pp. 87-8.

15. E. Hopkins, 'Were the Webbs Wrong about Apprenticeship in the Black Country?', *West Midlands Studies*, vol. 6 (1973), pp. 29-31.

16. Barbara Kerr, *Bound to the Soil* (1968), p. 134, for the prosperity of rural craftsmen in the late nineteenth century; for horses and carriages, see F.M.L. Thompson, 'Victorian England – the Horse Drawn Society'. Inaugural Lecture at Bedford College, 1970 (from 1830 to 1900 the number of cabs in London increased tenfold, and the number of buses increased from 1,000 to 4,000; nationwide, the number of large carriages increased from 30,000 to 120,000 and of small from 40,000 to 250,000 between 1840 and 1870; growth continued thereafter, only more slowly).

17. Printed census papers, 1891, 1901, 1911.

18. R.H. Tawney, 'The Economics of Boy Labour', *Economic Journal*, vol. 19 (Dec. 1909); R.A. Bray, *Boy Labour and Apprenticeship* (1911); J.A. Hobson, *The Evolution of Modern Capitalism* (1896), p. 255 ('The absence of any true apprenticeship in modern factories . . .').

19. Lee, *Deskilling and the Labour Market*, p. 7.

20. S. and B. Webb, *Industrial Democracy* (1920 edn), pp. 419-22.

21. Booth, *Industry*, vol. 1, pp. 182-5.

22. Based on comments by Mr N. Tiratsoo, in an Institute of Historical Research seminar, 12 Jan. 1979.

23. See Chapter 9 for a discussion of the implications of these changes for skill levels.

24. Booth, *Industry*, vol. 1, p. 100.

25. H. Llewellyn-Smith (ed.), *New Survey of London Life and Labour* (1931), vol. 2, p. 80.

26. Thompson and Yeo, *Unknown Mayhew*, p. 335.

27. Report of an Enquiry by the Board of Trade into the Conditions of Apprenticeship and Industrial Training (printed but not published, 1915). There is a copy of this report in the British Library of Social and Economic Science. Furthermore, some London trades had been recruited for many years from semi-skilled workers, notably the bricklayers who were recruited from labourers; D.B. Viles, 'The Building Trade Workers of London', unpublished MPhil thesis, University of London, 1975, p. 41 (referring to the mid-century).

28. Booth, *Industry*, vol. 1, pp. 41, 69, 101-2. Booth's sample of 124 builders was too small to draw reliable inferences about the difference between different age groups. *Report of an Enquiry into Apprenticeship and Training in 1925-26* (7 vols., HMSO, 1927-8), vol. II, p. 17.

29. There was a fall between 1909 and 1925 in most occupations, 1925 Report, vol. VII, p. 34. Mr W.W. Knox tells me that there was, however, increased interest in indenturing apprentices at the end of the nineteenth century, as compared with the mid-century.

30. E. Austin, *The Law Relating to Apprentices* (1890), pp. 17-18, 1915 Report, p. 55.

31. R.A. Bray, 'The Apprenticeship Question', *Economic Journal*, vol. 19 (1909), p. 410.

32. N.B. Dearle, review of 'Boy and Girl Labour' by Tawney and Adler, *Economic Journal*, vol. 19 (1909), p. 565.

33. George Howell, 'Trade Unions and Apprenticeship', *Contemporary Review*, vol. XXX (1877), pp. 833-57. Webbs, *Industrial Democracy*, pp. 463-73 in particular.

34. Webbs, *Industrial Democracy*, pp. 477, 479-80.

35. Ibid., pp. 463, 465-7, 470.

4 SOURCES AND METHODOLOGY

The purpose of this chapter is simply to outline the sources and methodology that will be used in the subsequent two chapters — Chapters 5 and 6 — on the acquisition of skill.

The Measurement of Skill

We should first examine in more detail the question of measuring skill, since we are concerned not only with the question of acquiring skill, but also with how much was acquired. Our working definition of skill has taken it as being roughly proportional to the training time needed to acquire it, but it is worth enquiring whether we can use some more exact measure, or whether we can refine our existing one.

We must first consider whether we can use wage rates as a measure of skill. Although labour economists would recognise a number of influences on wages, the latter have on occasion been taken as a proxy for labour force quality.[1] In other words, the amount a man earns has been taken as a direct function of his skill, physical efficiency and so on. Could wages be used as a measure of skill by itself in the period we are concerned with?

One immediate objection to this method of measurement is that if skill, and hence wage differentials, are socially constructed through the segmentation of labour markets by unions, or through other means, wages will not be an effective measure of genuine skill, which is what we are interested in. Obviously if we were to use only wage differentials as a proof of genuine skill, this objection would be insurmountable; if we showed the latter's existence by some other means, then wages might still act as a valid measure. Unfortunately there are so many other objections to using wages that they cannot be taken seriously even as a measure.

Excepting skill itself, whether genuine or socially constructed, there were three main influences on wage differentials in this period. One was effort:[2] it could certainly be argued that in any general assessment of labour force quality, effort should be taken into account, since it depends partly on physical efficiency and labour discipline; but from the point of view of measuring skill alone, the very existence of effort as a factor in wage determination vitiates wages as a measure of skill. The existence of differentials in wages due to effort differences can be very easily demonstrated. In agriculture, for instance, Dr Hunt has argued that wage differentials between northern and southern England were partly due to differences in effort resulting from the lower level of food input of southern labourers.[3] In engineering, the introduction of piece rate payment schemes resulted in gains in wages of 15 per cent or more; while some of this may have been due to the development of extra manual skill by workers, the literature of wage incentive schemes suggests that the major improvement in output and wages stems from higher effort, and possibly more effective use by workers of their working time.[4]

This brings us to the second factor which could distort wage differentials: differences in 'X-efficiency'. This is described by H. Leibenstein as efficiency which depends, not upon the correct allocation of resources in the total economy, but upon effective use by individual firms of factors already present; inefficiency might result from managerial ignorance, lack of competition or simple inertia.[5] In large sectors of the economy that were more or less secluded from competition, and had a partially 'captive' workforce that only responded sluggishly to the opportunity of higher wages elsewhere, there was room for inefficiency to creep in. Agriculture was one such sector; and Dr Irving's important study of railway efficiency implies that since efficiency increased rapidly in the Edwardian period, it must have been unduly low beforehand. Agriculture was a notoriously badly paid occupation, while railway pay was by no means high.[6]

Finally we have to take account of the enormous regional variations in wages, which resulted fundamentally from long-standing variations in the location of industry. The high wage areas were mainly those in which were concentrated some of the major industries, such as cotton, shipbuilding and the greater proportion of mining and engineering. Although differences in skill were undoubtedly one of the factors helping to maintain regional differentials, there were many others such as different factor endowments and lower management and external costs due to economies of scale.[7]

It seems, then, that we should dismiss wages as a serious measure of skill in this period, and try to approach the subject more directly. One measure which has been used in recent studies is that of investment in education — education provides knowledge, which as we have seen can be regarded as a component of skill.[8] A point which will immediately strike the reader is that since so much skill in this period was not acquired by means of formal education, but by on-the-job training, there will be problems because measuring such investment is likely to be difficult, and the methodology has never been worked out. For reasons which will become clear as our description of the acquisition of skill unfolds, these problems are practically insuperable.[9]

If we come back to our original working definition of skill as being proportional to learning time, however, we realise that it is unlikely to yield a result not dissimilar to that given if we could measure investment in education, while being more practical. The result will not be dissimilar because in general an increase in the length of learning time will increase the cost of acquiring the skill in question, although it is true that the cost might be affected by other factors such as the intensity of learning. It should be noted that we have substituted 'learning time' for 'training time', the phrase used by Renold, but it is clear from Renold's description that he is not necessarily referring to a course of systematic instruction, such as the word 'training' connotes;[10] we will therefore use the term learning time, as a neutral expression which does not imply the use of any particular method of acquiring skill. Even a measure so apparently straightforward as learning time, however, poses questions of considerable methodological complexity which we must now try to answer.

First of all, we must try to discover the criteria we should use to judge when a worker has learnt his job. It is not sufficient to take traditional apprenticeship times, or the length of time it took for a worker to be promoted in non-apprenticeship industries. To do this would be to beg the whole question of social construction which, at least if worker-initiated, depends on limitation of entry of some form or other. The only standard we can meaningfully adopt is the time a worker took to become efficient at his job, assuming that he had reasonable opportunities for learning it. Industrial psychologists call this Experienced Worker Standard, or EWS, and it has been defined by the British Standards Institution as 'the rate of output which qualified workers will naturally achieve without over-exertion as an average over a working day'.[11] Such a definition is rather more helpful for assessing repetitive jobs than other kinds, but the basic concept is clear enough, and the definition could easily be widened to include, for instance, maintenance workers or process workers. One further problem with EWS is that there are usually two standards, for day rate workers and piece rate workers.[12] As we have already noted, however, it seems likely that a large part of the latter's increased output can be accounted for by differentials in effort input and more effective management of working time, rather than by differentials in skill. Furthermore, in our period the ambiguities introduced by this dichotomy are further reduced because most major industries were conducted on either day rate or piece rate lines: thus building and process industries were predominantly day rate; cotton and shipbuilding predominantly piece rate; only engineering and woodworking fell between two stools.[13] In general, therefore, the concept of 'Experienced Worker Standard' is a useful one to keep in mind when assessing learning times.

The problem still remains of how we are to actually assess them. Fortunately there were a number of studies of apprenticeship and training in our period, and it is on these that we must largely base our conclusions. In general, the compilers of these studies were well aware that the apparent training times of traditional apprenticeships often concealed a different reality, but a full discussion of the credibility of these sources will be carried out in the next part of this chapter.

Having established some standard of assessment of learning times, and that there are some means for assessing them, we now have to consider the different methods of learning. These may be divided into three: formal education, which is not intended to train workers for specific jobs but does provide necessary prerequisites, such as literacy, for certain work; training, which provides either knowledge of a specific job, or manual skill, through systematic instruction; and experience, or on-the-job learning, by which workers might acquire either knowledge or manual skill. It may be asked first whether these methods can be meaningfully compared. With regard to education, this is problematic, because so much education will not be relevant to work at all. An important exception is basic literacy, which has undoubtedly become increasingly important as more and more work has become subject to rules and written instructions. It is a defect of this study that it does not consider literacy, but the problems of doing so are considerable: it is not always clear what work at this time actually required literacy as a *sine qua non*; and it is extremely difficult to assess exactly how to compare several years at school which might be spent acquiring literacy, with training for work during adolescence and adulthood. General education, therefore, will not be considered; nor will technical education be considered when assessing learning times, because in spite of its apparent relevance the evidence suggests that it was not essential to the great majority of jobs.[14] It will, however, have a separate chapter devoted to it.

It might be thought that training is more akin to education than to experience, because the former both involve formal instruction. On the other hand, a moment's consideration of how manual work is learned will show that the manual skill, as opposed to knowledge required, can only be learned by practice, since by definition manual skill involves co-ordination of sensory information and motor activity, and only practice can improve this co-ordination. On the face of it, the practice needed can be just as effectively carried out on the job as during formal training sessions, and thus experience and training can be equated. Furthermore, since knowledge could also be absorbed in a variety of ways while working – through observation of other workers, discussion during necessary breaks in work and so on – it would seem that training is not necessarily more effective than experience in the imparting of knowledge. Modern research, however, has shown that carefully designed training programmes are more effective than learning on the job in enabling workers to reach EWS, for a variety of reasons: for instance there are optimum lengths of time for practice, and optimum distributions of practice periods.[15] These improvements apply to skilled work with a high knowledge content, as well as to what are known as semi-skilled jobs, which require the mastery of a limited number of basic tasks, or only one, and usually necessitate the acquisition of more manual skill than knowledge: thus the time taken to learn a typical semi-skilled task – the operation of a series of machines producing wood screws – was reduced from nine weeks to four weeks after the introduction of a training scheme; a fully skilled job – the setting and maintenance of semi-automatic machines in an electronics works – was learnt in fifteen weeks by already skilled workers against the previous fifteen to eighteen months.[16]

The task of assessing the time taken to master jobs is made that much harder by the difference which alternative approaches to learning make to learning times. In investigating learning times in the period under consideration, therefore, we will have to take account of how much formal training there was, and how much learning by experience, if we are to assess these times objectively.

A Note on Skill and Semi-skill

It will have become apparent from the preceding discussion that there is no qualitative difference in the skill required of workers of any kind: it is always some combination of knowledge and manual skill. It remains useful to distinguish semi-skilled work as involving the mastery of only a limited amount of knowledge, or number of manual tasks, such as can be learnt in weeks or months, rather than years.[17]

Sources

The existence of skill among workers is usually taken for granted; the histories of firms and industries, while they often tell us about pay, trade disputes and annual excursions, rarely say much about skill or how it was acquired. Historians of trade unions, while saying even more about the two former subjects, are usually equally unforthcoming on the one we are interested in. Our evidence has therefore to come largely from other sources.

My first source has been the testimony of workers themselves on their training. This is partly based on the 'Family Life and Work' survey of some 440 Edwardians, people who had been born during or before, and for the most part were brought up and started work during, the Edwardian period.[18] These Edwardians, of whom some 140 were male manual workers in non-agricultural occupations, were selected to give a distribution corresponding to the average in terms of sex, social class and place of dwelling, the latter being divided into rural, town and conurbation; the working class, with whom we are concerned, were then divided into skilled, semi-skilled and unskilled.[19] The obvious problem of classification of occupations, and the relatively small sample size, suggests that we should treat any statistical findings based on the survey as merely indicative of general trends, rather than definitive. The Family Life and Work (henceforth FLW) respondents were asked about a number of subjects, work being only one, and inevitably they never tell us as much as we would like; but their testimony provides us with insights into what workers themselves thought of work which we do not find elsewhere.

I have also read as many working-class autobiographies of the period, and indeed for the whole nineteenth century and early twentieth centuries, as I have been able to find. The problem with these is that the writers are by definition untypical, since working-class people are not in the habit of writing autobiographies. Where evidence from FLW respondents or autobiographies is used, I have not usually given references unless a quotation is involved; the autobiographies are listed in the bibliography, and the whereabouts of the material in them on training and work is generally fairly obvious; references are given where this is not the case.

The other main groups of sources have been reports and books by various organisations and individuals who concerned themselves with training. There are five of these in particular. The first chronologically are the *Industry* volumes of Booth's *Life and Labour of the People of London*:[20] where Booth (or his co-writers, but the work will be referred to as Booth) strays into the field of historical comparison he is apt to be misleading, as we have seen; where he sticks to factual description of the existing state of affairs there is no reason to suppose that he is inaccurate, the more especially as the subject of industrial training was hardly likely to arouse the same sort of emotive response as, say, poverty. The manuscript notes on which *Life and Labour* is based are difficult to use, partly because they are so extensive, and partly because they are classified according to the different editions of Booth for which they were collected, as well as into subjects. Since the printed work does not aim to spare the reader by its brevity, it can be assumed that most of what is valuable is incorporated in it; where I have come across something interesting in the notes, I have used it. The main drawback of Booth is that he deals only with London, a drawback he shares with another source, N.B. Dearle's book of 1914 on *Industrial Training*.[21] There are three points which can be made in connection with this. The first is that large sections of industry, such as cotton-processing and shipbuilding, were wholly absent from London, and hence any distortions arising from London peculiarities in Booth's and Dearle's account of training cannot affect our view of occupations in these industries, since Booth and Dearle do not deal with them. The second is that evidence from other sources cited below suggests that capital-intensive industries such as grain-milling had very similar methods of recruitment and training in all parts of the country, and in these cases Booth's and Dearle's accounts can be taken as representative. The third point is that during our period about one in six of all workers in manufacturing industry worked in London, so that we can hardly reject evidence from London as only being representative of a small minority of workers.[22] It remains true that there were London peculiarities in training, which will be discussed later; but they were fairly well known, and indeed were made explicit by Dearle, and so can be corrected for.[23] Apart from this Dearle's book seems to me, from the degree of consistency it has with the other sources, to be objective, and in addition it provides a very useful analytical framework which I have adopted and which is discussed below.

Of the two pre-war national surveys, Jackson's *Report on Boy Labour* provides quite extensive details for a number of industries.[24] The other is a report on apprenticeship and training compiled by the Board of Trade over a number of years, and printed, although not published, in 1915 (henceforth 1915 Report).[25] The basis for its statistical findings, such as they were, was fairly narrow, although on the number of apprentices they can be supplemented by the Board of Trade enquiries into wages of 1906;[26] on the other hand, its investigations were wide-ranging and covered most industries. They can be supplemented by a report on similar lines conducted by John Hilton in 1925-6 (henceforth 1925 Report).[27] The chief problem with using this is its post-war date. It has already been suggested, however, that the degree to which the war permanently affected the organisation of the engineering industry can be greatly exeaggerated; since there is even less reason to suppose that it led to dramatic changes in other industries, I conclude that this report, together with its extensive statistical findings, can be used, albeit with caution as thirty years separated it from the Booth report. Some of the material on which the report was based, which is in the Public Records Office, has also been used where appropriate.

There are numerous other minor sources which have been used for particular industries, and which will be cited when used. The labour records of invidiual companies are extraordinarily hard to find, and when found usually unrevealing: certain records have been useful, however, which again will be cited when used.

Arrangement of the Material

Dearle classified the methods of learning skilled work into three: Regular service, Migration and Following-up. Semi-skilled work was learned by Picking-up.[28]

The method of regular service covers most, though not all, of the groups of workers who acquired a skill through apprenticeship. It also covers some non-apprenticed workers. It denotes workers who underwent a certain period of service, which was formally dedicated to learning, in one firm; the usual method of teaching was to attach them to another worker, but the variations will be discussed in due course. The occupations learned by this method included:

Engineering: patternmakers; millwrights; most fitters, turners and erectors; some more skilled machinemen; some smiths; some moulders; some gas fitters and electrical installation workers.
Building: carpenters and joiners; most masons, some bricklayers and high-class painters.
Shipbuilding: shipwrights, ship carpenters and joiners; drillers; some platers.
Printing: high-class bookbinders; stereotypers; lithographers; type-

founders; most compositors; some machine-managers.

Textiles: overlookers (weaving); carpet-makers.

Woodworkers: wheelwrights; coach-builders; wet coopers; high-class cabinet-makers.

Old crafts: bespoke shoe and tailoring workers and hatters; high-class watch and jewellery manufacture; 'Sheffield Trades' (cutlery etc.).

Transport work was often learned by a method which can only be described as 'regular service', although it is not really comparable with the methods of learning in the trades listed above.

The method of migration denotes the learning of a trade by moving round from firm to firm, or from machine to machine or process to process within a firm. It had a number of variations, but was a common method in industries where the work was highly subdivided, but parts none the less required considerable skill: these included in London silversmithing, machine woodworking, machine boot and shoe making, and light engineering. As we shall see, however, it could be extended to the method of learning in a number of process and other industries.

The method of following-up denotes the learning of a trade by working, either as a member of a gang, or as a mate to a skilled worker. In some instances, as sometimes with plumbers, the mate might be an apprentice; riveters and glassblowers, too, served their apprenticeship while working in a gang. In many cases, as with engine-drivers and firemen, many plumbers and gasfitters, and steel and tinplate workers, there was no apprenticeship. Other occupations where the process of learning was analagous, and which were likewise non-apprenticed, included cotton-spinning, where the 'little piecers' and 'big piecers' were the mates, and coalmining, where in some districts the face-workers were in pairs or groups, with one or more of their number hewing, and the other, or others, filling the tubs; these fillers would eventually hope to become hewers. Picking-up, as its name implies, was learning in a more casual way, which might have elements in it of all the other three methods.

In the next chapter, Regular Service will be discussed, and in Chapter 6 Migration and Following-up, with a brief section of Picking-up.

Notes

1. R.L. Raimon and V. Stoikov, 'The Quality of the Labour Force', *Industrial and Labour Relations Review*, vol. 20 (April 1967), use the wages of occupational groupings as a basis for measuring quality, which they imply is is virtually identical with skill. C.G. Williams, *Labour Economics* (New York,

1970), pp. 41-2, in reply to these and other attempts to measure quality by wages, raises objections similar to those raised in this chapter.

2. Effort, in this context, I take to mean the physical input of labour, which would be a function of physical efficiency, willingness to work, management's ability to utilise labour efficiently and other factors.

3. E.H. Hunt, 'Labour Productivity in English Agriculture, 1850-1914', *EcHR*, 2nd ser., vol. XX (1967).

4. The average earnings of piece rate workers in engineering were at least 18.5 per cent higher in 1906 than those of day rate workers in the same occupations: M.L. Yates, *Wages and Conditions in British Engineering* (1937), pp. 98-9. On wage incentive schemes, see for instance J.P. Davison *et al.*, *Productivity and Economic Incentives* (1957), esp. pp. 33-7, 38-41.

5. H. Leibenstein, 'Allocative Efficiency versus "X-Efficiency" ', *American Economic Review*, vol. 56 (June 1966), pp. 391-415.

6. R. Lennard, *English Agricultural Wages* (1914), pp. 49-60; R.J. Irving, 'The Profitability and Performance of British Railways, 1870-1914', *EcHR*, 2nd ser., vol. XXXI (Feb. 1978); see esp. pp. 60-3. For railway pay, and the recruitment of railway workers from agricultural areas, see J.W.F. Rowe, *Wages in Practice and Theory* (1928), pp. 43 and 169.

7. E.H. Hunt, *Regional Wage Variation in Britain, 1850-1914* (1973), see esp. Ch. 1 and pp. 356-61.

8. G.S. Becker, *Human Capital* (New York, 1970); see also E.F. Denison, *Why Growth Rates Differ* (Washington, 1967), Ch. 8.

9. Mincer has used data on earnings/educational differentials to arrive at some conclusions for the US, but this data is not available for other countries; Mincer admits that some costs, such as firm's costs for training, are very hard to estimate: J. Mincer, 'On-the-job Training: Costs, Returns, and Some Implications', *Journal of Political Economy*, vol. 70 (1962, Supplement), pp. 50ff. For other objections see below, Chapter 8.

10. H. Renold, 'The Nature and Present Position of Skill in Industry', *Economic Journal*, vol. 38 (1928), p. 593.

11. W.D. Seymour, *Industrial Skills* (1967), p. 92.

12. Ibid., p. 120.

13. In 1906 building had hardly any piece workers; printing was also predominantly time rate; in cotton weavers and spinners were all piece workers, and other trades were usually either all piece or all time; the same applied in shipbuilding – some trades predominantly piece, some time; woodworking had about 20 per cent piece workers, engineering about 30 per cent. Source see note 26.

14. See Chapter 10.

15. Seymour, *Industrial Skills*, pp. 95-6.

16. Ibid., pp. 267 and 271.

17. Ibid., pp. 159-60.

18. I am grateful to Dr Paul Thompson, who organised the original survey, for allowing me to look at the records. See P. Thompson, *The Edwardians* (Paladin edn, 1977), pp. 17-18, for some further details on the survey. The answers of the respondents were recorded, which accounts for their sometimes repetitive and hesitant character, which I have not altered.

19. The number of male manual non-agriculture workers is my own estimate; I worked first from the codings given by Dr Thompson's team, selecting those who were coded as working class before the First World War. (Members of the mercantile marine have not been included.) I have not subjected the findings to any statistical tests, because once the sample is broken into subgroups (skilled, semi-skilled etc.) the number in each group becomes too small

for such tests to be useful.

20. Charles Booth *et al.*, *Life and Labour of the People of London*, 2nd series, *Industry* (5 vols., 1903, mainly incorporating material from the 1895 edition).

21. N.B. Dearle, *Industrial Training* (1914).

22. The proportion rose from somewhat under one-sixth (of England and Wales) in 1861, to slightly over in 1921; P.G. Hall, *The Industries of London since 1861*, 1962, p. 21.

23. Dearle, pp. 36-43.

24. C. Jackson, *Report on Boy Labour in London and Certain Other Towns*, PP 1909, XLIV. Henceforth Jackson Report.

25. Report of an Enquiry by the Board of Trade into the Conditions of Apprenticeship and Industrial Training (printed but not published, 1915). There is a copy of this in the British Library of Social and Economic Science. A note at the beginning states that 'Some preliminary information as to the number and wages of apprentices was obtained in connexion with the Enquiry into the Earnings and Hours of Labour of Workpeople in 1906, and this was afterwards supplemented by more detailed returns from a large number of firms and companies' (and also from employers associations and trade unions). So no precise date is given as to when the survey was carried out. Henceforth 1915 Report.

26. PP 1909, LXXX; PP 1910, LXXXIV; PP 1911, LXXXVIII; PP 1912-13, CVIII. Estimates of apprentice numbers partly based on these sources are given in Chapter 5, Appendix 1.

27. *Report of an Enquiry into Apprenticeship and Training in 1925-26* (7 vols., HMSO, 1927-8). This survey was conducted on the same lines as the 1915 one, but on a larger scale; about 30 per cent of all apprentices were covered. Henceforth 1925 Report.

28. Dearle, *Training*, pp. 20-7.

5   THE METHOD OF REGULAR SERVICE

Apprenticeship and Learnership

There were, at a very rough estimate, over 340,000 apprentices in any one year in the early years of the twentieth century.[1] The internal evidence of the figures themselves, as well as the evidence of our other sources, suggests that apprentices formed the greater part of the recruits to the two key engineering occupations of fitting and turning, and also to pattern-making; in engineering they also formed a substantial proportion of the recruits to moulding and smithing; in shipbuilding, platers and riveters, as well as the subsidiary trades of caulking and holding-up, were largely recruited by apprenticeship; in building and woodworking, carpenters and joiners, wet coopers and some cabinetmakers, as well as a proportion of bricklayers, masons and painters; in printing, many compositors, as well as such subsidiary occupations as lithographers and stereotypers.

If we attempt to discuss apprenticeship as a method of learning, we are faced with a number of problems, the first one of which is the variety of occupations, and of types of apprenticeship. Only some of the occupations which recruited through apprenticeship are listed above; to add to their variety, we have artisan apprenticeship, which existed in almost as many trades as ordinary apprenticeship – even engineering workshops could have only two or three workers.[2] Furthermore there were the various ways of binding an apprentice – by indenture, by simple written agreement, verbally, or by what was known as 'learnership'. The latter was a development which was still inchoate before the war. Thus Dearle divided the types of apprenticeship and learning agreement into four: apprenticeship with a definite binding agreement; learnership, which was sometimes called apprenticeship, with a verbal agreement; 'Employment during Good Behaviour' – including a tacit agreement that the boy was given an opportunity to learn a trade; and 'working and learning', meaning that if the boy was capable he was left to pick up the trade himself.[3] After the war, however, the 1925 Report clearly distinguished learnership from verbal agreement; the latter it, and the 1915 Report, considered to be almost on a par with written agreement or indentured apprenticeship, as we shall see; learnership it characterised as appertaining to 'a worker who, not being an apprentice, is specifically engaged by the employer for a recognised period of training in the capacity of a learner, and is provided by the employer with instruction or with definite facilities for learning a branch of process of the industry'.[4] This really corresponds with the third type which Dearle distinguished — Employment during Good Behaviour — and not with what he called learnership.

Given that the definitions of learner and apprentice were somewhat uncertain, and therefore that returns using these classifications must be used with a degree of caution, two things are clear from such figures as are available. First that learnership tended to be concentrated in subdivided industries where in practice learning was by migration, that is by moving from machine to machine or process to process. Thus in 1909, when much of the data used for the 1915 Report was collected, 26.1 per cent of all trainees were learners, but in pottery the proportion was 66 per cent, in boot and shoe manufacture 49 per cent, and in clothing 42.4 per cent.[5] The second point to bear in mind is that in 1925, when rather more trouble was taken to separate the two groups, learnership outside such industries does not seem markedly different from apprenticeship in length of training or rates of pay; in engineering, training took an average of 6.1 years against 5.7 years for apprenticeship, and pay was 11s 1d per week against 10s 7d per week.[6] It also seems likely that there were inaccuracies in the returns, perhaps more so in 1909; the 1915 Report did not itself clearly distinguish learners, and the figures given above were presumably compiled in 1925 from the 1909 returns, so it seems likely that they enjoyed, or suffered from, the benefit of hindsight, and it would be unwise to put too much trust in them. Therefore I will make no attempt to particularly distinguish learnership, at least until we come to discuss learning by migration.

But as well as not distinguishing learners, we will not distinguish other groups, such as artisan-type apprentices. The reasons for adopting a blanket approach are twofold: first, if we subdivide apprentices into groups, we would not know where to stop, since they could be classified according to so many different criteria; second, and more important, because by treating them together, we will bring out the fact that, even including artisan apprenticeships, there was an essential similarity between all types of apprentice training. At the end, when we sum up, we can point out the more important differences.

Recruitment

To start at the beginning: recruitment. Almost certainly the largest single source of recruits was, as in many non-apprenticed trades, the relatives of workmen in the same firm or occupation. Evidence for the adoption by employers of this method of recruitment comes from numerous sources: Booth mentions it in connection with general engineering and railway workshops; at Crewe railway workshops it went so far that 'the chance of becoming apprenticed to a skilled trade were very small unless one's father was already employed by the company'; the 1925 Report instances it also in textile and marine engineering, and ironfounding; the 1915 Report found that most firms in engineering gave the sons of employees preference.[7]

We can add some statistical weight to these comments, first from Crossick's study of Kentish London: the table below is abstracted from Crossick's figures, which were based on a sample of 3,886 marriages in 1851-3, and 4,310 from 1873-5.[8]

Table 5.1: Percentage of Fathers in Same Trade as Son

	1851-3	1873-5
Engineering crafts	41.2	42.7
Building crafts	57.9	45.6
Shoemakers	37.6	49.1*
Tailors	45.3	50.0*

*Fathers *either* shoemakers or tailors.

Crossick's figures can be supplemented by two surveys of young men in trade or continuation schools; because these were unlikely to include many unskilled workers, they may slightly overstate the degree of self-recuitment; they do, however, show that the very high figures in Crossick were not unrepresentative of the situation in other districts and later in the century. Dearle, also in London, found that 30 per cent of a sample of 87 had followed in their father's trade, about 10 per cent had followed relatives' trades, and another 10 per cent had followed trades cognate to their father's. Chapman and Abbott had the benefit of a much large sample in a Lancashire survey in 1912, but the problem here was the dominance of the textile industry, and to a lesser extent of mining, although we must remember that since many areas had some dominant industry the situation was not so unusual as all that. They found that 61.7 per cent of textile workers had followed their father, and 36 per cent of miners; of more significance were the 33.3 per cent of metalworkers, and 24.2 per cent of builders and woodworkers, who had done likewise; the proportion of fathers in these trades was 16.3 and 9.7 per cent, so in both cases these was a tendency to go into the trade far stronger than might have been expected if the occupations had been entered without any family influence being brought to bear.[9] Finally, the Family Life and Work respondents show the following pattern:

Table 5.2: Family Life and Work Respondents

Occupation**	Total entry	Father's occupation cognate	Father in firm*	Artisan apprenticeship in relative's firm*
Engineering	16	6	2	—
Woodworking	9	5	2	2
Metal conversion (includes smithing)	9	7	5	3
Other skilled	14	2	—	—
Total	48	20	9	5

*Included in previous column.
** The list includes all those in named occupations, whether apprenticed or not. 'Other skilled' includes a miscellany of minor crafts; occupations like mining and railway work are omitted.

Put together, the figures we have suggest that in occupations with a large number of workers such as engineering, building and woodworking, between a quarter and a half of children followed their father, although not necessarily into the same firm. While self-recruitment was extremely important, therefore, there were still likely to be more recruits to a trade from outside it than from within it. Dearle suggests that recommendations of head teachers were one source; but quite definitely high educational qualifications were not; they are very rarely mentioned, and the great majority of FLW respondents in this category went to elementary schools.[10] Nevertheless, by the end of our period some of the big engineering firms did pay some attention to preliminary education: the 1915 Report gave a number of examples, such as Vickers of Barrow, which went further than others in insisting upon a knowledge of algebra and geometry; Armstrong Whitworth at Manchester, which insisted upon Standard VII level at entry; and Barr and Stroud at Glasgow, which paid general attention to educational standard and extra-curricular activities.[11] But these were exceptional, and as late as 1925 the agricultural machinery and machine tool firms replying to the questionnaire sent round in connection with the Report often had no criteria for selection beyond the obvious ones of an elementary education and local residence — or in other words no apparent criteria at all.[12]

It would be going too far, however, to say that there were no actual criteria. No doubt all firms took some account of the 'likeliness' of a boy, and local residence implied that they had, or could obtain, some knowledge of his background. There was frequently, too, some form of probation: the 1915 Report stated that formal probation was rare, informal frequent, but in 1925 36 per cent of engineering apprentices went through a formal probation.[13] On the other hand only three of the 36 FLW apprentices, or 8 per cent, spoke of a probation, although in some cases it may have been missed in the questioning. What probation usually meant was that the lads acted as errand boys about the works, taking tools around, or like J.T. Murphy, acted as check-boys, whose task was to return the brass tokens which acted in lieu of a clocking-on machine to the men. How many boys failed their probation we do not know, but from the descriptions it is clear that it was primarily a test not of aptitude, since no serious work apper-taining to the trade was performed, but of willingness to work.

Some boys might not have originally intended to be apprentices, and come in through errand boy type work in the shop, although the dis-tinction between this and probation is shadowy. There is some disagree-ment about how frequent the practice was. The Jackson Report thought that it was quite frequent in engineering and printing, although the report may have been referring to what was in reality probation. Dearle also instances it in printing, where indentures, especially for machine-hands, were often dated back after a few years service if a boy had proved satisfactory. On the other hand, the Webbs claim that there was a sharp division between apprentices and other boys in shipbuilding.[14] Shipbuilding was a peculiar industry, as we shall see later; the problem can be put in context by noting that in a very large sample of engineering firms, in 1906, there were 57,400 apprentices and 19,150 'other lads' and improvers.[15] Given that improvers, who will be discussed in a moment, must have formed a large proportion of these, it seems likely that in most branches of engineering there was little room for odd-job boys, so the question of whether it was customary to recruit from them does not arise. This ratio of three apprentices to every one 'boy' or improver in engineering, which overestimated the proportion of boys because of the inclusion of improvers, may be compared to a ratio of 5.7:1 in building; in printing, on the other hand, the ratio was 1:1 precisely, and in ship-building 2.8:1.[16] Given the point made by Dearle, it seems likely that only in printing was there much recruitment from existing boy workers.

We can conclude from this survey that apprenticeship, although the route to a skilled trade, did not require the apprentice to show beforehand that he possessed any extraordinary intelligence or manual dexterity. And now that we have surveyed the mental criteria for entry, we can conveniently deal with the material. Premiums, as we suggested earlier, were rare, except for apprenticeship which was intended as an entrance to management. Jackson found that nine engineering firms out of 85 demanded them, or 11 per cent, although the returns on which the 1915 Report was based found that 18 per cent of firms took them; but most premiums were small − £5 or so. And in printing and building only 4.3 per cent and 4.7 per cent of firms, respectively, asked for premiums, and Jackson found that they were rare in cabinet-making also. By 1925, even fewer firms asked for them.[17] Only one of the 32 FLW apprentices recorded paying a premium, a joiner who was apprenticed to a small firm owned by a relative; his premium of £20 was quite large, but his apprenticeship should probably be classed as artisan-type rather than 'premium' *per se*. There may possibly have been some instances where the wages were so low that they acted in lieu of a premium; for instance another FLW respondent, who significantly left school as late as sixteen, did not pay a premium to the boatbuilder to whom he was apprenticed, but obtained an all-round training, including draughtmanship and clerical work; his wages were only 1s per week, raised by 6d per week for every year of his six-year apprenticeship. These were well under the usual apprentice rates, which will be discussed more fully later; but the very fact that the average wages for apprentices were far above this shows that it was an exceptional situation. It also seems that where premiums were paid for trade apprenticeship there might be special circumstances. In Norwich, for instance, there were a number of apprenticeship charities, and because the money was available firms tended to demand premiums: thus premiums did not form a pecuniary barrier to entry, although they were a nuisance because they tended to restrict entry to those whose relatives had contact with a charity trustee.[18] But in general, we can conclude that premiums were not important.

Duration of Apprenticeship

There is no particular problem in estimating the length of apprenticeships, since there is a substantial amount of statistical data. The problem, as we have already seen, is to decide whether their length depended on the amount of knowledge or skill imparted, or on some other criteria such as custom or union influence. At this stage no attempt will be made to discuss this issue in detail, and I will confine myself to presenting the statistical data and making some preliminary comments.

Table 5.3: Length of Apprenticeships (Percentage, 1909)[19]

	3 yrs	4 yrs	5 yrs	5-7 yrs*	6 yrs	7 yrs
Engineering	0.1	0.9	53.5	10.0	8.0	27.5
Shipbuilding	0.2	—	53.0	0.6	18.0	28.2
Building	0.7	5.1	33.8	12.1	21.4	26.9
Furniture	2.3	15.2	39.9	15.7	16.9	10.0
Printing	—	—	4.2	6.6	4.8	84.4
Boot and shoe**	1.4	32.2	25.1	20.8	8.5	12.0
Electricity supply**	17.8	17.3	58.9	5.4	0.6	—
All industries (including some not shown above)	1.2	5.9	38.9	10.0	13.4	30.6

*According as apprentices commenced at 16, 15 or 14 years of age.
** The last two occupations have been put in to enable comparison between the major apprentice trades, a subdivided industry with a residue of craft work (boots and shoes) and a new occupation where union influence was weak (electricity supply).

On the basis of this data, some tentative remarks can be made which might help to clarify it. The influence of custom seems to have been very strong: as the fourth column (5-7 year apprenticeships) shows, many firms were willing to adjust the length of apprenticeship according to the age of entry; as it also shows, the reason for this was to preserve the traditional finishing age of 21.[20] This strongly suggests that, since some firms had apprenticeships for the same jobs which could last between five and seven years, the length of apprenticeship bore no particular relation to the amount of training; and this in turn suggests that the most popular period, five years, was itself a product of custom; this is borne out by the fact that even in a new industry, electricity supply, five years was the most favoured time, although three or four years were also popular. In general, comments by employers suggests that seven-year apprenticeships were falling out of favour because in many industries boys of 14 were not yet strong enough to even make an attempt at learning a trade; in industries where strength was not so important, like printing, apprenticeships could start earlier. The data above suggests, incidentally, that the figures published by the *Boy Labour* scaremongers should be taken with an even larger pinch of salt than was earlier suggested, because even in many apprenticed trades entry was not encouraged before 16. As a result, many boys who meant to become apprentices might at first take apparent blind-alley jobs: it is interesting in this context to note that at least 15, or 42 per cent, of the FLW respondents who were apprenticed had a full-time job beforehand, lasting usually between six months and two years. We might finally note the length of the FLW apprenticeships.

Table 5.4: Length of FLW Apprenticeships

Less than 5 yrs	5 yrs	6 yrs	6 or 7 yrs	7 yrs	No details
8*	10	3	3	7	5
26%	32%	10%	10%	23%	
(19% without learners)					
1909 data					
7.1%	38.9%	13.4%	10% (5-7 yrs)	30.6%	

*Including possibly two learners. There was also a possible learner in machine-made boots and shoes, who has not been counted.

These figures do suggest that the FLW apprentices are by no means unrepresentative, although the sample is small.

Improvership

When an apprentice in certain trades, notably in engineering and woodworking, had served his time, he was likely to become an improver, and it is important to understand the nature and scope of improvership so as to gain a full understanding of apprenticeship. There were two different types of improver: on the one hand, there were workers who moved around from firm to firm during the learning process; on the other, time-served workers who earned less than full wages.

We are not primarily concerned with the first group here. Dearle uses the term improver to denote workers in a number of London trades who learned by migration, and this use of the term seems to be warranted, as George Acorn, a cabinet-maker who learned in this way, used it in just this sense;[21] improver was also used, however, in reference to trainees in building work who moved from firm to firm; in this sense, although not in Dearle's sense, use of the term could be compatible with apprenticeship, since building firms were willing to transfer indentures. There is little evidence, however, that it was a common method of training in building at that time, and its use in other industries more properly comes under the heading of learning by migration.[22]

Time-served workers who became improvers are of more interest to us at this stage. The excellence of first-class London work was generally recognised, but as had already been suggested London was a poor training ground for apprentices. As a result, there was a constant demand in London for 'country workmen' — which in fact seems to have meant anyone from a reasonably small shop who had an all-round training. These workmen were not immediately able to reach London standards of excellence, and therefore their first two years or so of apprenticeship were spent as improvers, in Booth's day at 50-75 per cent of the full rate.[23] The demand for such workers was especially high among cabinet-makers in the piece-masters' shops, which were midway between the high-quality West End trade and the sweated trade, but in all woodworking and building trades London was considered to be unrivalled for the highest quality work; in engineering, too, London, had some very high-quality workshops.[24] The reasons for preferring country workmen were different in the different industries: in building and woodworking, the all-round training of the country workshops was a good base for the specialisation London demanded; in engineering, the extent of repair work meant that all-round workers were in demand for their versatility.[25]

Just how common such London improverships were, and just how long payment at under full wages lasted, we do not know. Both Booth and Dearle refer to the practice as if it was common, and it is perhaps significant that two engineering workers who were later to become famous, George Barnes and Tom Mann, both moved to London early in their careers, although neither actually mention improvership. Booth suggests that the payment of less than full wages lasted for one to three years in engineering; [26] perhaps in cabinet-making, where subdivision was the rule outside the West End, a man could go on working at under the full rate for much longer, since there must have been doubt as to what was the accepted rate for subdivided work.

Improvership was by no means confined to London, however. When a man finished his apprenticeship, or when a young worker just released from his time applied for a job at another firm, it was a frequent practice in some industries to offer him relatively low wages, as Table 5.5 shows.

Table 5.5: Improvership (1925)[27]

Industry	% of apprentices and learners required to serve improvership
Engineering	90.3
Furniture	38.2
Building	30.4
Shipbuilding	15.9
Printing	10.7

In firms in the machine-tool and agricultural engineering industries, which together cover a fairly wide spectrum of engineering, improvership in 1925 lasted usually from one to two years, and wages in most cases rose from 80 to 100 per cent during that time.[28] There is little doubt that improvership was common from an early date in some industries. Thomas Wood of Bingley, an engineering apprentice in the 1840s, was offered 14s by his employer, instead of the standard rate of a pound, when his time was up; he went on the tramp, but returned to his original master and in two years or so was earning the full pound.[29] Only two of the FLW respondents in engineering actually mention serving an apprenticeship, in both cases for two years, but the respondents were not actually asked about it so more may have done so. Two of the nine woodworkers also mention improverships.

The Jackson Report had the impression that most apprentices in engineering left their firms when their time was up in order to gain wider experience. It was only an impression, and it is not wholly borne out by the evidence. As we shall see, there were firms where the worker was trained to specific, which did not necessarily mean low-skilled, jobs, and it was advantageous to neither the firm nor him to leave. And of the agricultural machinery and machine-tool firms in 1925, only two stated that they encouraged apprentices to leave; most of the others, by failing to reply to the question asking them how they recruited skilled workers if not by apprenticeship, imply that they kept their own workers.[30] Of the FLW respondents in engineering, the two who mentioned improvership both stayed with their firm; but two others left immediately after their apprenticeships, and it may well be that they served improverships. Sometimes, one does not know how often, a firm had a policy of improvership, but an able worker escaped it: Harry Pollitt, apprenticed to boilermaking in a locomotive works just before the First World War, left to earn full money after his apprenticeship, rather than work for two years as an improver; after the two years was up he went back to his original firm.

Wages

The fundamental principles of apprentice wage setting were very simple. Apprentice wages usually stated at around 5s per week at the beginning of the century, a figure that applied to most districts and occupations. They rose by annual increments of between 1s 6d and 2s 6d per week, depending on district, occupation and length of service, to reach anything between 10s and £1 at the end of apprenticeship, although the middle of the range would be more common; some of the shipbuilding trades were exceptional, and paid much better at the end.[31] These figures compare with an adult skilled man's wage of 30s to 40s in most areas and occupations – lower in some remote country districts, higher in certain shipbuilding trades.

The average wages for apprentices can be conveniently tabulated alongside the average wages for other boys in the same industries, and in other industries. We have no data on the ages of these boys, but in textiles and tinplate boys undoubtedly started young – probably younger on average than in apprenticeships, since as we have seen many boys had left school for a year or two before starting an apprenticeship, and in the North-West they often worked in textiles.

Apprenticeship did not require a large pecuniary sacrifice, and in some trades apprentices apparently earned higher wages than non-apprentices; this finding should be treated with caution, however, as many of these 'other boys' would be official or unofficial probationers, who would become apprentices, and were therefore by definition younger than the average apprentice. According to Dearle, there was general agreement that differentials between 'learners and earners' had narrowed in recent years, although there is no firm statistical evidence on this; Dearle's interpretation of it was that the rising value of learners' earnings made employers less concerned with actually teaching them. But Dearle himself also noted that out-and-out exploitation was less common than formerly, and this apparent contradiction suggests that there could be other explanations for the decline in the cost of apprenticeship in terms of foregone wages – if decline there was.[32]

One partial explanation might simply be the growth of skilled or semi-skilled occupations learned by other methods, which will be

Table 5.6: Juvenile (Under 20) Wages (UK, All Districts, 1960)[33]

Occupation	Apprentices	Other Boys
Building Trades	8s 5d	10s 4d
Sawmilling	9s 4d	9s 10d
Cabinet-making and allied	7s 10d	10s 6d
Engineering and boilermaking	9s 2d	12s 10d
Rly. carriage and wagon	11s 10d	11s 9d
Shipbuilding	Omitted. See note 32	
Printing	9s 3d	8s 6d
Bookbinding	9s 4d	8s 6d
Paper stationery	9s 0d	8s 5d
Tailoring (bespoke)	6s 3d	8s 10d
Tailoring (ready-made)	9s 5d	9s 11d
Boot and shoe	9s 4d	10s 4d
Paper manufacturing	10s 9d	11s 9d
Cotton		12s 8d
Woollen		10s 1d
Tinplate		11s 11d

discussed in the next chapter; although trainees in such occupations did not have the formal status of apprentices, they had a reasonable expectation of learning a skilled job and these trades were therefore in competition with apprenticeship; thus juvenile wages in two industries which provided opportunities for progression, textiles and tinplate, were significantly higher than apprentice wages. This might have had two effects on apprentice differentials: either they remained unchanged when compared with totally unskilled occupations, but declined relative to all non-apprenticed occupations, which included many where skill was acquired; or the competition of such occupations forced employers of apprentices to utilise the latter more efficiently, a development which might be quite commensurate with the maintenance of standards of education since, as we shall see, apprenticeships often included periods which for various reasons were not used very profitably for either education or productive work. Dearle's comments about the decline of exploitive apprenticeships suggest that this interpretation might have some validity.[34]

Apprentice Contracts

If we are to take apprenticeship seriously as an educational institution, we must be sure that apprentices took it seriously as well. One test of this is the extent to which apprenticeship agreements were broken, and all the evidence suggests that this was rare. The 1925 Report found that the apprentice failure rate was 10 per cent in shipbuilding, 9 per cent in engineering, and 2 per cent in woodworking, printing and building.[35] It seems unlikely that there had been significant changes since before the war, and the 1915 Report provides some confirmation of this. In a discussion which was particularly about engineering apprenticeships, but by implication about apprenticeship in general, it said, 'In practice an apprentice is seldom discharged except for gross misconduct or incompetence and (when serving a regular apprenticeship) seldom breaks his engagement.'[36]   By a regular apprenticeship it meant any engagement that was recognised as an apprenticeship, whether written or not.

The experience of the FLW respondents would seem to confirm these findings: out of 41 apprenticeships which were started, there were eight failures, although some were not permanent. They are tabulated in Table 5.7, as they were probably typical of the contingencies which could lead to failure.

The overall failure rate was 19.5 per cent, although this includes the boatbuilder who was hardly a 'failure'. This evidence certainly does not contradict the general impression that most apprentices took their careers seriously enough to persist with them.

There is only one piece of evidence contradictory to the general pattern outlined above: apprentice riveters in shipbuilding, in at least one firm which there is no reason to think was atypical, had a very high turnover rate, some 50 per cent failing to complete their apprenticeship in the late nineteenth century, rising to 80-90 per cent before the First World War.[37] The implications of these very high figures will be discussed in Chapter 7, but it should be reiterated that the evidence strongly suggests that they were unusual. Most occupations which apprentices entered did not experience anything like this sort of turnover.

There were some sanctions on errant apprentices. Indentures, in theory, provided a legal redress for employers (and for apprentices, if the employer failed to keep his side of the bargain). Written contracts had the same legal status as indentures, which were indeed merely a more solemn and detailed version of the former, although verbal contracts did not.[38] In practice, however, there was no real distinction between any of them, for two reasons. The first was that, even if an apprentice broke an indentured or written agreement, 'the employer has no remedy in law worth taking'; unless parents were a party to the contract they could not be sued; even when they were party, there is no evidence that employers attached importance to legal sanctions.[39]

Table 5.7: Apprenticeship Terminations (FLW Respondents)

Apprenticeship	Time served	Reason for termination	Was app. eventually completed?
Electrical engineer	9 mnths	Wanted to go to sea	No
Engineering worker (turner/fitter)	3 yrs	Sacked (probably unfairly) — alleged misconduct	Yes — at another employer
Motor repair	1 yr (? learner)	Low pay	Returned to employer; not clear whether app. formally resumed
Shoemaker (hand-sewn)	1 yr	Trade learned	No
Boatbuilder	4 yrs (out of 6)	Family moved	Taken as complete; two years improvership at another firm
Fancy leather work	2 yrs	Father died — had to support family	No. Became export packing case maker
Coppersmith	1 yr	Did not like job	No (see below)
Sheet iron worker (same respondent as above)	2 yrs	Did not like job	No (became apprentice tile-fixer — served time)

Note: The careers of all workers, including semi or unskilled, were searched for apprenticeships, since ex-apprentices would not necessarily be found only among skilled workers.

The second and much more important reason why verbal agreements were as good as others was that if the apprentice left he risked forfeiting his 'lines' — his certificate at leaving which showed that he had served so many years: 'The importance attached to the possession of "apprenticeship lines" which can be produced when asked for is said to be of much more binding effect on the apprentice than any signed agreement at the outset of apprenticeship.'[40] Employers, except in the building trade where as we have noted there was a recognised, although small, class of migratory apprentices known as improvers, reinforced this sanction by generally refusing to take on apprentices who had been sacked by other firms.[41] The FLW respondent who was sacked from a Tyneside firm was 'stopped' by other firms all over the river, and was very lucky to find a friendly employer who let him finish his time.

A discussion of the extent of indentured apprenticeship is therefore almost otiose. In 1909, it formed a proportion of total apprenticeship ranging in the major apprenticed trades from 29 per cent in engineering and 37 per cent in building, to 51 per cent in shipbuilding and 64 per cent in printing. Within engineering, in particular, there were sharp variations both in different sectors, and in different areas. Thus in 1925, when a more detailed breakdown is given, 49 per cent of trainees had indentures or written agreements in marine engineering, but only 2 per cent in textile engineering; not surprisingly, therefore, the North-East had 48 per cent of engineering trainees under such agreements, and Lancashire, where the textile machinery industry was concentrated, less than 5 per cent, with most under verbal agreements; but these latter were also predominant on the Clyde, where they formed 69 per cent of the total, in spite of its marine engineering bias.[42] Thus although indentures, at least in engineering, bore some relation to the difficulty of the work to be learnt — marine engineering being relatively skilled compared with textile engineering — there also seem to have been regional differences which bore more relation to the custom and practice of the locality than to anything else.

Apprentice Training

The most important thing about an apprenticeship was not length of service, wages or security, but what was learnt during it.

When an apprentice started work, he had to acquire some elementary but important information, such as the names of tools and materials. Most commentators on the subject suggest that it was usual to start an apprentice on 'errand-boy' work, and that this sort of work had some value as giving the boy an opportunity to acquire such knowledge, although it could easily be overdone; Dearle thought a reasonable period was six months.[43] Although two of the FLW respondents in engineering did start their apprenticeship in this way, the majority did not, most from their description starting on serious work right away. One reason for this, of course, was that some had already served a probation; while others, especially in the textile districts, had worked full time for a year or two and experienced something of industrial discipline. In general we can conclude that some sort of errand-boy work in the factory in which the apprenticeship was served was a fairly frequent introduction to an apprentice's career, but that it might well form part of his probation, rather than his apprenticeship proper. It is important to note, however, that there is no evidence from either the surveys and reports, or the biographical material, that apprentices spent a large part of their time in making tea or getting beer for the workmen, as legend sometimes has it. This does not mean that the work they did was necessarily educative, but merely that it was not wholly trivial.

Once this sort of work was over, an apprentice's training would depend partly on the size of the firm. The hallmark of an artisan-type apprenticeship was that the teaching was done by the employer. In a small firm, for instance the moulder's shop in Bolton which one FLW respondent served his time at, the foreman was able to give personal attention to the apprentices. In most firms, however, this actual teaching was done by a journeyman: just over two-thirds of the engineering firms responding in 1925 regarded this method of training as predominant, while most of the rest reported that the boys were primarily in charge of the foreman, or possibly the works manager or employer, although still working with a journeyman.[44] The actual method of training, not just in engineering but in most occupations, could be summed up by saying with Dearle that the detailed teaching was done by the journeyman, but that the foreman was 'in the front line' — responsible for seeing that the boy was being taught properly, and for moving him around if necessary to different types of work.[45]

As Dearle said, training connotes systematic instruction, but in fact this was rare; so how did the apprentice acquire his knowledge and manual skill?

The educational value of an apprenticeship would depend on three things: how good a teacher the journeyman was; how effectively the foreman supervised the apprentice's work to see that he was getting all-round experience; and how willing a pupil the apprentice was. And the apprentice's education had to ensure that he acquired both manual skill, and the knowledge appropriate to his future job.

Manual skill can only be acquired by practice at manual operations. Therefore it was necessary that the apprentice should spend much of his time practising. The acquisition of knowledge, on the other hand, requires, if not systematic instruction, at least opportunities for observation and asking questions. The amount of knowledge needed might vary: thatching, for instance, required mainly manual skill, and a sort of 'craft knowledge' of the materials and suchlike which could only be obtained by actually working; engineering, on the other hand, needed increasingly larger amounts of formal knowledge, for instance of how to read blueprints. By the 1890s the opportunity to acquire some of this knowledge through technical education was becoming increasingly widespread, although a discussion of how far this opportunity went, and how far it was used, will be deferred until Chapter 10. Nevertheless, there was a wide gap between the classroom and workshop practice, and hence it was still important for apprentices to have the chance to acquire as much technical knowledge from the journeyman as possible. One obvious limitation on this was the amount and type of knowledge the journeyman actually possessed: the knowledge content of tasks probably changed more quickly than the manual skill content, and there was less chance for an older worker to adapt to the former if the new knowledge was not widely available. It is, however, extremely difficult to assess how far this limited apprentices' education; most apprentices do not seem to have perceived it as a problem.

According to the 1925 Report, the engineering apprentice was usually given an opportunity to acquire this knowledge, insofar as the journeyman possessed it: 'during the first year or more of the training period it was usual for the apprentice to spend a large part of his time watching the skilled man performing the operations incidental to the job in hand, and he might be allowed to undertake simple pieces of work; he also gradually learnt to read blueprints or working drawings and to appreciate the importance of certain fundamental principles of engineering practice, e.g. the need for extreme accuracy of measurement and strict attention to the detail given in the working drawings'.[46] While the biographical material does not usually go so far as to tell us the details of what an apprentice did while learning, the impression given by it is that the Report was rather too optimistic, although possibly, with the spread of technical knowledge and the wider use of blueprints, there was an increase in this sort of instruction in the post-war period.

Thus a number of apprentices, far from 'watching a skilled man', started work on automatic machines of one sort or another. Two of the FLW respondents started on this sort of work — although it is true that they soon progressed to working with a journeyman, and their early work might be regarded more as a sort of probation. J.T. Murphy started by working relatively simple machines: W.G. Riddell spent several months on a nut-facing machine; and Wal Hannington became so fed up with the repetition work he was doing that he left his apprenticeship after two years — although one reason for his disillusionment was that friends of his at other firms were doing much more varied work. This suggests that one should not exaggerate the extent to which apprentices were put on such repetition work. Murphy and Riddell both escaped from this sort of work after complaining, while Riddell also admitted that his initial lack of interest in engineering did not help him: most boys would not have started an apprenticeship as he did, with a total ignorance of what was entailed, because they either lived locally — he came from the country — or had relations in the firm or industry. In general, the FLW respondents imply that they got down to work with a journeyman quite quickly or immediately. We can conclude that while many apprentices, at least pre-war, did not necessarily enjoy the year of observation which the 1925 Report alluded to, and while their opportunity for acquiring any very deep technical knowledge from their journeyman was limited, they did not in general simply provide cheap labour. Finally, it should be stressed that in many apprenticeships in the older crafts such as thatching, coopering and smithing, very little formal technical knowledge was needed, as opposed to craft knowledge which could only be acquired while actually doing the job.

Given that there were limitations on the amount of technical knowledge that the average apprentice acquired from a journeyman, it was obviously crucial that the manual skill and craft knowledge he *did* acquire were of the highest quality, if his apprenticeship was to be worthwhile. Three factors were important here: the helpfulness of the journeyman, the journeyman's actual skill, and his aptitude as a teacher.

In the 1840s Thomas Wood had found his workmates in an engineering shop 'thoughtless, vicious, and selfish'; but few other commentators shared his gloom.[47] Dearle thought that with hourly paid workers there was no problem in getting them to teach the boys: as already noted, most workers in building, printing and woodworking were hourly paid, and many engineering workers were too.[48] The 1925 Report also referred favourably to the 'readiness with which journeymen and foreman assisted young workers to gain a knowledge of the trade'; and even today, when piecework is much more prevalent in engineering, the help received from the 'blokes on the shop floor' is usually spoken highly of by apprentices.[49] While there is not that much comment in the biographical material, most of it is reasonably favourable. In the 1860s Thomas Wright remarked that the men in engineering workshops took a kindly interest in the apprentices. In the 1880s Alfred Herbert, also in engineering, was particularly impressed: 'my shop-mates, without exception, were most kind and friendly. They answered my innumerable questions, and did their best to teach me something of the rudiments of my trade.'[50] W.F. Watson, writing about the Edwardian period, provided striking testimony to the interest the men took in their apprentices, without glossing over the roughness and crudity of workshop life:

Wherever he went, the apprentice was placed under the charge of a craftsman who, although he might accompany tuition with kicks, cuffs, and livid language, took very great pains with his pupil. The mechanic proudly boasted of 'my pupil' if he was particularly apt, and the apprentice would frequently make small presents to his tutor.[51]

George Barnes also remarked favourably on his workmates' helpfulness, and some of the FLW respondents commented in generally favourable terms, while none made the sort of allegations that Thomas Wood did. One of the respondents thought his journeyman very strict, and others remarked similarly about foremen or employers; strictness, however, might be an attempt to foster learning — the journeyman mentioned above administered corporal punishment if the apprentice did not learn; only in one autobiography — that of a cabinet-maker in a small shop after the First World War — is there an account of generally unhelpful and even positively unpleasant workmates: the firm was run by an ignorant bully who later replaced the journeymen with apprentices, thus confirming the former's fears that by teaching apprentices they would lose their own jobs.[52]

Pieceworkers might be expected to be less willing to teach apprentices, since on the face of it they had much more to lose than day-workers through inattention to their own work. But there were ways of making up for this loss, and Dearle thought that in most cases a monetary allowance was made to pieceworkers.[53] What evidence there is from other sources tends to confirm this: coopers, for instance, were credited with part of their apprentices' earnings; the same was the case with the fancy-leather worker in the FLW survey.[54] Direct payments to the journeyman were often made: George Howell notes them in the case of printing-machine minders, lithographic printers and glass-makers.[55] In the case of surgical-instrument makers and some other minor but highly skilled London trades, there was an unofficial artisan-type apprenticeship to the 'chamber masters', who worked independently: men 'are not regularly apprenticed, but agree to work three to five years at a very low wage'; since the 'apprenticeship' was purely a matter between the journeyman and the trainee, both were presumably satisfied.[56] Direct payments were also made in trades which did not have apprenticeship, but which were learnt by some form of regular service: in the tanning industry, labourers who worked in the lime-pits would pay the more skilled unhairers and fleshers to teach them;[57] in the carpet industry, similar payments were made — 2s 6d per week for a year at Kidderminster, and a lump sum of £3-4 for a rather shorter period of training at Paisley and Bonnyrigg in Scotland; and in the Nottingham lace trade a youth promoted to adult work did not at first receive the adult wage, the surplus being divided between the machine-minder and the employer.[58]

We can conclude that there were no real obstacles to effective training from the attitude of the journeymen. But whether or not their attitude was favourable, there was no real advantage to be gained from an apprenticeship if the journeyman had not some real skill to impart. Biographical evidence shows that apprentices perceived their journeyman's skill as forming an integral part of the learning process.

L.T.C. Rolt wrote of his time in a locomotive factory in the late 1920s, 'I can only feel humble in the presence of a man who is doing his job superlatively well and in 1928, there was no lack of such craftsmen at the California works ... The men I was privileged to work beside were craftsmen as surely as were Sturt's wheelwrights.'[59] His opinion was echoed by some of the FLW respondents: a joiner who commented that the work at his shop was 'as good as you'd get anywhere in England'; a boatbuilder reckoned that his workmates were 'damned good craftsmen', while a moulder commented that his firm 'were a well-noted place to learn', partly because it had a 'good foreman ... he learned you and you learned your trade', and partly because there was a variety of good-class work.[60] Thomas Okey, a basketmaker, summed up the advantages of working with a good journeyman: his man, Dan Murphy, was 'generally reputed to be the best craftsman in London ... He was a rapid, as well as an economic and excelling worker ... The value of such a pacemaker and master hand to me was inestimable'; his comments were echoed by an FLW respondent, a blacksmith — not himself an apprentice, but in a trade often learned by apprenticeship: 'You became qualified by practice you see ... and I had a very good blacksmith.'[61] Arthur Gill, a signwriter, perhaps expressed what was necessary most concisely: 'I was lucky to be working among real good craftsmen, as it gave me the chance of becoming one myself.'[62] This had its corollary: Paul Evett, a printer who learned in a provincial shop, 'became as good a display comp [compositor] as the others — nothing special';[63] but a negative comment such as this is unusual; most people, if they commented, did so favourably.

The journeyman's willingness to teach the young worker, and the value of the skill he had to impart, are not therefore in serious doubt. What is more questionable is his ability as a teacher. Given that there was no particular hurry to learn the work, so long as apprentices were prepared to put up with five to seven year apprenticeships and perhaps a spell as an improver afterwards, the slowness of learning by working with a journeyman might not seem to matter. It is true that research has shown that in repetition work special training, rather than on-the-job practice, not only cuts learning times but improves the workers' quality by preventing the picking-up of bad working habits; but it would be much more difficult to demonstrate this with skilled workers.[64] Nevertheless, the obvious truth remains that the established ways of doing things are not always the best ways; to this might be added the suggestion that 'learning by doing' fosters an exaggerated respect for established methods, and a reluctance to adopt new ones.

So far we have examined the importance of the journeyman in relation to the apprentices' education. The foreman's attitude, however, was also important. In many cases the apprentice might need to be moved around to different journeymen, and at some stages he would need to start working by himself. An apprentice ought to be moved around, for instance, if his journeyman specialised in certain work; or in engineering, some apprentices were taken on with the explicit understanding that they were to be given an all-round education, and would thus need to work in the turning and fitting shops;[65] more often turning and fitting were regarded as separate trades, of which the apprentice only learned one, but even then a turner, for instance, would ideally need to work on specialised machines, as well as on a variety of lathes.

Much work imposed a logical progression on the learner. Simple machines were mastered, and it was then natural to move on to more complex ones: occupations where this was the case included wood-cutting machinists, printing machine managers, and engineering turners.[66] Even so, an inefficient or ill-willed foreman might prevent this progression: as we noted J.T. Murphy, J.G. Riddell and Wal Hannington all spent some time on elementary machines, and the first two had to complain in order to obtain a move, while Wal Hannington simply left. Other work, such as joinery and compositing, did not impose a logical progression on the learning process, and this put the onus even more on the foreman – or in a small shop the employer – to ensure that the apprentice was fairly treated.

In spite of the complaints noted above, there is no evidence that there was widespread exploitation of apprentices, in the sense of using them as cheap labour to do elementary work. As we shall see when we come to explore the attitudes of firms towards apprentices, it was not necessarily in the firms' interests to do this. Furthermore foremen themselves were by no means always – in fact probably rarely – ill-willed towards apprentices. Only two FLW respondents record unpleasant memories of them, and this was because of their strictness, which was at least better than slackness. Foremen were often members of unions: there is widespread evidence of this on the North-East coast, while in London during the Edwardian period W.F. Watson records it as a natural state of affairs that the foreman should be an ASE member.[67] Given the unions' hostility to over-specialised apprentice-ships, such foremen must have had a beneficial effect on training.[68] It is not surprising, therefore, that Dearle found little evidence of any deliberate exploitation of trainees, and thought that the habit of putting them to repetition work early on was far less common than it had been, a verdict borne out by the FLW respondents, who as we have seen mostly quickly moved on to work alongside a journeyman.[69] Dearle thought that there was more danger that a boy would fail to get an all-round training because the firm he was with specialised in certain processes, although he does not say how frequent this was.[70] In some cases, failure may have been due to lack of communication rather than anything else − a factor which possibly accounts for Murphy's and Riddell's problems. One of the FLW respondents provides a striking instance of this. He was taken on by British Westinghouse in Manchester, a firm that was noted for having one of the earliest special training schemes for apprentices, complete with a separate apprentice school. But in spite of this, his training was 'quite haphazard'; there was little effective supervision, and although apprentices were meant to be moved in accordance with a plan of training, they could simply ask and be moved.[71]

Given that an ideal scheme might not work out in practice, there is evidence that firms did try to move their apprentices around. Thus Clayton and Shuttleworth, a big agricultural machinery firm in Lincoln, reported that they gave their apprentices an all-round training; the Elswick works of Armstrong, the armament firm, reported that their apprentices started in the plan-room, then made simple gauges, moved to lathes, and then on to fitting, marking-off and erecting − thus gaining a width of experience that was perhaps unusual.[72] W.F. Watson, who although he was not apprenticed became a skilled mechanic and worked at a large number of firms, thought that apprentices often ex-perienced a large variety of work, although more by chance than design: 'Circumstances often decided the branch of trade a lad would follow. He might spend a time with the fitters, and then be shifted to the machine-shop to work with the turners and machinists − planers, millers, shapers and slotters.'[73] In carpentry and joinery, the 1915 Report thought that many firms made an attempt to teach boys both hand and machine work.[74]

Watson's remarks point up another important factor in apprentice training. Since an apprentice's career was rarely the result of a carefully thought out plan by management, the apprentice himself should not be regarded as merely a helpless pawn. If he was dissatisfied he could complain — as Murphy and Riddell did: and it is worth noting that their complaints were successful — they both obtained a move to better-quality work. Many apprentices, as we have seen, had relations in the trade or even in the firm; these boys did not enter their apprenticeship knowing nothing of what it entailed; while their family, too, was in some position to monitor their progress. Finally, working and learning at the same time had a more positive side for the apprentice. In France, where apprenticeship survives alongside more purely technical training, the former is held to have some distinct advantages over the latter, one of which is that adolescents like to feel part of an adult team.[75]

Given that there were both advantages and disadvantages to educating an apprentice in the time-honoured way, alongside a journeyman in the shops, it would be interesting to know if apprentices were often segregated in separate training establishments. Such a practice, however, seems to have been extremely rare. British Westinghouse's scheme was regarded by contemporaries as unique, and even in that much of the training was in the shops; there had been a much earlier scheme started by the Lancashire firm of Mather and Platt, but this was more in the nature of technical education, and did not include a separate establishment for training the apprentices in the actual work process.[76] In 1925, just 26 engineering firms out of 1,573 surveyed had separate 'apprentice masters' whose sole duty was to train apprentices, and even this does not necessarily imply that the latter were trained outside the shops.[77] Dearle also referred to the practice of giving apprentices a separate room, but implied that it was rare, and certainly the biographical material has nothing to say about it.[78]

Perhaps the best short summary of the actual content of apprenticeship, and the philosophy behind it, comes from a well-known employer, Sir Benjamin Browne of the shipbuilding and engineering firm of Hawthorn Leslie. What it shows most clearly is the essential unity in apprenticeship of learning and working; the proximity of a skilled journeyman was a vital part of an apprenticeship, but his function was as much, or more, to act as an exemplar as to teach. As Sir Benjamin Browne saw it, after the errand-boy stage the lad started on simple work; he 'must keep at this until he can really do it well' — because even the simplest work should contain high-class workmanship. Then, 'a little reflection shows that as the boy is one degree better than when he came, he can now, with a very slight effort, undertake rather more difficult work, while a new boy can be brought in to undertake the first, or simplest, position'. And so the process went on. Browne thought that the great merit of practical workship training was this:

> the most important thing for an apprentice to learn is to know *good work from bad* ... Now, for this, it is necessary to see an enormous amount of work about and around him, on every side, all excellently done. Then he must learn to do this himself, and to do it with the greatest possible efficiency and economy ... Next ... he needs to see numerous examples of good workmen all about him whom he can imitate.[79]

Dearle summed up the implications of these remarks: 'actual teaching often plays a smaller part than the knowledge which a boy instinctively acquires by continuously being among skilled men and seeing them at work'.[80]

Artisan Apprenticeship

Before moving on to a discussion of other methods of learning manual work, certain specific aspects of learning by regular service should be considered.

So far no attempt has been made to distinguish artisan-type apprenticeships, and indeed some of the comments quoted above originate from workers who learned their trade in artisan workshops. On the face of it, artisan apprentices had two sorts of advantage over other apprentices. They were taught, not by a paid journeyman, but by their employer; and they received a more all-round training. As we have seen, however, the Webbs' view that journeymen were unwilling to teach apprentices seems to have had no foundation. The Webbs argued that journeymen did not like apprentices because the latter represented a potential threat to the journeymen's livelihood, although of course just the same argument could be applied to small employers. The evidence shows that in practice most of those who taught apprentices, whether journeymen or small employers, did not act out of Hobbesian motives of self-interest or fear, but, subject in the case of journeymen to their employer not attempting to make excessive use of apprentices, were perfectly willing to teach the latter.

What does seem probable is that a higher proportion of the apprentices taken by small employers were members of a latter's family, and thus may have benefited from extra personal attention. Out of 36 apprenticed and non-apprenticed FLW respondents in engineering and metals, woodworking, and miscellaneous skilled occupations, who were not artisan-type workers, seven seem to have had a close relationship with their father or another relative while learning their work, while out of the 13 artisan workers six seem to have had a similar connection.[81]

It could be more forcibly argued that an advantage of artisan-type appreticeship was that a small country shop was likely to have a wider variety of work, although this would seem to be less likely in a large town, where the employer might act as a sub-contractor and specialise; as we have seen there was a preference in London for 'country-trained' carpenters and joiners for this reason. But the importance of the small shop can be exaggerated: Table 5.8 suggests that, in engineering in particular, shops with less than 20 workers, which was probably the practical upper limit for the owner to also be able to work in the shop, or even concern himself with the details of manual work, only employed a small minority of apprentices. In building the influence of the small firm was considerably greater, but in woodworking, it was limited.

Three comments can be made about these figures. First, there was no doubt some increase in concentration between the 1900s and 1925, and thus the small shop was probably rather more important before the war; the difference, however, is unlikely to have been very great. Second, the samples may be inaccurate: in engineering, all firms with more than 100 workers were circularised, but only a 'substantial proportion' of the others;[82] nevertheless, the discrepancy between the number of apprentices employed by the small and large firms is so great that even if the former number was doubled or trebled it would not make a great deal of difference; and in building and woodworking it was stated that 'the sample covered by the inquiry may confidently be taken as representative of the whole industry'.[83] Third, as an influence tending the other way, Liepmann has pointed out that no such great discrepancy in the worker/apprentice ratio between different sizes of firms was apparent in the 1950s; she suggests that small firms which did not employ apprentices may not have replied to the 1925 survey;[84] whether or not this was the case, it does not alter the basic point that only a minority of apprentices were trained in very small shops, except in building. Here the small shop, with its — rather hypothetical — advantages was undoubtedly fairly important even if Liepmann's point is correct.

Table 5.8: Number of Apprentices by Firm Size

	Engineering		Building		Woodworking	
Size of firm	1	2	1	2	1	2
Less than 5	47	2.3	957	2.4	40	1.9
5-10	111	3.4	1,225	3.8	50	4.2
10-20	384	4.8	1,586	5.0	77	5.8
20-30)						
30-40)	1,307	6.6	670	6.9	177	5.9
40-50)						
50-100	2,509	6.9	1,190	10.0	161	9.0
100-200	5,268	8.4	1,321	12.4	259	11.8
200-500	9,518	9.4	1,113	15.5	395	14.1
500-1,000	7,482	12.5	494	19.4		
1,000-3,000	11,820	11.9				
3,000+	5,477	18.9				
1,000-5,000			377	27.5		
a) Total apprentices	43,923		10,206		1,159	
b) Total apprentices in firms with less than 20 workers	542		3,768		167	
b) as % of a)	1.2%		36.9%		14.4%	

Column 1: Number of apprentices.
Column 2: Ratio of all male workers in firm to male apprentices.
Source: 1925 Report, vol. VII, p.27.

In the older crafts, of course, which were not covered very systematically in 1925, we would expect small workshops to be much more predominant. The 1906 Wages Census is not much help to us, because although it gives figures for apprentices in the bespoke branches of boot and shoe making and tailoring, the internal evidence of the figures makes it clear that the Census did not attempt to cover artisan-type workshops.[85] The evidence of the FLW survey and other oral evidence, as well as the findings of Eric Hopkins for Stourbridge, certainly suggests that small employers in old-established trades *did* take apprentices, and some guesstimates of their numbers are made in Appendix 1 to this chapter. Since the number of workers in such old trades declined quite slowly, we can conclude that artisan-type apprenticeships were still very much a reality in early-twentieth century Britain.

A surprising number of these craft skills could be utilised in new industries after the war. Carpenters and joiners, of course, could transfer to many industries, even, as one FLW respondent did in the First World War, to aircraft manufacture; watchmakers could become precision toolmakers, as another respondent did during the war; leather workers could find jobs in the motor industry — a respondent joined

Leylands in 1936;[86] carriage-builders could turn to motor-vehicles, and blacksmiths were always useful and necessary, in large-scale industry as well as small. Some occupations, such as basket-making or coopering, had little long-term future, but in general the old craft skills seem to have had a useful part to play in the new industries.[87] This was mainly a post-war development, however, and what is most striking is their persistence until the First World War.

Maintenance Workers

Against this slow decline in old crafts can be set a probable increase in the number of workers concerned with the maintenance of large plants. Whether maintenance workers have increased in numbers faster than the workforce as a whole has grown is a theoretically interesting question, which has not been subject to much empirical investigation. Since investment is as likely to be capital as labour saving, and since there is no necessary reason why the productivity of maintenance workers should not increase as fast as the productivity of other workers, there would seem no necessary reason for the proportion of maintenance workers to increase as a proportion of total workers. A fairly recent survey on the introduction of highly automated plant, however, suggests that the proportion of maintenance workers does in general increase slightly.[88] It seems likely that labour productivity in maintenance (and repair) work does not in fact increase as rapidly as labour productivity in other work, because the former is less easy to routinise; even where a large plant is designed to facilitate easy maintenance, the ageing of the plant will increase the maintenance and repair load again.

Clearly empirical investigations into secular changes in the proportion of maintenance workers are necessary before we can make any definite statements about them; we can say something, however, about the proportion in our period. The 1906 Wages Census gave the number of 'mechanics' in various industries, and the 1921 Census was the first to give a detailed breakdown of non-production workers in each industry. Some of these figures are shown in Table 5.9, although it should be noted that they are not directly comparable, as the 1906 figures almost certainly included some semi-skilled workers, while in the 1921 figures I have excluded all such workers, as well as some minor groups of skilled workers; thus this total includes only the major groups in each industry, such as smiths, fitters, carpenters and electricians.

Table 5.9: Proportion of Maintenance Workers (Various Industries)[89]

Industry	1906 % of all workers	1921 % of all workers	1921 absolute nos.
Gas	3.8)	7.6	7,361
Electricity	9.3)		
Pig-iron		8.8	2,762
Chemicals	10.0	12.3*	2,042
Cotton (carding, spinning)		1.9	1,758
Grainmilling	4.0		
Paper	8.1	5.9	1,937
Brewing	6.9	5.1	3,251
Mining		2.9	32,975

*Heavy chemicals

As the figures indicate, the proportion of maintenance workers varied, with the more capital intensive industries, or those like chemicals and steel which imposed heavy wear on their equipment, employing a higher proportion. In total, there were certainly a considerable number, and the 1915 Report makes it clear that many of these workers were recruited by apprenticeship within the factories or works concerned.[90] Finally, individual figures for one firm, interesting for illustrative purposes, are shown in Table 5.10.

Table 5.10: Maintenance Workers in a Papermill[91]

Date	Total workers (approx.)	Millwrights/ engineers	Apprentice ditto	Joiners	Black-smith	Hammer-men
1871	40	2		1		
1881	70	2	1	1		
1891	85	3	1	1		
1901	80	1	4	1	1	1
1911	85	2	3	2	1	1

Given that there was probably some increase in the proportion of maintenance workers to total workers, and that many maintenance departments took apprentices, what implications does this have for apprenticeship as a whole?

It would seem likely that maintenance work provided good conditions for effective apprentice training. The position of maintenance workers was a strong one, both tactically because of their knowledge of the factory they worked in and strategically because of the increasing demand for their services, and they were unlikely to feel threatened by apprentices. Furthermore, there was likely to be a wide variety of work, because of the varying age of the machinery in most factories, unless the maintenance department was itself large and specialised; and perhaps most important, maintenance workers, although relatively independent, were in a position of considerable responsibility because of the machinery under their care, and therefore had to make sure that their apprentices were properly trained. Thus the social relations in maintenance departments were perhaps more akin to those in artisan workshops than to those in large factories, while at the same time both the opportunities for training, and the incentive for the training to be performed efficiently, were possibly greater than in either workshops or factories.

Non-apprenticed Workers

Although most of the skilled work which was learnt by regular service involved apprenticeship, there were types of work, both skilled and less-skilled, which did not. Some of the artisan workers in the FLW survey, for instance, do not seem to have had a formal apprenticeship, especially where they entered the firm of a relative who could be expected to give them personal attention. Informal apprenticeship to one's father also obtained in some non-artisan trades, notably some of the Sheffield trades and stonemasonry; the Webbs distinguished it as patrimony, and pointed out that it had the distinct feature that the boy was not apprenticed at all, or apprenticed to the journeyman — that is his father — rather than to the employer.[92] Nevertheless, since the actual method of teaching was presumably the same as if the trainee had been regularly bound, and as most fathers could be expected to teach their sons as well as they could, it seems sensible to classify patrimony as essentially the same as apprenticeship.

Certain types of learning, while they fall into the category of regular service, exhibit features which mark them out from apprenticeship. Instead of allowing the apprentice to gradually absorb his skill from working with a journeyman, instruction, usually of a fairly limited skill, was intensive but lasted for a much shorter period. Particularly characteristic of this method were transport occupations. Electric tram drivers required four weeks' training if they were converting from horse trams;[93] horse carmen converting to lorries — although few would have done this before the First World War — required six weeks' 'fairly constant training'; experienced motor-vehicle drivers required an extra four weeks' training to become bus drivers.[94]

As we shall see, experience of horse-drawn vehicles was initially acquired by some combination of following-up, migration and picking-up, rather than regular service, and the same applies to railway work. Nevertheless, grades such as guard and signalman required from two to four weeks' training, although presumably in this case the training was mainly to acquire knowledge, rather than manual skill.[95]

Short intensive training was also characteristic of certain occupations mentioned earlier, in particular tanning and carpet-weaving, where the trainee paid an experienced worker to teach him the job; certainly training was relatively brief in the case of the latter, lasting for a year at most, and we can infer that any training which required a worker to part with ready cash was expected to give a fairly rapid return. As with railway work, however, the trainees in both these occupations had some acquaintanceship with the industry already.

One branch of work which required much more skill was not learnt by apprenticeship. This was gas-fitting, where at least two London companies had long and carefully arranged training schemes. One of these, shown in the 1915 Report, incorporated some instruction which would have been available at any technical class, such as in drawing and mathematics, but its special character lay in its emphasis on direct instruction in the workshops, which can be contrasted to the *ad hoc* acquisition of skill which was characteristic of apprenticeship.[96] Nevertheless, the important thing about this scheme was its uniqueness; even the much-vaunted British Westinghouse training plan did not, as we have seen, give the apprentice much systematic direct instruction of this kind.

Notes

1. See Appendix 1 to this chapter.
2. L.T.C. Rolt started his engineering career in the 1920s at a country jobbing shop with seven workers: L.T.C. Rolt, *Landscape with Machines* (1971), p. 66.
3. N.B. Dearle, *Industrial Training* (1914), p. 20.
4. 1925 Report, vol. VII, p. 8; 1915 Report, p. 55.
5. 1925 Report, vol. VII, p. 34.
6. Ibid., pp. 158-60.
7. Charles Booth *et al.*, *Life and Labour of the People of London*, 2nd series, *Industry* (5 vols. 1903), vol. 1, pp. 312-13; K. Hudson, *Working to Rule*, 1970, p. 61; 1925 Report, vol. VI, pp. 15; 1915 Report, p. 57.
8. G. Crossick, *An Artisan Elite in Victorian England* (1978), Tables 6.4 and 6.5.
9. Dearle, *Training*, p. 240; S.J. Chapman and W. Abbot, 'The Tendency of

Children to Follow their Fathers' Trades', *Journal of the Royal Statistical Society*, vol. LXXVI, (1912-13), pp. 509-604. (This covered a total of 4,196 children.) Trade and continuation schools are discussed in Chapter 10.

10. Dearle, *Training*, p. 193. Other minor sources of recruits were Apprenticeship and Skilled Employment Associations, set up in various towns in the 1900s in response to fears about the decline in apprenticeship. Their placement figures of 600 to 700 in the period 1910-11, or about 1 per cent of the annual recruitment to apprenticeships, illustrate their lack of importance compared with traditional methods of recruitment. Other placement institutions (The National Institution of Apprenticeship and the Jewish Board of Guardians) were similarly unimportant, although the latter may have made a real contribution in the limited area in which it operated. 1915 Report, pp. xviii-xix.

11. 1915 Report, pp. 92-111; Standard VII was the highest grade in elementary schools, and only a few children reached it.

12. PRO, Lab. 41:200.

13. 1915 Report, pp. 56-9; 1925 Report, vol. VI, p. 87.

14. Jackson Report, pp. 1082 and 1078; Dearle, *Training*, p. 60; S. and B. Webb, *Industrial Democracy* (1920 edn), p. 456.

15. PP 1911, vol. LXXXVIII, p. 117. It should be noted that in some minor branches of engineering the ratio of apprentices to other boys was much lower.

16. PP 1910, vol. LXXXIV, p. 13; PP 1912-13, vol. CVIII, p. 354; PP 1911, vol. LXXXVIII, p. 160. In calculating the ratio in building, improvers have been added to apprentices, as they were akin; see this chapter, below.

17. Jackson Report, pp. 1078-82; 1925 Report, vol. VII, pp. 18, 36, 170.

18. C.B. Hawkins, *Norwich, A Social Study* (1910), p. 194.

19. 1925 Report, vol. VII, p. 179; this apparently covers apprentices only, and not learners.

20. As an illustration of this, a Board of Trade handbook on Yorkshire trades stated that apprenticeship in engineering *always* ceased at 21; *Handbook on Yorkshire Trades* (HMSO, 1914), p. 4.

21. Dearle, *Training*, pp. 92ff; George Acorn, *One of a Multitude* (1911), pp. 156-7.

22. 1915 Report, pp. 8 and 18; the ratio of ordinary apprentices to improvers in building in 1906 was 5.3:1; PP 1910, vol. LXXXIV, p. 13.

23. Booth, *Industry*, vol. 1, p. 299; this refers to engineering; Booth did not give the ratio in other industries.

24. Ibid., pp. 182 and 41.

25. Dearle, *Training*, pp. 42-3.

26. Booth, *Industry*, vol. I, p. 299.

27. 1925 Report, vol. VII, p. 180.

28. PRO, Lab. 41:200.

29. John Burnett, *Useful Toil* (Pelican edn, 1977), p. 309.

30. Jackson Report, p. 133; PRO Lab. 41:200.

31. In 8 of the first 12 groups shown in Table 5.6, less than 2 per cent of apprentices earned under 3s per week. Low wages might be paid in out-of-the-way areas − for instance de Rousiers found that engineering apprentices in Galashiels started at 3s per week, rising by 1s per week per annum. Dearle concluded that 4s 6d to 5s was the most common starting wage in most areas. 1915 Report, pp. 56 and 68 (for shipbuilding); P. de Rousiers, *The Labour Question in Britain* (1896), p. 314; Dearle, *Training*, pp. 245-53.

32. Dearle, *Training*, pp. 248-58, 264.

33. From the 1906 Wages Census. Shipbuilding has been omitted because of the peculiar nature of shipbuilding apprenticeships (see discussion in Chapter 7; apprentices' wages were higher than those of other boys). Cotton and woollen

wages have been adjusted to exclude half-timers.

Dearle gave estimates of juvenile wages based on the Wage Census (pp. 250-1), but his figures were not always considered consistently; mine have all been calculated on the basis of the full-time earnings of time and piece workers, weighted according to their respective numbers.

34. The Jackson Report notes (p. 133) that one employer accounted for the increase in the wages of *all* boys that had taken place over the past few years by citing better education, which increased their adaptability and hence their value to the employer. This explanation would certainly square with declining relative (but not absolute) differentials, since the investment in elementary education was roughly equal for all boys, apprenticed or not.

35. 1925 Report, vol. VII, p. 61.

36. 1915 Report, p. 55; turnover rates in some occupations may have been somewhat higher before the war; in printing, Musson refers to the continued existence of 'turnovers' – apprentices who had broken their engagement after two or three years – up to the war; A.E. Musson, *The Typographical Association* (1954), p. 211.

37. Sylvia Price, 'Clyde Riveters Earnings, 1889-1913', unpublished paper, p. 24; I am extremely grateful to Mrs Price for allowing me to look at this paper.

38. E. Austin, *The Law Relating to Apprentices* (1890), pp. 17-18; 1925 Report, vol. VII, p. 15.

39. 1915 Report, p 55; 1925 Report, vol. VII, p. 19.

40. 1915 Report, p. 55.

41. Ibid., p. 55; confirmed in the Board of Trade, *Handbook on Yorkshire Trades*, p. 4, where exactly the same thing is said.

42. 1925 Report, vol. VII, p. 34. Mr W.W. Knox has suggested to me that indentured apprenticeship was valued by employers because it increased their control over apprentices who could be used, for instance, as strikebreakers. While I would not disagree with this interpretation, the fact that indentured apprenticeships were in the minority suggests that this cannot be used as a general explanation of the existence of apprenticeship. It is important to note in this context that the 1925 Report found that there was no less likelihood of an indentured apprentice *failing* to complete his contract than of an unindentured apprentice doing likewise; ibid., vol. VII, p. 61.

43. Dearle, *Training*, p. 266.

44. 1925 Report, vol. VI, p. 39.

45. Dearle, *Training*, p. 260.

46. 1925 Report, vol. VI, pp. 39-40.

47. Burnett, *Useful Toil*, p. 308.

48. Dearle, *Training*, p. 271.

49. 1925 Report, vol. VI, p. 39; favourable comment in more recent years is noted in D.J. Lee, 'Craft Unions and the Force of Tradition: the case of Apprenticeship', *British Journal of Industrial Relations*, vol. XVII, no. 1 (March 1979), p. 41.

50. Thomas Wright, *Some Habits and Customs of the Working Classes* (1867), pp. 91 and 99; Alfred Herbert, 'Memories', *Machine-Tool Review*, XLI (Sept.-Oct. 1953), pp. 97-8.

51. W.F. Watson, *Machines and Men* (1935), p. 18.

52. Burnett, *Useful Toil*, pp. 347-55 for the last reference cited; FLW nos. 48, 102, 140, 146, 339, 41, 296, 134, 56 for various references to training; one respondent (181) recorded unfavourable comments, although not specifically about the quality of training. Tom Bell, a moulder, also commented negatively about journeymen's attitudes: 'the apprentices were left to shift for themselves and looked upon [by the workers] as cheap competitive labour'; T. Bell,

Pioneering Days (1941), p. 62.

53.　Dearle, *Training*, p. 271.

54.　In fact, the method adopted by coopers, and apparently with the leather-worker alluded to as well, was for the journeyman to receive the joint earnings and give the apprentice a few shillings at the end of the week. When the apprentice was proficient he earned 'thirds' — that is a third of the normal wage — and the employer then received a share, as a return for his patronage. It was obviously in the interest of the journeyman to teach the apprentice properly, and for the employer to ensure that this was done, because the apprentice was of more value to them as a skilled worker than an unskilled boy; K. Kilby, *The Cooper and His Trade* (1971), p. 169.

55.　George Howell, 'Trade Unions and Apprenticeship', *Contemporary Review*, vol. XXX (1877), pp. 845 and 847.

56.　Booth, *Industry*, vol. 2, pp. 38-9, 66.

57.　Ibid., p. 127.

58.　1915 Report, pp. 189, 193-4.

59.　Rolt, *Landscape with Machines*, pp. 87 and 104.

60.　FLW respondents nos. 41, 438, 134.

61.　T. Okey, *A Basketful of Memories* (1930), p. 27; FLW respondent no. 425.

62.　Burnett, *Useful Toil*, p. 343; Arthur Gill was not formally apprenticed, but was given the opportunity to learn the trade.

63.　Ibid., p. 332.

64.　W.D. Seymour, *Industrial Skills* (1967), p. 163.

65.　Thus an FLW respondent in a North-Eastern marine engineering firm learned turning, but also worked on erecting engines in ships; see also comments below.

66.　Dearle, *Training*, p. 268.

67.　Watson, *Machines and Men*, pp. 19, 31, 80-2; J.F. Clarke, 'Labour Relations in Engineering and Shipbuilding on the North-East Coast in the Second Half of the Nineteenth Century', unpublished MA thesis, University of Newcastle, 1966, pp. 225-30.

68.　Webbs, *Industrial Democracy*, Ch. X, section a. In recent years, unions like the printers and engineers seem to have copied what was at that time only a practice of the Boilermakers, in insisting upon a rigid demarcation between separate trades (e.g. riveting and plating). But even such recognition of the inevitability of specialisation, which is then turned to the union's own ends, is not incompatible with insistence upon an adequate training. As Turner argues, it is always in the unions' interests to insist upon this.

69.　Dearle, *Training*, pp. 264 and 275. The problems of relying, as commentators on apprenticeship tend to, on a limited range of autobiographical material which they happen to be acquainted with, are illustrated by comparing the evidence of T. Jackson with the comments of Dearle; Jackson, an apprentice in a large London printing firm in the 1890s, considered that apprentices provided cheap labour (*Solo Trumpet* (1953), p. 10). Dearle said of printing trade apprenticeships: 'A certain number of complaints there must be, but they are far fewer than in other trades. More than one of the men's leaders, indeed, informed me that there was little reason to complain of the way in which the boys were taught, whilst the employers do far more than employers in most industries to encourage attendance at Trade and Technical Classes.'; Dearle, *Training*, p. 179. Jackson's comments are no doubt perfectly fair in relation to his firm, but Dearle had a much broader conspectus.

70.　Dearle, *Training*, p. 275.

71.　FLW no. 127; the scheme is described in detail in A.P.M. Fleming and

J.G. Pearce, *Principles of Apprentice Training* (1916), pp. 141ff.
72. 1915 Report, pp. 95 and 99.
73. Watson, *Machines and Men*, p. 18.
74. 1915 Report, pp. 12ff.
75. G. Williams, *Apprenticeship in Europe* (1963), pp. 90ff.
76. See Chapter 10.
77. 1925 Report, Vol. VI, p. 39; the Report also referred to a 'few' firms with special apprentice schools, but only for the first six months or so; ibid., p.40.
78. Dearle, *Training*, p. 263.
79. 1915 Report, p. 127.
80. Dearle, *Training*, p. 265.
81. Non-artisan: FLW respondents nos. 219, 339, 12, 134, 307, 340, 94.
     Artisan: FLW respondents nos. 10, 41, 186, 360, 276, 257.
82. 1925 Report, vol. VI, pp. 5-6.
83. Ibid., vol. II, p.6.
84. K. Liepmann, *Apprenticeship* (1960), pp. 58, 60-1.
85. See Appendix 1 to this chapter.
86. FLW respondents nos. 41, 94, 56.
87. Although wet coopering, the most skilled branch of the trade, remained surprisingly buoyant until the 1940s; Kilby, *The Cooper*, p.16.
88. J.R. Bright, *Automation and Management* (Boston, 1958), pp. 185ff; of the firms Bright specifically studied, seven registered increases in the proportion of maintenance operatives, two declines, and four no change; there was no pattern in the size of plants – plants in each of the three categories were large and small; ibid., pp. 196-7.
89. 1906 Wages Census; 1921 printed census papers.
90. 1915 Report, pp. 133 (iron and steel works), 135 (tinplate works), 324 (corn mills), 342 (breweries), 386 (gasworks – maintenance, not gas fitting), and note p. 171 (cotton): 'among the numerous mechanics employed in the mills and factory apprentices are common', and p. 254: 'apprentices are found in the mechanics' and millwrights department of every large paper mill'.
91. These figures were recorded from a papermill's wages book at the beginning of each year – papermill employment was very stable, so they accurately reflect the pattern throughout the year; they come from a Scottish mill, Jas. Lovell and Co.; SRO, GD. 272/36 onwards.
92. Webbs, *Industrial Democracy*, pp. 458-62.
93. J.P. McKay, *Tramways and Trolleys* (Princeton, 1976), pp. 236-7 (figures from Germany).
94. *New Survey of London*, vol. VIII, pp. 38 and 85.
95. P.W. Kingsford, *Victorian Railwaymen* (1970), p. 54.
96. 1915 Report, pp. 386-7; discussed further in Chapter 10.

Appendix 1: Apprentice Numbers

The number of apprentices (males only) in 1906 has been calculated mainly from the 1906 Wages Census, with some help from other sources. The computation is only intended as a very rough guide, and some of the problems with it are pointed out in the notes below, which refer to the various columns and occupations. No attempt has been made to distinguish learners from apprentices; given the confusion, which has been discussed in Chapter 5, between the two, it seems probable that learners were usually counted as apprentices in 1906.

Columns 1 and 2. These columns are intended to establish the number of male workers (including apprentices) in the various industries in 1906, where no figures at all are given in the Wages Census; and, where figures are given, but it is not clear what percentage of workers in an industry are covered, an estimate is put in Column 2 so that this percentage can be established. The figures in Column 2 are calculated from the mean figures of the 1901 and 1911 England and Wales Censuses, plus 20 per cent for Scotland and Ireland.

Column 3. Where the Wages Census unambiguously gives the percentage of workers covered in an industry, these percentages have been used. Otherwise they are calculated from Column 1 as a percentage of Column 2.

Column 4. This column is self-explanatory.

Column 5. This is calculated in most cases by simply multiplying Column 4 by the approximate figure to bring it up to 100 per cent. In a few cases where the Wages Census does not cover the occupation, other methods have been used, as detailed in the marginal notes.

Column 6. Figures from 1925 Report, vol. VII, p. 37. The number of apprentices *and* learners has been given, as it is probable that in 1906 learners were counted as apprentices. Where the figure for 1925 is roughly comparable with that for 1906, no further comment has been made. Where is it substantially different, a marginal note is added.

Table 5.11: Number of Apprentices, 1906 and 1925

	1 Nos. in 1906 Wages Census	2 Nos. in industry in 1906	3 % covered by Census	4 No. of apprentices in Census	5 Total no. of apprentices (nearest 100)	6 No. of apprentices and learners in 1925	
Engineering			61%	57,402	94,100	97,000	a
Shipbuilding			78%	14,082	18,100	42,500	a
Railway carriage and wagon			75%	3,387	4,500		a
Iron and steel					5,000	4,600	b
Other metal					20,000	28,000	c
Wire drawing etc.	7,491	19,240	39%	452	1,200		
Gold, silver, electroplate	5,367	35,959	15%	298	2,000	2,250	
Electrical and telegraph	11,507	59,995	19%	443	2,300	7,500	d
Building			12%	12,019	100,200	80,000	e
Printing, lithography, paper stationery	47,549	139,277	34%	5,538	16,300	18,000	f
Bookbinding	4,720	14,468	33%	680	2,100		
Various textile			44%	1,821	4,100	4,650	g
Tailoring			29%	1,195	4,100	12,000	h
Shoemaking			33%	1,103	3,300	4,000	h
Hatting			32%	238	700		
Utilities			100%	668	700		i
Railway work			100%	1,175	1,200		j
Pottery	10,157	45,955	22%	733	3,300	2,750	
Glass	6,761	32,723	21%	420	2,000	1,500	
Baking and confectionery	17,920	86,969	21%	1,328	6,300	5,000	k
Leather-makers, saddlers, harness		51,828			3,800	1,100	l
Cabinet-making	21,678	117,416	18%	2,996	16,600	8,500	m

Table 5.11 (continued)

	1 Nos. in 1906 Wages Census	2 Nos in industry in 1906	3 % covered by Census	4 No. of apprentices in Census	5 Total no. of apprentices (nearest 100)	6 No. of apprentices and learners in 1925	
Sawmilling	20,660	42,344	49%	1,751	3,600	4,500	m
Coach-building, car-body making	10,429	34,813	30%	1,228	4,100		n
Wheelwrights		27,665			2,100		n
Coopers		17,854			1,400		
Brushmakers	2,685	10,384	26%	209	800		n
Basket-weavers		11,011			800		
Other artisan (shoemakers, tailors)	110,000				8,500		o
Miscellaneous maintenance workers					10,000		p
TOTAL					343,200	368,500	q

Notes

a) The 1925 figures for shipbuilding also include marine engineering. The combined total for engineering, shipbuilding and railway carriage and wagon in 1906 is 116,500, or 14.6 per cent of all workers in the industries concerned; the combined total for the first two in 1925 is 139,500, or 10.4 per cent of all workers. Given the growth of the lighter sectors of engineering, which used more semi-skilled labour, this decline seems plausible.

b) Probably all maintenance workers. Since more iron and steel was produced in the 1900s than in the 1920s (12-16m tons against a maximum of 13m), the figure of 5,000 apprentices for 1906 is possibly conservative.

c) The 1925 figures probably comprises wire drawing and part of the electrical and telegraph industry, plus (probably) estimates for motor repair shops, tinsmiths, coppersmiths, blacksmiths, watchmakers etc. My estimate, based loosely on the 1925 figure, is exceedingly uncertain; given the decline in artisan workshops, it is probably conservative.

d) The 1925 figure is for electrical contracting only. Although this industry was in its infancy in 1906, it is probably underrepresented in the Census as there were large numbers of small firms.

e) The main defect of this estimate is that it is extrapolated from a small percentage of the industry. The 1925 figure is from an industry that was some 20 per cent smaller, but with an apparently lower ratio of journeymen to apprentices (see below), implying that the number of apprentices in 1925 should be similar to the number in 1906. The figures in the 1925 Report should be treated with caution, however.

f) The industry was much the same size in 1925 as in 1906, but in this case the journeyman/apprentice ratio had apparently risen, implying that the number of apprentices should have fallen, or that the 1906 figures are too low. Again, the comparison with 1925 should be treated with caution.

g) Apprentice overlookers and other apprentices in minor trades. Also presumably apprentices in maintenance work.

h) The internal evidence of the figures suggests that the number of tailors and boot and shoe makers was greatly understated by the Wages Census, presumably because it omitted artisan workshops. Thus the Wages Census figures compared with 1901 Census figures for employees and own account workers (not employers) show:

	a) Wage Census	b) 1901 Census	a) as % of b)
Tailors	58,839	105,675	56%
Boot and shoe	86,404	164,821	52%

This suggests that on a conservative computation some 40,000 tailors and 70,000 boot and shoe makers should be added (see note o). It also helps to account for the discrepancy between the 1906 and 1925 figures. See also note o.

i) Probably maintenance work.

j) This is a puzzle. It was probably partly accounted for by apprentices to signal-fitting, and perhaps premium apprentices.

k) Food, drink *and* tobacco in 1925. There was probably a decline in the number of small bakeries which were more likely to take apprentices.

l) The decline is plausible. Saddlery and harness-making were still substantial industries in the 1900s, but not by the 1920s; general leatherwork was affected increasingly by mechanisation. See note n for calculation of apprentice numbers.

m)   My category of cabinet-making probably includes some trades which were counted under sawmilling in 1925. The overall decline can be accounted for by the mechanisation of cabinet-making. Although there were apprentices to the trade of woodcutting machinist, more of the work was semi-skilled and would not be recruited by apprenticeship.

n)   All these trades were ones where the future must have seemed uncertain. As a result I have applied to them the low worker/apprentice ratio of brush-makers, a similarly slowly declining artisan trade. The use of the term 'apprentice' in these trades is problematic, because many boys were probably not bound, even by verbal agreement, simply because they learned from their own relatives. To all intents and purposes they were apprentices.

o)   As described in note h, there were a large number — I have estimated 110,000 — artisan-type workers in these trades not covered by the Wages Census. I have adopted the brushmakers formula — see note n) for estimating the number of apprentices. This figure is subject to considerable uncertainty.

p)   The 1925 Report gives figures of 2,500 apprentices for chemical, and 750 for brick and tile; most of these must have been learning maintenance work. There were large numbers of maintenance workers in e.g. coal, brewing and papermaking (38,500 in these industries in 1921 — see Table 5.9). But my figure of 10,000 apprentices is a guess, although it seems to me unlikely that it is too high.

q)   The 1925 total includes a large number of unclassified apprentices; 1906 and 1925 exclude distributive and mercantile marine apprentices.

As a final check to the figures, the ratio of journeymen to apprentices in certain trades in 1909 and 1925 can be compared (see Table 5.12). The 1909 figures do rest on a small sample (16,863 apprentices in *all* industries), and insofar as they indicate decreases or increases in individual categories should be treated with caution. But taking one with another, the figures for the two dates are roughly comparable, some categories changing in one direction and some in another; this suggests that the impression given by direct comparison of numbers, that there was no major *overall* change, is correct.

It is interesting to estimate the proportion of apprentices to all young workers. The problem is that we cannot estimate the number of apprentices at one year of age — say 17, when practically all apprentices would have started and few if any finished. We only have the total number of apprentices of *all* ages, in one year (1906).

As we have seen, the modal duration of apprenticeships was five years (Table 5.3); more recorded apprenticeships were over five years than under, but many artisan apprenticeships may have lasted less than five years. If we take five years as the mean duration of apprenticeships, then we can compare the number of apprentices in 1906 with the total number of young workers.

The latter figure has been estimated by taking the arithmetic mean of the Census figures of 1901 and 1911 for males aged 15 to 19 (incorporating England and Wales, Scotland, and Ireland). The result is shown in Table 5.13.

Table 5.12: Journeyman/Apprentice Ratio, 1909 and 1925

Industry	Occupation	No. of Journeymen per apprentice or learner	
		1909	1925
Building	Bricklayers	5.3	3.8
	Masons	5.2	4.5
	Carpenters and joiners	4.3	3.8
	Painters and decorators	4.2	3.9
	Slaters and tilers	3.4	3.1
	Plasterers	3.9	3.2
	Plumbers	2.0	1.7
Printing	Compositors	3.7	4.1
	Stereotypers	2.8	4.6
	Letterpress machine minders	2.9	4.0
	Lithographers	5.0	5.0
Shipbuilding and marine engineering	Platers and boilermakers	4.0	3.6
	Riveters	6.1	3.7
	Shipwrights	2.0	2.0
	Fitters	2.0	2.2
	Machine tool workers	2.0	3.1
	Joiners	4.5	1.2
	Plumbers	4.1	1.0
Engineering	Fitters and erectors	2.4	2.8
	Turners and machinists	2.6	2.0
	Pattern-makers	2.3	1.3
Furniture	Cabinet-makers and joiners	4.3	4.8
	French polishers	4.0	3.9
	Upholsterers	2.9	3.1
	Woodcutting machinists	3.9	1.5

Source: 1925 Report, vol. VII, pp. 43-4.

Table 5.13: Proportion of Apprentices, 1906

Estimated number of occupied males aged 15-19	1,882,855
Estimated number of all males aged 15-19	2,088,068
Estimated number of apprentices and learners	343,200
No. of apprentices and learners as % of occupied males aged 15-19	18.2%
No. of apprentices and learners as % of all males aged 15-19	16.4%
Add distributive and mercantile marine apprentices (13.3% of total in 1925; calculated on same basis for 1906)	52,500
Total	395,700
Total as % of all occupied males aged 15-19	21.0%

Appendix 2: Premium Apprenticeship

There seems little doubt that premium apprenticeship developed from the same root as ordinary trade apprenticeship – that is from apprenticeship in the high-class trades like cabinet-making and coach-building. In the days when workshops were small and every man could expect to eventually become a master (even if many did not), an ordinary apprenticeship encompassed all that needed to be known of the trade. As time went by, industrial units grew larger and their organisation more complicated, while the amount of technological knowledge needed in order to run a large factory successfully also increased: these developments were particularly marked in engineering.

Premium apprenticeships therefore grew up as a special type, in which an all-round training was given, designed to fit the apprentice for management. Clearly this was much more expensive to the employer than an ordinary trade apprenticeship, and as a result premium apprentices paid quite large sums of money at the outset; how their wages compared with those of ordinary trade apprentices is not very clear, but given a payment of £50-100 even quite substantial wages, for which there is no evidence, would barely have covered the initial outlay.[1]

Evidence for the wide use of such apprenticeships in the engineering industry, as opposed to the profession of civil engineering, is scattered, but what is there is suggestive. A short article in the *Journal of Careers* for 1928 stated that: 'Premium apprenticeship as a method of training, especially for the engineering profession and for the merchant service, is not nearly so widespread as it was some years ago . . . in many other occupations, not only professional, but business, where a premium of £100 or more was at one time rigidly enforced for all new entrants, boys are now accepted without charge, and given moderate pay from the outset . . . In engineering the drop in the proportion of premium apprentices during the last twenty years has been very considerable. Though some of the leading firms still retain the system, it is now used most by firms operating on a moderate scale.'[2]

This excerpt implies that premium apprenticeship was widespread in industry, as well as in the professions, before the First World War. Even after the war, it still existed, although the evidence bears out the *Journal*'s assertion about its decline: from 1926-30 eight engineering firms out of 36 surveyed charged premiums; from 1931-5 only two out of 41; and from 1936-9 only one out of 17.[3] The fact that even in the motor industry the system was quite widespread suggests, however, that it was still flourishing when many of these firms were founded just before the First World War: motor firms accepting premium apprentices included Daimler, Humber, Leyland, Rolls-Royce and Vauxhall.[4] The level of premiums in some firms surveyed in 1928 ranged from 100 to 300 guineas, suggesting a rather lower level before the war.[5]

Evidence from biographical material bears out this interpretation. Thus one of the FLW respondents served part of his time at Parsons, the famous turbine-makers: he commented that he was one of only a few trade apprentices, since the firm mainly took premium apprentices. In complete contrast to this up-to-date firm was Jessops of Leicester, a medium-sized jobbing shop; yet when Alfred Herbert served his apprenticeship there in the 1880s, there were four or five other premium apprentices.[6] L.T.C. Rolt served a premium apprenticeship at the California locomotive works in the late 1920s, and he was not the only such apprentice there at the time.[7] Both Rolt's and Herbert's training consisted largely of work on the shop floor like any other apprentice, thus providing that practical and empirical training so prized by the British. But the apprentice did also gain an all-round acquaintanceship with the work which was denied to most trade apprentices: Herbert's indenture provided for him to be instructed in the arts of a turner, a fitter and a draughtsman, and to the latter end more common, although the basic principle was the same; more adven-

The system of premium apprenticeship deserves much more attention than this brief survey has given it, and its saliency to the question of management education is obvious; less obvious, but also important, are the implications it has for attempts to measure social mobility.[8]

Notes

1. Alfred Herbert's wages were 5s per week, rising by annual increments of 2s 6d per week; this was probably rather more than a trade apprentice would receive in the 1880s, but not significantly so; Alfred Herbert, 'Memories', *Machine-Tool Review*, vol. XLI (Sept.-Oct. 1953), pp. 97-8; L.T.C. Rolt mentions that his premium of £100 was repayable in the event of his successfully completing his apprenticeship; even so, the value of the capital to the firm would not be insignificant, but the repayment of premiums is not mentioned in other sources; L.T.C. Rolt, *Landscape with Machines* (1971), p. 85.

2. Unsigned article, 'Premium Apprenticeship – a Decaying System', *Journal of Careers* (Oct. 1928), p. 9.

3. M. Anderson, *The Universities and British Industry* (1972), p. 294.

4. B.G. Robbins, 'Motor Engineering as a Profession for Well-Educated Boys', *Journal of Careers* (Sept. 1928), p. 12.

5. *Journal of Careers* (1928, various issues).

6. Herbert, 'Memories'; Jessops employed about 150 men.

7. Rolt, *Landscape with Machines*, p. 86.

8. See the important suggestion by D.J. Lee that apparent changes in the rate of upward mobility achieved by early leavers from school may be distorted by the declining proportion of such leavers who are middle class, since these are likely to be the most mobile. D.J. Lee, 'Class Differentials in Educational Opportunity', *Sociology*, 2 (1968), pp. 293-312.

6 MIGRATION AND FOLLOWING-UP

Introduction

In apprenticeship, a worker accepted a somewhat lower wage than he could have earned in other jobs in order to avail himself of the opportunity to work with a journeyman, on the understanding that he should receive instruction. Many types of work, however, were learned by workers who made no such overt sacrifice, and were promised no such reward. I have followed Dearle's separation of these other types of learning into migration, following-up and picking up a semi-skilled occupation. Before examining these in more detail, it will be helpful to discuss their common elements.

There was in apprenticeship an almost inevitable progression from apprentice to skilled worker, and this obtained unless the worker was exceptionally incapable, or was prevented for some reason from finishing his apprenticeship. In some of the occupations learned by other methods, as we shall see, this inevitable progression did occur, albeit in a different way. But in many of them it did not, and the progresssion of the learner to more skilled work depended on his own abilities. Whether or not there was guaranteed promotion to more skilled work, learning by progression differed from apprenticeship because there was no specific time set aside for the learning. The trainee was expected to obtain his knowledge and skill by observation and imitation of other workers while he was himself working.

If skill is regarded as a social artefact, then occupations not subject to apprenticeship certainly show signs of attempting to close the trade by controlling entry and thus constructing skill. Almost inevitably, the method adopted was the institution of seniority rules, that is rules by which vacancies in a higher grade were filled by strict rotation from the next grade below it, thus preventing the employer from gaining unilateral control of the labour supply. The classic operators of such rules were the spinners; but the steel-smelters were busy constructing them in our period, the tinplate workers seem to have had them already, and they also appear to have been accepted on the railways.[1] But it is important to note that in many industries whose members learned by some form of progression rather than apprenticeship, such as the boot and shoe industry and a variety of process industries, there were no such rules.

Migration

Dearle identified various groups of London workers as learning by migration. Among them were time-served apprentices who had become improvers; they have already been discussed. There were also exploited apprentices, who needed to move if they were to have a chance to learn anything, but as already noted Dearle thought that out-and-out exploitation was rare. Finally, in the apprentice or ex-apprentice group were 'improvers of the casual fringe' some of whom had broken their apprenticeship to earn more money, and some with the deliberate intention of learning more.[2] Where a lad had character and pertinacity, this might be an acceptable method of learning, at least in London where there were many small firms with work which shaded from the simple to the most complex; and since there was such a variety of work and of firms, there was always room for a worker with some experience, while the strict control over the movement of apprentices which obtained elsewhere seems not to have existed in London. Wal Hannington is a classic example of this group, leaving his apprenticeship after two years but nevertheless becoming a skilled toolmaker by the time he was 21. And W.F. Watson managed to become a skilled engineering worker without any apprentice training, although he admitted that he was very lucky to start on the route to skill by working a very simple lathe, with a helpful foreman.

The most important group of migratory workers which Dearle identified were not ex-apprentices, however, but learners in certain industries which required skill, but not the highest degree of skill, and which were highly subdivided. These industries included machine-made boots and shoes, silversmithing, the East London cabinet-making trade, sawying, woodworking by machine and French polishing; in engineering, migration was common in electrical engineering and the lighter branches of general engineering. By migration, Dearle pointed out, could be meant movement from shop to shop, which might be necessary in cabinet-making to master the different branches; but also movement from machine to machine in one shop as the learner grew competent to handle more difficult work. The latter was probably the more common, although the basic principle was the same; more adventurous boys might benefit from moving firms, but Dearle noted that where boys stayed in one firm they were 'given ample opportunity' to work their way up; this method of learning was often supplemented by technical education in the relevant subject.[3]

An example of how jobs were minutely broken down and thus

provided opportunties for gradual progression upwards is given below.
A boy learning French polishing would expect to start as a 'boy for
polisher's shop' — that is an errand boy; from there he would rise to
the position of a 'boy to help polishers', then a 'boy who knows a little
polishing', a 'boy who undertakes polishing' and so on until he could
claim to be a 'polisher's improver', going on to become an improver
who 'will do' in lieu of a polisher, until he could at last claim the full
rate.[4] A particularly good example of this sort of progression is provided by George Acorn, a cabinet-maker in the East End around the
turn of the century. Acorn started at 13 at a shop-fitters as an errand-
boy; in spite of his lowly position he learned to plane up wood and
employ trade terms — much the same as would be learned by an
apprentice in his first few months.[5] After a short period of dead-end
messenger-boy work, he joined a cheap workshop making wardrobes;
although he does not specify his position he obviously had the opportunity to learn, for he related that 'I was rapidly learning to do a few
things — could use a saw pretty well, could plane and paper up'; but
he also came to the conclusion that 'the wardrobe branch of cabinet-
making was unpromising to say the least of it'.[6] He was sacked anyway
after three years as a result of an argument with his boss, and could
now claim to be an improver, in which position he got a job at an oak
furniture specialists; by now, at about 17, he was earning 15s per week,
or about 5s more than an apprentice could expect to get; he left again
and went to two more firms in quick succession, each time obtaining
slightly higher wages. It is clear that such mobile young workers were
common, for not only does he mention friends of his doing the same
thing, but he related how such jobs were found: 'I inspected various
ironmongers' shops to see if any bill-heads were displayed announcing
that a "chap" was wanted. The grades are distinct: first one is a "Boy",
then a "Lad", after that a "Chap", and finally a "Maker".'[7] By this
time he was earning 5d an hour, or about 23s per week, and was still
a youth; his apotheosis was complete when, dismissed through slack
trade, he applied for and obtained a maker's job, which he soon left
to set up in a very small way for himself.

Learning by migration was not, however, just a London phenomenon. It obtained wherever the division between apprenticed and
unapprenticed workers had broken down, as well as in trades that had
never been learned by apprenticeship. In many of these trades, it is
difficult to distinguish learning by migration, or for that matter
following up, the other method of learning skilled work, from picking
up a job casually; as we have seen, neither migration nor following up

allowed the learner any specific period for instruction, and therefore the actual method of learning was by necessity fairly casual. Perhaps two distinctions can be drawn. The first is that we would only apply these two terms to jobs which, when the process of learning was complete, did involve the possession of a reasonable degree of skill. And the second, and since skill is so hard to judge perhaps the more satisfactory, is that jobs learned by migration or following-up involved a reasonable expectation on the part of the learners that he would advance up the ladder of promotion, even when this ladder was not strictly specified by formal seniority rules; whereas someone who picked up a job casually would also obtain promotion casually or by chance.

Learning by migration — by which, it must be remembered, is meant moving from machine to machine in the same shop or works, as well as moving from one shop to another — was most common in machine-tending occupations, rather than in process work. The latter will be discussed in more detail later, but as an introductory distinction it might be said that machine-tending operations involve work requiring some manual skill on machines each of which perform a discrete operation, while process work involves the control of processes involving materials which flow from one part of the plant to another, and requires more knowledge than manual skill.

Learning by migration in machine-tending industries, apart from the London industries already mentioned above, encompassed a vast number of trades. Probably the largest single one was boot and shoe making. Mechanisation in this industry had begun in the 1860s and 1870s, and the variety of machines had steadily increased. The work was highly subdivided, but some of it did require quite considerable skill: Fox quotes extracts from a report made in 1920 by the Industrial Fatigue Research Board which used phrases like 'requires great skill' (clicking), 'some operations almost automatic, but others demand great skill' (closing), 'requires much skill' (pulling-over) and 'requires skill and judgement' (edge-trimming).[8]

There is considerable evidence that in other parts of the country besides London the method of acquiring skill in this industry was to move from the simpler to the more difficult operations. Thus in the finishing room in Northampton a boy started with elementary unskilled work. But

> as soon as he has got the hang of the room he may be put to inking the parts of the sole requiring less precision . . . If he is a fairly smart

lad he may before long be set to use the honecake and sand-paper, which prepare the rough sole for the inking and colouring. From this he may get on to heel-scouring, in which the heel is given its correct shape by being pressed against a rapidly-rotating machine ... Owing to the length of practice required in order to know the exact amount of pressure to be applied and for how long to apply it the work is really men's work [although boys sometimes did it].[9]

The men doing this earned 28s per week, and the most skilled workers in the room, the edge-trimmers and setters, and the getters-off, earned from 30s to 36s per week, the latter a similar wage to that a skilled engineering worker might expect outside the big centres.[10] Although there were frequent complaints in the boot and shoe industry that much of the work was relatively unskilled, and this led to the over-stocking of the labour market by boys, progress was undoubtedly possible for boys who made an effort to get on. As C.B. Hawkins said of Norwich, another shoemaking centre, if a boy was anxious to improve himself, he 'moves on to another process, involving slightly more skill or allowing more scope for learning higher branches of the trade'. Allied to technical education, 'It is the modern substitute for apprenticeship, and it serves the purpose better perhaps than critics are sometimes willing to allow.'[11]

A classic example of learning by migration which was documented by FLW respondents was biscuit-making; although it was not clear how much skill was involved at any part of the process, there was a definite progression. Thus one respondent, starting with a variety of odd jobs around the factory, moved to warehouseman, preparation of biscuit ingredients and working on a mixing machine, eventually becoming an assistant foreman. The possibility of acquiring some skill in the industry is suggested by the testimony of another respondent, who recalls that he 'learnt an awful lot about the machines', while the 1925 Report mentioned that many workers left at 16 or 17, and only those who were intended for more skilled positions remained.[12]

Some textile work could possibly be classified as an instance of learning by migration, although there was perhaps not enough skill in it to deserve the appellation: many of the boys who entered the spinnning and weaving departments, as little piecers or doffers, left the departments in their late teens as they had little chance of promotion and moved to another section. In the sense that they acquired some familiarity with the materials while in the spinning or weaving departments this could be regarded as an example of the transference of skill from one job to form a basis for another, but in the sense that they started as more or less unskilled in the departments they moved to it was not. In these departments and other branches of the industry, such as printing, bleaching, dyeing and finishing, trainees moved from machine to machine and therefore did acquire such skill as there was by migration.[13] In the lace industry, as we have already seen, some formal instruction was given when men's work was started, but before that there was a system of progression, from shop lad to threading: then, 'While at this work for a few years, he picks up, generally, sufficient knowledge of brass winding to go to it, if he desires, without any probationary period at all. Otherwise, if opportunity occurs and if his ability warrants it, he is promoted — sometimes straight from threading, sometimes from winding — to being a minor in either lace-making or warping' (that is to learning adult's work).[14] The reference to ability implies that this progression was not merely formal or customary, but did relate to some genuine skill which needed to be acquired; the reference to picking-up suggests that this skill was not so great as to require any defined period of instruction.

Migration was also the characteristic method of learning the so-called Birmingham trades — light metalwork of all kinds. In the precious metal and jewellery trades, there was increasing subdivision and recruitment from learners rather than apprentices;[15] in anchor and chainmaking, boys started on small chains, or else as strikers on medium-sized chains, and progressed to striking on large chains, eventually becoming welders;[16] in light chain, nut, bolt and nailmaking, in some of which training was required for as long as seven years on the various machines, the same sort of methods applied;[17] in cycle works, boys were paid entirely according to skill, and if they showed promise were given new work as opportunity arose;[18] in brass-casting and moulding, described as skilled work, the method of learning in Birmingham was by genuine migration from firm to firm, while the same applied to iron-moulding, or founding, in London.[19] Tinsmithing and sheet-metal working was another class of metalwork often learned by migration in other areas besides Birmingham, even though the work was usually described as skilled.[20] Booth found that of 15 zinc and tin works surveyed, nine said that the work was skilled, but only three had apprentices, while in others the work was 'picked up'; of eleven coppersmiths and brassfounders, nine also said the work was skilled, but only five had apprentices, while again in others the work was 'picked up'.[21]

In some of these and the other occupations described above, there was a formal system of learnership, which meant as we have seen that there was an agreement to at least give the trainee an opportunity to learn, even though no especial provision was made for a defined system of teaching. From the figures for the numbers of learners in the 1925 Report, however, it seems likely that even in trades where this did obtain, such as precious metal and jewellery, and boots and shoes, there were many young workers who learnt without necessarily being recognised as learners.[22] And in many industries, such as cycle manufacture, there was no formal system of learnership, let alone apprenticeship, at all, while of course a formal system of learnership could not be established where workers actually migrated from one firm to another.[23] As a generalisation, it might be said that the more skilled an occupation, as in boot and shoe making, precious metals and light engineering, the more likely it was to adopt a formal system of learnership; but the fact that some skilled occupations like cabinet-making or brass-moulding were learned by moving from firm to firm precludes this generalisation from having much predictive value.

The problem of workers in heavy or medium engineering learning by migration, whether within the firm or between firms, was one which considerably exercised the minds of ASE officials and time-served engineering workers, especially in the 1900s. While the agreement between the union and the Employers Federation following the 1897-9 lock-out theoretically gave the latter the power to employ anyone they liked on any machine, it seems doubtful as to whether there really was much upward progression to fully skilled work.[24] W.F. Watson and Wal Hannington both learned in this way; but the latter had had a two-year spell of apprenticeship and the former enjoyed a lot of luck, while they were obviously both rather exceptional people. Of the 17 FLW respondents in skilled engineering jobs, excluding moulding, only two seem to have had no apprenticeship at all: one became a fitter doing maintenance work on buses, and the other progressed via work as a boiler-fireman to become a maintenance engineer. Significantly, one respondent who had a short and informal apprenticeship was also in motor repair, which as a rapidly growing industry with no established standards must have been a relatively easy business to break into. The 1915 Report instanced certain specified kinds of work, such as moulding by machine, and shops with a high proportion of simple repetition work, as employing non-apprenticed journeymen.[25] It would require an extensive sample to find out how common such work was before the war, and the material for it is probably not there, if it ever was. As we have seen, however, the agricultural machinery and machine tool firms in the 1925 Report mainly recruited from their own apprentices or learners, and very little promotion of labourers was mentioned. Sir Benjamin Browne, the chairman of Hawthorn Leslie, the sort of heavy engineering firm — it was in shipbuilding, marine engineering and locomotive building — which was typical of British engineering at this time, said in 1907,

> in our trade, the semi-skilled man is the man who was on the floor, that is a shop labourer. If he is any good at all, he is taken to a small machine, say a drilling machine: then if he is any good at that, he goes to a planing machine and so on to a slotting machine and other things, *but not to lathe work usually*.[26]

This and the other evidence adduced above tends to suggest that the amount of promotion of labourers to fully skilled work in engineering which went on can be exaggerated. Undoubtedly migration from machine to machine in heavy engineering was important as a channel for recruitment to semi-skilled work: Browne said that 'Planing, drilling and slotting are usually worked by semi-skilled men who get higher and higher wages.'[27] There is some evidence, which will be discussed in Chapter 9, that the proportion of such work was increasing, albeit slowly; it may be that it was the perception that craftsmen's work was under indirect threat from such developments which led a heightened importance to be given to the occasional instances where labourers were promoted to fully skilled work, via work on such specialised machines.[28]

Other factory occupations where migration was an accepted method of learning lay on the boundary between process work and machine-tending work, while the method of learning lay on the boundary between migration and following-up. Candle-making and soap-boiling, for instance, both recruited their more skilled workers from those lower down. Thus in a Nottingham firm the progression was from soap-stamping or cutting to soap-boiling and then to perfumery.[29] In London such progression also applied, both in these occupations and also in rubber works and floor cloth and linoleum factories. In most of these occupations there was general agreement that the highest that could be aspired to was semi-skilled work, the rate of wages in the latter, for instance, being 26s per week in the 1890s.[30] In paperstaining, or in other words wallpaper manufacture, boys in the machine branch of the industry 'are engaged upon leaving school, and those who are suitable are given an opportunity of working in the printing shops or at colour mixing. The apt ones are then made back tenters or printers, or assistant colour mixers, and eventually printers upon the smaller machines and colour mixers.' The degree of selectivity implied by the use of the phrase 'the apt ones' suggests that, as in the lace trade, some genuine skill was needed; in this case it may have been quite considerable, for we are told that 'No boy of ability need ever leave this factory without having been thoroughly taught a well-paid trade.'[31]

Although, in process industries proper, following-up was almost a necessity where a considerable amount of skill was required, learning in some process industries also involved migration. It might be argued that moving from one part of a process to work on a completely different part did not lead to the acquisition of any further useful skill, since unlike movement from machine to machine there might be no similarity between the work. But it should be stressed that process skills particularly require the acquisition of knowledge, including knowledge of the materials used, and hence there might be a real educational value in giving workers an acquaintance with different kinds of work and thus enhancing their knowledge of the whole. Furthermore, even when this was not the case, learning several parts of the process might have considerable value because process plants are typically capital intensive and often employ only a few workers on each part of the process; thus it is useful, in case of illness or accident, to have a number of workers who possess an all-round acquaintance with the work.

Migration seems to have been particularly prevalent in grainmilling, or rather in the roller mills that were playing an increasingly large part in the industry. Both Booth and the 1915 Report testify that the usual method of recruiting the more skilled process workers was from the labourers, although some labourers remained as such. Thus at a Nottingham firm the process workers 'start ... as youths at sack mending or packing. Those showing ability are moved to departments until they have been through each (wheat cleaning, purifiers, centrifugals and rolls), becoming eventually competent flour millers.' At a London firm the progression was from sweeper to cleaner to packer to machineman; once on the machines, the progression was purifierman, silksman, rollerman, or silksman, purifierman, rollerman. The degree of skill actually needed is not clear: Booth reported that

on the one hand, we are assured that any man can master the duties from the modern operative in a few weeks, while from other sources — masters as well as men — we are told that much of the work is of a most responsible character, and that no man can, for instance, be trusted as a rollerman until after years of experience in a mill.[32]

Perhaps the apparent contradiction can be resolved by suggesting that while the basic techniques and principles of the work did not take long to learn, the finer points of the work, and the ability to react in the appropriate way to malfunctioning, took much longer to acquire.

Papermills also utilised the system of migration, particularly in the early stages of the worker's career. The 1915 Report suggests that in some mills boys were kept to certain departments, selected boys being in a sense 'apprentices' to the machinemen, the most skilled branch, although unlike apprentices in other industries they were not automatically entitled to the full skilled man's rate at 20 or 21, or indeed until there was a vacancy. In other mills, and usually in all departments except papermaking itself, progression, either by migration or following-up, was the rule. Thus in a Yorkshire mill work on the machines was learned by 'apprentices', but 'cuttermen or reelermen begin as boys helping in the finishing department and later as packers etc.'; but in another mill, boys started at the paper-cutter, and then moved anywhere where a vacancy occurred. Although the 1915 Report considers that men and boys tended to be kept to one department, the fact that there were very few apprentices shown in the 1906 Wages Census — and some of these must have been apprentices to maintenance work — suggests that there was rarely a hard and fast rule about this.[33]

Chemical works also moved men about from process to process. The skill needed here should not be overestimated, however, because processes were 'invariably carried out under the supervision of professional chemists'; nevertheless, 'A certain amount of intelligence is demanded of chemical labourers, and, once they are accustomed to the manufacturing processes, they have a practical value for many varieties of chemical production in bulk.'[34] This comment bears out my earlier suggestion that migration from one process to another might genuinely enhance the skill of the worker by widening his knowledge of the materials and giving him a more all-round ability.

Outside both machine-tending and process work were other jobs learnt by methods which included an element of migration, although as in other cases it is sometimes difficult to distinguish this from other methods. Thus where trainee coal-hewers started work right away with adult hewers, as in South Wales, the method of learning might properly be described as following up or even regular service; where, as in the North and Midlands, 'they commence work . . . on the surface at the picking belts and tables or underground as door boys or incline boys, opening and shutting doors or coupling and uncoupling tubs', their progression to other work might be better described as migration, although how useful the knowledge they acquired in their preliminary activities was to the work they eventually did is not clear; presumably there was some gain in becoming acquainted with life underground, the dangers of the pit and so on.[35] On the borderline between migration and following up was the North-Eastern practice of setting lads at the age of 17 or so to 'putting', that is hauling loaded tubs from the coal face to the nearest siding on the underground haulage system. Following-up proper means working in a gang all the members of which are engaged in the same task, although they have different roles to play in actually fulfilling it, whereas putting and hewing are separate tasks; nevertheless, putters learned the rudiments of hewing by being 'in constant contact with the hewers at the face, and whenever they have any spare time they are allowed to hew', and in this their method of learning was analogous to that adopted in following-up.[36] Coalmining cannot, of course, be regarded as highly skilled work, although undoubtedly there was both skill and knowledge involved; there seems to be fairly general agreement that two years was the time it took to make an efficient hewer.[37] But it seems reasonable to class the method of learning coalmining, and for that matter ironstone mining and stone quarrying as well, as some combination of the formal methods of regular service, migration and following-up rather than merely casual picking-up, because there was a definite expectation among most learners that they would progress upwards.[38]

Very similar in this respect was railway work. As we have seen, there were short periods of formal training for guards and signalmen; but basically railway work was learned by moving from a lower grade to a higher. Thus porters usually became passenger guards or signalmen, shunters and greasers became goods guards or signalmen. Furthermore within these grades themselves there were a myriad of different subdivisions, the lower leading to the higher.[39] Of railway jobs, only engine-driving could be regarded as really skilled, and this was learned by following-up and will be considered under that heading. Nevertheless, there is a fair amount of knowledge, as of the rule book and the line to be travelled, needed in most railway jobs, and some manual skill particularly among shunters and goods guards, who had to couple and uncouple trucks; migration was therefore genuinely useful in that it enabled knowledge which was transferable to be acquired gradually. The division of railwaymen into grades was not merely an artificially constructed seniority ladder.

Following-up

Following-up, as has already been indicated, was the method of learning in which a man was attached to a gang, or as a mate to a more skilled worker, and while carrying out a full-time job himself also learned that of the man above him. It was such jobs, in particular, which were most likely to have a system of progression formalised by seniority rules, but these did not apply to all occupations of this kind. As the foregoing comments have indicated, in papermaking or grainmilling, in both of which there was following-up as well as migration, promotion was largely by ability. Some work learned by following-up was also subject to apprenticeship; this will be indicated where appropriate. Following-up was used in a wide variety of occupations, and all that can be said to unite them was that they all involved the accomplishment of a particular task by the teamwork of two or more men.

In machine-tending industries, cotton-spinning was the classic exampler of following-up. Boys became little piecers at 14 or so, graduated to 'big piecers' in the late teens, and became fully fledged spinners round about their mid-twenties — although after the First World War when the industry was depressed they were liable to remain as big piecers for longer.[40] As we have already seen, however, spinning was not a highly skilled occupation, and if it were not for the institution of seniority rules, would hardly deserve the label of following-up, as opposed to merely picking-up. Cotton-spinning is somewhat exceptional among machine-tending occupations in requiring work in gangs, and because of this following-up is at least usual within machine-tending occupations. Outside the cotton-industry, and apart from work attending various subsidiary processes in the metal industries, which lie on the borderline between machine-tending and process work and will be dealt with under the latter category, only the minding of printing presses really comes in the former.

Printing press minding, or machine managing, was an occupation which was also recruited via apprenticeship; but Musson documents the failure of the Typographical Association, the main provincial printers' union, to institute strict apprenticeship in the press, as opposed to the compositing section of the trade.[41] Musson's comments are borne out by the 1915 Report, which states that rotary machine minders were largely apprenticed in London, but not outside. It was on rotary machines that learning by following-up, rather than merely casual picking-up, was possible, because they required a number of workers of different grades. Thus a labourer could become a carrier, 'fly' hand, 'brake' hand and finally a manager.[42] Machine managing was a skilled task, and especially so on the rotary machines. A manager

> must have a thorough understanding of the different machines, so that if any hitch occurs he may be able to put it right. He must also exercise much skill and judgement in order to get a perfect impression ... when illustrations or diagrams occur great skill is required in producing the correct effects of light and shade.[43]

Following-up was much more common in process industries. Process work involved material which flows rather than moved in discrete stages; it therefore usually necessitates limited manual skill, as the material itself is often not handled at all by the operator; what is needed are what have been called 'control skills', that is the ability to identify, and react correctly to, malfunctionings in the process;[44] before instrumentation – and as we shall see there was little instrumentation in process industries at this time – the duties of operators also frequently included the actual formulation of the material, and the monitoring of the subsequent stages of the process as the material became modified by chemical or mechanical action. To fit the skills needed in process work into our simple typology of useful qualities – knowledge and manual skill – we can say that process operatives need a considerable amount of knowledge – the actual amount depending of course on the operation; this knowledge has to encompass the details of the process plant itself, the nature of the materials, and possibly the behaviour of the materials when undergoing change. The latter sort of knowledge, in particular, could in our period only be acquired by experience, since in the absence of instrumentation there was no way of monitoring what changes were taking place except through the knowledge of the process operator himself. Finally, we might add that there is no hard and fast distinction between process and other work; nowadays in many factories material 'flows' along conveyor belts and is handled by automatic machines which require monitoring, rather than non-automatic machines which require manual tending. Before the First World War conveyor belts were non-existent, but as we have already noted there was some work which lay on the boundary between process work and machine-tending work.

Process work which involved genuine and considerable skill and which was learnt by progression through a series of grades is best illustrated by the iron and steel industry. On open-hearth furnaces the progression was from chargewheeler, which was basically a labouring job, up through third and second to first melter; samplepassers, the equivalent of foremen, were recruited from first melters. Progression on blast furnaces and Bessemer steel furnaces was similar.[45] One of the interesting questions connected with this method of learning is how the learner acquired his initial knowledge; it is not difficult to see how, once he starts to actually take part in the work, he acquires further knowledge; similarly it is not difficult to see how, in jobs where boys are employed, they can get acquainted with the work because their own duties are not very onerous; but in work like steel-melting the chargewheeler was an adult labourer fully employed in heavy manual work, mainly bringing materials up to the furnace. Patrick McGeown, who started work in 1914, recalls that 'During the long break I used to go on the melting shop to talk to any furnacemen I knew' (his father, who was not at that time at the same works, was also a melter).[46] When he became a chargewheeler, as distinct from a yard labourer, he notes that 'Strictly, the chargewheelers provided the material and left the rest to the melters, but it seldom worked out that way. We dived into the fettling to give the sweating melters a lift, and the same with the charge feeding, we lashed in the iron ore with the rest'; and so on . . . 'We were preparing for the day when we would take our first third-hand shifts, and they would be hectic if we hadn't the knowhow.'[47] The chargewheelers opportunity for this would come at first when third hands were absent on rest shifts or for some other reason; then they would gain promotion to a regular third-hand position. Promotion to first hand often took ten years or longer.[48]

The steel-melters' skill — and that of leading hands in other departments of the iron and steel industry — was undoubtedly high:

> The old craftsmen had 'measured' temperatures, alloy contents and qualities of steel by a glance at the molten metal, his judgement so refined by long years of experience that given normal conditions he could tell the heat of a melt to a tenth of a degree, an alloy content to a decimal place, and the proper operation of a furnace by the 'feel of it' . . . He had in effect complete control and responsibility during operations, 'making up' to the desired specifications on his own initiative and controlling the entire working of the furnace.[49]

An FLW respondent who worked as a furnaceman producing armour plate, and who also learned by following-up, could estimate temperatures so accurately that during the 1930s depression he was able to find a job at a gasworks which no one else could do, because it involved the estimation of temperatures by 'feel'. And Harry Brearley, a chemist, recalled that when he submitted a collection of fractured ingots to a number of teemers (workers employed in the making of crucible steel; see next paragraph), each one arranged them in the same order of hardness, and the men's grading corresponded with the amount of carbon as determined by laboratory analysis; two who knew about carbon percentages gave the figures to within 0.03 of the percentage determined in the laboratory.[50] Steel-melters, furnacemen and teemers all had a precise sense of measurement, needing years of experience to acquire, because of the lack of instrumentation until after the First World War.[51]

Another highly skilled steelmaking process was crucible steel manufacture, which was concentrated in Sheffield. Here there was opportunity for boys' work, and this gave the boy, called a 'cellar lad', the chance 'at once to learn something of the properties of the materials with which he has to work, and to accept responsibility for an appreciable part of the furnace tools'. Cellar lads would also learn by imitation: the 'pullers-out' pulled the pots out of the heated furnace, and the boys would pull out cold, empty pots.[52] Harry Brearley, who described the cellar lads' life, was a chemist who started as a cellar lad himself: he related how when he helped to set up a steelworks in Russia he saw grown men who were trained to the job of pulling-out, but none had the same flair for it as a full-grown cellar lad.[53] As the boy progressed, he would reach more responsible positions such as that of the teemer, who judged the right moment for pouring the molten steel and actually poured it from the crucibles, which were small enough to be handled: this, unlike much process work, needed great manual skill in putting the molten steel into the right place in the mould, at the correct angle. But teemers also needed considerable knowledge, acquired only through experience: Brearley, who as a chemist might be expected to favour scientific methods, said, 'let me restate the belief that the reputation of Sheffield tool steel depends more on the accurate observation of workmen, or managers who have been workmen, than anything else'.[54]

Iron and steel manufacture was probably the most important type of process work where skill was widely spread among the operatives. As we have noted, chemical works tended to concentrate expertise in the foremen, and not surprisingly also made use of the trained chemist earlier than other industries; none the less, experienced operatives did acquire some useful skills, although part of the value of these skills was acquaintance with a number of different processes, acquired by migration as well as following-up. The same applied, perhaps to a greater extent, to breweries, where few of the workers had to have any very considerable skill, if we except ancillary workers such as coopers and maintenance men;[55] grainmills and papermills also required, for most of their workers, a diffuse rather than deep knowledge of operations. But in all these cases the workers had to have some chance to acquire knowledge of how the processes themselves worked, even if the knowledge needed was not very great; learning by migration was not wholly adequate. The method of acquiring knowledge was informal as compared with steel mills: in grainmilling 'picked suitable youths and young men work as assistants to skilled men with a view to ultimately occupying the positions themselves'.[56] As we have seen there was some disagreement about how skilled process workers in grainmilling had to be; in papermaking the machineman, and the beaterman 'on whose judgment the quality of the paper ultimately depended' were generally recognised as skilled, in contrast to other operatives who were not so skilled — although, again, the latter by moving from process to process may have acquired all-round ability.[57] Beatermen and machinemen, like steel-melters, had a say in deciding the right mix of materials in the process, as well as controlling the process itself, while instrumentation was rare till after the First World War; an experienced mill manager has suggested to me that machinemen and beatermen, in terms of skill, could be compared with craftsmen who had served an apprenticeship. While they might move round at first, they would also need to learn by 'following-up' on the machines and beaters.[58]

On the boundary between process work and other work were a number of other occupations in the iron and steel and allied industries. In rolling mills

> boys enter in various capacities, such, for instance, as door lads at the heating furnaces, and to take minor positions at the rolls. As they get older and stronger and prove themselves capable, they work into better positions, as these become vacant, so that it is quite possible for a youth to rise to the position of a roller or become a heater.[59]

Heavy forge work, that is work with big steam hammers or presses, was similarly recruited.[60] L.T.C. Rolt described the skill involved in the latter operation:

> The making of a heavy forging called for perfect coordination

between the master smith, who was in charge of the operation, his hammer driver who stood behind the hammer and worked the steam valve handle which caused the hammer to strike a hard or soft blow, and the men who, clinging to long chain-supported tongs, manipulated the glowing billet on the anvil as the smith directed ... long experience in his craft had given him powers of judgment that seemed almost uncanny.[61]

Tinplate and galvanised sheet manufacture were also progression industries, and promotion in these and copper manufacturing was strictly by seniority.[62] There was an element of migration in such promotion, in that boys passed from one department to another; but this only happened once or twice, and was not a permanent feature of their career. Boys started in the cold rolling department, learning various stages of the process. In their late teens they were promoted to behinding in the mill gang on the hot rolls, 'and usually rise in regular progression to second helper at the age of twenty years or over, first helper, furnaceman, doubler and rollerman'. A few went on to become shearers. There were also alternative careers in the pickling department, where they could rise to be annealers, on in the tin house, working with the tinmen before being promoted to this position in their mid-twenties or so; a few went on to become assorters. As with other branches of the iron, steel and related industries, tinplate work was reckoned to require considerable skill.[63]

One other industry which required a somewhat similar progression was baking. In London, at least, there was little or no apprenticeship, and men rose from third to second to first hand; young boys were not employed because of the hard physical work required, and legislation preventing their employment on night work, but the 1906 Wages Census does suggest that there were a fair number of apprentices in the country as a whole. Booth thought that 'A considerable degree of skill is required to produce uniformly good bread day after day.'[64]

Finally we come to a host of miscellaneous but important occupations which cannot be fitted into the categories of machine-tending or process work. Among the most important were the shipbuilding and boilermaking trades of plating and riveting. Most shipbuilding trades, whether in ironwork like caulkers and anglesmiths, or wood and iron like shipwrights, did not involve gang work to any large extent and were learnt by regular service. But platers and riveters both worked in gangs; while, as we shall see, platers did not strictly learn by following-up, they did have a large number of helpers; riveters did not have so many helpers, but their method of learning was more definitely that of following-up.

Platers' work was basically to cut and shape plates and place them in position: their apprentices

> generally start as marker boys and assist platers in making templates at the ship, and in making plates and bars either from templates or from working drawings. It is also common in the early stages of apprenticeship for boys, working in squads of two or more, to do the simpler work of beam knees, brackets, wash plates etc. Gradually the apprentices are advanced to more complex and heavier work.[65]

It is probably true to say that the actual method of learning in plating was in some ways more akin to regular service: the plater's marker learned various techniques which the unskilled members of the gang did not; and Dearle noted that the boys were taught by the foreman, rather than gradually acquiring the skill as in following-up proper.[66] Riveters joined the plates, bars and so on together by rivets, and their task was to strike the heated rivets sharply and effectively so as to mushroom out the ends and lock the plates together; they also worked riveting machines when these were used. In riveting the method was more definitely following-up, since the boys began as rivet-heaters, whose work was self-explanatory, or rivet-catchers who caught the rivets thrown to them by the rivet-heaters and gave them to the holder-up — another grade of workman, who might be an apprentice or who might be an adult, who held the rivets while the riveter struck them. A gang would consist, at least in shipbuilding, of a minimum of four, that is two riveters, a holder-up and a heater, with additional catchers if necessary. It is important to note that not all the latter were apprentices: some were adults, although it was a poorly paid job.[67]

Platers' work was skilled, whether in shipyards or boiler shops, encompassing a number of different activities and entailing considerable responsibility.

> Instructions as to the shapes to which the plates and bars are to be cut and given on working plans or are indicated by templates. According to these instructions the platers mark the plates and bars ready for punching and shearing by electric or hydraulic machines. In some cases platers and bars have to be shaped by the platers at furnaces.[68]

They were also responsible for erecting the plates and bars in position ready for riveting. Rolt describes the flanging of a plate for a loco-motive boiler as 'a spectacular demonstration of skilled manual team-work', with split-second timing being necessary.[69] The 1925 Report does note, however, that in shipyards men often specialised in only one of these tasks. Riveting, on the other hand, with its one basic operation of striking, needed only strength and a specific manual skill; furthermore, because the strength of a ship depended on its design rather than on each individual rivet, ship-riveting could be done to relatively low standards; boiler riveting was a more skilled job, because each individual rivet had to withstand the pressure of the boiler. In the case of ship-riveting, apprentices very quickly learnt to do the work of tradesmen, and went on to piecework after six months.[70]

Plating and riveting were therefore rather peculiar occupations. Plating was undeniably a skilled trade: yet unlike other sorts of gang work, often highly skilled as in the case of steel-melting, it was learnt by apprenticeship; it is true that the apprentice received a certain amount of definite instruction, but the remark by Rolt that plating involved 'skilled manual team-work' suggests that the platers' helpers, although paid as unskilled, were not necessarily so; indeed they could hardly fail to pick up a considerable knowledge of the processes. Riveting was much less skilled, and ship-riveting would count as no more than semi-skilled in terms of the knowledge and manual skill needed. It too involved gang work; yet it too required a five-year appren-ticeship in most areas.[71] The implications of these strict apprenticeship requirements will be explored in Chapter 7.

One other group of workers which employed the gang method coincidental with apprenticeship were glass-workers, especially the high-class flint glass makers. There was a hierarchical ladder, from apprentice to footmakers to servitor to workman, and at least where the union was strong seniority rules were strictly enforced.[72] The glass-makers therefore combined apprenticeship with seniority rules, but in this they were atypical, if not unique; in general apprenticeship excluded seniority rules, and vice versa.

Two groups of workers who were recruited by a combination of mateship and apprenticeship were smiths and plumbers, although neither occupation was at all analogous to platers or riveters. The two latter had a number of assistants who were paid far less than them-selves, and who were unable to gain promotion because they had not been apprentices; smiths' strikers, or hammermen, were quite well paid in their own right, and furthermore both smithing and plumbing required a considerable amount of genuine skill, unlike riveting.

There is some disagreement about how often hammermen had the opportunity to move up to smithing. The 1915 Report thought that apprenticeship was usual, but promotion occurred in some cases, particularly railway carriage and wagon shops in the Midlands.[73] Booth said that there was no apprenticeship in London, but lads were destined from an early stage to be either smiths or hammermen depending on ability and influence, and that once established the latter were unlikely to rise further.[74] On the other hand, of the four FLW respondents who were smiths, none were apprenticed. It is true that two were taught by their fathers in small workshops, and obviously experienced conditions similar to apprenticeship. The other two, from Reading and South Wales, both started as strikers; the latter respondent, who worked with a smith in the maintenance department of a tinworks, commented that 'You became qualified by practice you see . . . And I had a very good blacksmith.'[75] In a trade which depended very much on manual skill allied to a slow culmination of experience, practice was really the only method of learning: when smiths *were* formally apprenticed, they became strikers for other apprentices when strong enough, and then had their own fire; in other words, they replicated the career of a promoted striker in microcosm.[76]

Plumbing seems to have been recruited by apprenticeship outside London, and mateship in London, although there were also improvers − which in the building trade meant mobile young workers who had a semi-formal status − in the provinces.[77] Even more than in smithing, however, there was no real distinction between plumbers' mates and apprentices, because the latter in fact acted as mates. Thus there were few if any workers in the trade who were excluded from a chance of promotion. Because of this the training of plumbers had some paradoxical features. Plumbing was a skilled trade, the 1915 Report thought a highly skilled trade because of the 'modern development of sanitary science, and the increasing stringency of building bye-laws'.[78] But because every plumbers' mate was a potential plumber, it was also a trade, Dearle thought, which was quite exceptional in that plumbers were often reluctant to teach it to their assistants.[79] In spite of this, the mate/apprentice could hardly fail to learn a considerable amount: 'They become familiar with the different kinds of material and their uses and learn how to saw, bend, and cut screw threads on pipes.'[80] They also, of course, became familiar with the plumbers' tools. Although a plumbers' mate could become fairly well acquainted with this work through following-up, its technical nature meant that it was an early candidate for technical instruction. The Worshipful Company of Plumbers started a registration movement in the late nineteenth century, and there were City and Guild exams in connection with this. According to the 1915 Report, technical education in London was compulsory for plumbers' apprentices, although since there were hardly any in London this didn't mean very much.[81]

We have already noted that coalmining and quarrywork were learnt in a variety of ways, the methods used in the former, in particular, depending very much on the locality. In this it reflects the fact that it was not highly skilled, and a great deal of the skill needed was knowledge — of safety rules, formal and informal, of the state of coal seams and the best methods of working them and so on — which was acquired by simply being in the mine and in reasonable proximity to experienced miners. Whether or not the trainee was a member of a gang, attached to one hewer, or moving about from task to task, did not really matter. In contrast, one other occupation which was learned very definitely by following-up was that of engine-driver. The process of learning is very well described in a book by Michael Reynolds, an ex-driver.

The first step was to become, as a boy, an engine-cleaner. No great skill was required in this, but the boy did learn something about locomotives. The next step, which because of the strength required would not come until the lad was fully grown, was to become a fireman on a shunting locomotive. Instruction depended on the driver:

> The driver is in charge of the engine, and it is his place to give the fireman a complete knowledge of his duties . . . It is a lesson to show him how to handle the shovel . . . how to prepare the engine . . . how to take the bulk of the momentum out of the train with the brake, and then to lower [sic] the train under control to the platform.[82]

What is interesting about this is that the fireman was not just learning to be a fireman, although this was the first task, and demanded no mean skill: he was also learning to be a driver; or rather the fireman's duties involved a considerable amount of work connected with actually controlling the locomotive, as well as merely feeding the fire. The fireman then moved up to a slow goods, where he had a chance to perfect his firing without mistakes mattering too much, and also to learn about oiling the engine, and feeding the boiler with water, as well as gaining experience of inevitable vicissitudes such as breakdowns.[83] Firemen finally progressed up to passenger work. It will be obvious that by this time they had had a chance to acquire considerable driving as well as firing skills, and naturally the next step was to become an engine-driver on a shunter, and follow the whole process all over again. It might be added that apart from acquiring the knowledge and manual skill needed to control the locomotive, the driver also had to 'know the road', while firemen and drivers had to have knowledge of signals and the rule book. Reynolds thought that 'a man is generally about five years before he is capable of taking the responsibility of a driver upon his shoulders'.[84]

Picking-up

It was suggested earlier that the distinction between migration and following-up on the one hand, and picking-up on the other, lay not so much in the actual method of learning or even the skill involved in the task to be learnt as in the chances the learner had of promotion. If his chance was low, or if promotion was a matter of luck or oppor-tunity, then the method of learning could better be characterised as picking-up. Hence some occupations which were often classed as skilled could be learned by picking-up. One of the most important was bricklaying: the 1915 Report considered that it was chiefly learnt either by picking-up, or by unofficial patrimony, the latter being facilitated by the prevalence of subcontract.[85] Unfortunately the 1906 Wages Census does not distinguish apprentices within different branches of building, so we are unable to authoritatively check this: the 1925 Report, on the other hand, treated bricklaying as an appren-ticed trade, but conditions may have changed rather more in building than in most trades in favour of apprenticeship between the two dates.[86] Undoubtedly simple bricklaying was easy to learn: an FLW respondent who picked it up just after the First World War claimed that he learned simple 'line work' in half an hour.[87] Dearle thought that many country building labourers, having learned the rudiments by observation, came to London where apprenticeship was weak and then proceeded by migration from firm to firm to master more difficult techniques. Both Dearle and the FLW respondent, however, pointed out that it was not nearly so easy to reach a high state of efficiency as it was to master simple work, and many who picked it up never got beyond the latter stage.[88] Somewhat similar comments apply to painting; it was, if anything, even easier to learn rough painting than bricklaying; but in some areas there was apprenticeship.[89] Builders' labourers, who often had specialised positions and were by no means an indifferentiated class, also acquired the skill of their particular branch by picking it up; Booth instances scaffolders and hoisters. One could add to these semi-skilled building workers in a variety of miscellaneous occupations, such as the tile-fixer and the marble-polisher who appeared in the biographical sample in Booth's survey.[90]

A large amount of semi-skilled work in engineering was picked up: work ancillary to moulding, that is work in and about foundries, particularly comes in this category. The 1915 Report's coverage of this was particularly extensive, since it surveyed 110 firms: core-making was often recruited from labourers, while dressers or fettlers of castings, casters, cupolamen and furnacemen were usually promoted labourers, as boys could not do the work; for that matter moulding itself was frequently recruited in the same way, although it was reckoned that a good moulder needed an apprenticeship.[91] Of the FLW respondents in moulding, two had been apprentices and one started as a boy in a 'repetition' shop, making simple castings.

Finally we could list a whole host of jobs which required some definite skill, but for which there was no defined method of training, and no regular channel of promotion. Dearle instances carmen, ware-houseman, crane-drivers and stationary engine-drivers, as well as other groups we have already mentioned.[92] The skill required in some of these occupations was by no means negligible: as anyone who has seen an overhead crane at work will know, the drivers have an almost uncanny mastery over their charges: as Rolt put it,

> in the hands of these men flexible chains and steel cables seemed to become rigid, such was the effortless precision with which they lifted their unwieldy loads aloft, moved them swiftly along and across the shop, both traverses working simultaneously, and then lowered them in the exact spot required.[93]

Van-drivers, too, acquired no inconsiderable skill in some cases. They became acquainted with the work as van boys, picked up a little bit of driving experience by, for instance, backing the van into the yard, and then progressed upwards to a light cart, light van work, and if they were capable to three or four horse vans, earning in London 34s to 38s per week, or nearer a fully skilled wage than an unskilled wage.[94] A general carman also needed considerable knowledge of his delivery area: an employer thought that 'It will take a man nearly three years to fit himself for a general carman.'[95]

We could multiply instances of semi-skilled work almost indefinitely, but the various one given above serve to illustrate the general point that, although casually acquired, the skill required was genuine and in some cases considerable, and might arise from quite a lengthy acquaintance with the work. It is now time to turn away from the question of how skill was acquired, and examine the implications of our findings.

Notes

1. For seniority rules in various occupations see H.A. Turner, *Trade Union Growth, Structure and Policy* (1962), pp. 127-8 (spinners); A. Pugh, *Men of Steel* (1951), pp. 89-90 (steel-smelters); 1915 Report, p. 135 (tinplate workers); the information for railways is harder to come by, although references suggest that seniority was generally accepted; F. McKenna, 'Victorian Railway Workers', *History Workshop*, 1 (1976), p. 47, suggests that seniority was one of the criteria in the classification system, which was really a system of artificial grades within grades; T.A. McCulloch, 'On the Railway' in J. Commons (ed.), *Seven Shifts* (1938), p. 253, refers to promotion by seniority as standard. According to the Webbs, seniority rules were only enforced locally and against the wishes of the unions, but Pugh's account shows that this was not the case with the steel-smelters, while the existence of seniority rules in tinplate works shows that they were more widespread than the Webbs implied; S. and B. Webb, *Industrial Democracy* (1920 edn), pp. 493-5. An important point to note about seniority rules is that they depend for their effective working on limiting entry only to those in the same firm or plant; otherwise the number eligible for any vacancy becomes effectively unlimited.

2. N.B. Dearle, *Industrial Training* (1914), pp. 92-5.

3. Ibid., pp. 98-110.

4. Ibid., p. 113.

5. George Acorn, *One of a Multitude* (1911), p. 113.

6. Ibid., p. 131.

7. Ibid., pp. 185-6.

8. A. Fox, *A History of the National Union of Boot and Shoe Workers* (1958), p. 360.

9. Jackson Report, Appendix VI, p. 187.

10. Ibid.

11. C.B. Hawkins, *Norwich, A Social Study* (1910), p. 187.

12. FLW respondent no. 98; 1925 Report, Vol. V, p. 87.

13. 1915 Report, p. 197.

14. Ibid., p. 189.

15. Ibid., pp. 136-44.

16. Ibid., p. 168.

17. Ibid., pp. 163-4.

18. Ibid., pp. 164-5; also mentioned by P. de Rousiers, *The Labour Question in Britain* (1896), p. 281.

19. R.B. Smirke, *Report on Birmingham Brass Trade* (HMSO, 1914); Charles Booth *et al.*, *Life and Labour of the People of London*, 2nd series, *Industry* (5 vols., 1903), vol. 1, p. 338.

20. 1915 Report, pp. 151 and 154.

21. Booth MS., 2nd series, A9 (in British Library of Political and Economic

Science).

22. Thus in precious metals there were about 45,000 male workers in 1925, but only a total of 2,250 apprentices and learners; in boots and shoes there were about 146,000 male workers, but only 4,000 apprentices and learners; 1925 Report, vol. VII, p. 37. The Report makes the same point about the boot and shoe industry in vol. IV, p. 121.

23. 1915 Report, pp. 164-5.

24. H.A. Clegg *et al.*, *A History of British Trade Unions since 1889* (Oxford, 1964), p. 167.

25. 1915 Report, p. 58.

26. Evidence of Sir B. Browne to the Royal Commission on the Poor Laws, PP 1910, XLVIII, Qu. 86334 (my emphasis).

27. Ibid.

28. See also the discussion in Chapter 2.

29. 1915 Report, p. 256.

30. Booth, *Industry*, vol. 2, pp. 116 and 357.

31. 1915 Report, p. 256.

32. Ibid., p. 325; Booth, *Industry*, vol. 3, p. 106.

33. 1915 Report, p. 255; 10 per cent of all boys in papermills were apprentices, but about 8 per cent of all workmen were 'mechanics', who would mainly be recruited through apprenticeship; so there can have been very few apprentices to the process side; PP 1912-13, CVIII, p. 340. See also Chapter 6, Appendix 1 for details of migration in a papermill.

34. 1915 Report, p. 300; the general points made are confirmed by Booth, *Industry*, vol. 2, p. 100.

35. 1925 Report, vol. III, p.4.

36. 1915 Report, p. 49.

37. Two years was enshrined in the Coal Mines Act of 1911 as the period during which a trainee had to work alongside an experienced hewer before he could work by himself; 1925 Report, vol. III, p.5; also see H.S. Jevons, *The Coal Trade* (Newton Abbott, 1969, reprint of 1915 edn), p. 622, who does not specify a period, but implies that mining should not be regarded as a highly skilled trade; de Rousiers, *Labour Question*, p. 124, thought that two years was adequate.

38. 1915 Report, pp. 51-2.

39. Booth, *Industry*, vol. 3, pp. 341-2; railwaymen in the FLW survey all report this sort of progression; e.g. nos. 20, 86, 266.

40. A.P. Wadsworth, 'The Cotton Operatives' in G.D.H. Cole (ed.), *British Trade Unions Today* (1939), p. 389.

41. A.E. Musson, *The Typographical Association* (1954), pp. 218-19. After the First World War the TA managed to bring machine-minding under apprenticeship agreements; ibid., pp. 338-39.

42. 1915 Report, p. 248.

43. Board of Trade Handbook on Trades: *Printing* (HMSO, 1914), p. 9. Child confirms both that a considerable degree of skill was needed, and also that progression through the grades was the standard method of learning the work; J. Child, *Industrial Relations in the Printing Industry* (1967), p. 111.

44. W.D. Seymour, *Industrial Skills*, pp. 306-9.

45. P. McGeown, *Heat the Furnace Seven Times More* (1967), p. 90; 1915 Report, p. 143; 1906 Wages Census, PP 1911, LXXXVIII, p. xxiii; see also the discussion on subcontracting in Chapter 7, and in Chapter 7, n. 48.

46. McGeown, *Heat the Furnace*, p. 78.

47. Ibid., p. 10.

48. H. Gintz, 'Effect of technological change on labour in selected sections of the iron and steel industry of G.B., the U.S., and Germany, 1901-39',

unpublished PhD thesis, University of London, 1954, p. 93.

49.   Ibid., p. 99.
50.   Harry Brearley, *Steelmakers* (1933), p. 78; FLW respondent no. 307.
51.   There was little instrumentation in the relatively modern mill in which McGeown worked until the 1930s, McGeown, *Heat the Furnace*, p. 143; the evidence of Brearley and the FLW respondent also suggests that instrumentation was rare.
52.   Brearley, *Steelmakers*, pp. 43 and 49.
53.   Ibid., p. 68.
54.   Ibid., pp. 70ff, and 85.
55.   Booth, *Industry*, vol. 3, p. 123.
56.   1915 Report, p. 325.
57.   L. Weatherill, *100 Years of Papermaking* (Guardbridge, 1974), pp. 32 and 39.
58.   Information from Mr R. Rowan; I would like to thank Ron Rowan for giving up his time to talk to me about this industry. See Chapter 6, Appendix 1, for details of following-up in a papermill.
59.   1915 Report, p. 133.
60.   Ibid., p. 61; Jackson Report, Appendix VI, p. 186.
61.   L.T. C. Rolt, *Landscape with Machines* (1971), p. 96.
62.   1915 Report, p. 135.
63.   1925 Report, vol. VI, p. 127; W.E. Minchinton, *The British Tinplate Industry* (1957), pp. 110-11; FLW respondent no. 380, a tinplate worker, reported experiences similar to those outlined in the text.
64.   Booth, *Industry*, vol. 3, p. 159.
65.   1925 Report, vol. VI, p. 69.
66.   Dearle, *Training*, p. 132.
67.   1925 Report, vol. VI, p. 71; Sylvia Price, 'Clyde Riveters Earnings 1889-1913', unpublished paper, pp. 3-4; in 1906 the average earnings of riveters on piece (the majority) were 47s 10d per week, although Price thinks this may be overstated; the contrast with the 15s 9d per week of adult rivet-heaters is remarkable, even if the riveters' earnings were less than shown; ibid., pp. 17-18.
68.   1925 Report, vol. VI, p. 69.
69.   Rolt, *Landscape with Machines*, p. 95.
70.   Price, 'Clyde Riveters', p. 24.
71.   Booth considered that apprenticeship in this occupation in London, was not necessary at all, and Dearle considered that only a short apprenticeship was necessary; Booth, *Industry*, vol. I, pp. 324-5; Dearle, *Training*, p. 133. London was, however, hardly an important centre for riveting.
72.   Webbs, *Industrial Democracy*, p. 490.
73.   1915 Report, p. 61.
74.   Booth, *Industry*, vol. I, p. 332.
75.   FLW respondent no. 425.
76.   1915 Report, p. 61.
77.   Ibid., p. 16.
78.   Ibid.
79.   Dearle, *Training*, pp. 123-5.
80.   1925 Report, vol. II, pp. 50-1.
81.   1915 Report, p. 16.
82.   Michael Reynolds, *Engine Driving Life* (1881), p. 17.
83.   Ibid., pp. 21-2.
84.   Ibid., p. 34. Engine-driving did not change much over the years; a driver who started in the last days of steam recently described his career to me; it was little different from that outlined by Reynolds almost 100 years ago.

85. 1915 Report, p. 9.

86. 1925 Report, vol. II, p. 43; building trade unionism was undoubtedly strengthened by the war, and this may have led to an increase in apprenticeship; J.W.F. Rowe, *Wages in Practice and Theory* (1928), p. 101. Many building employers are not averse to entry restrictions, which prevent undercutting; see K. Liepmann, *Apprenticeship* (1960), p. 169, and discussion of printing, where similar tendencies are exhibited, in Chapter 7.

87. FLW respondent no. 343.

88. Dearle, *Training*, pp. 138-9. Their comments are borne out by those of a building firm manager: the young unskilled man 'can become a bricklayer in twenty-five minutes, you might say'; but 'it requires five years to make a bricklayer who can cut arches, who knows the bonds and who can set out the work'; Charity Organisation Society, *Special Report on Unskilled Labour* (1908), p. 233.

89. 1915 Report, p. 21.

90. Booth, *Industry*, vol. 1, pp. 57ff. and 88-99.

91. 1915 Report, pp. 56-9.

92. Dearle, *Training*, pp. 143-4.

93. Rolt, *Landscape with Machines*, p. 94.

94. Dearle, *Training*, p. 147.

95. Charity Organisation Society, *Special Report on Unskilled Labour*, p. 187.

Appendix: Migration and Following-up in a Scottish Papermill

The following career patterns, taken from the wages book of a Scottish papermill, contain examples of both learning by migration and following-up. While no attempt was made in this study to trace careers over a number of contiguous years, some interesting patterns were apparent: for instance there was little movement between the labourers, the skilled maintenance workers and the process workers (shown here). There was some indication that some process workers were more favoured than others in promotion, but whether this was because of ability or family influence was not clear.

Examples 2 and 3 show how boys, who usually started on the machine, were moved around quickly to gain experience. This was the case practically every year. Example 6 shows a career in full — including decline due presumably to age.

1. Peter Duncan
1871 3rd hand beaterman
1872 2nd hand machineman
by 1881 1st hand machineman

2. William Kidd
1881 Boy on machine
1882 Boy on grass-boiler
1883 Assistant on press
1883 ”   ”   ”
1885 1st hand on press

3. William Merriwell
1881 Boy on machine
1882 Boy on grass-boiler
1883 ”   ”   ”   ”
1884 Assistant on press
1885 ”   ”   ”

4. J. McMeechan
1901 Assistant on machine
1902 ”   ”   ”
1903 2nd hand beaterman
1910 2nd hand beaterman

5. A. McDonald
1901 3rd hand beaterman
1902 2nd hand on press
by 1910 1st hand breakerman

6. James Harkness
1871 Assistant beaterman
by 1881 1st hand beaterman
1891 1st hand beaterman
by 1901 2nd hand beaterman
1910 Assistant on grass-boiler

Source: Jas Lovell and Co. (Penicuik) Wages Books; SRO, GD 272/36-41.

Part III

SOME IMPLICATIONS

7 SKILL IN THEORY AND PRACTICE

Introduction

The evidence we have assembled in the previous two chapters will now be used to test the theories outlined in Chapter 1. While we will be concerned in the chapter to which this passage forms the introduction with the idea of the social construction of skill in general, we will focus in particular on the ideas which are implicit in Turner's account of apprenticeship: viz. that apprenticeship was an institution which was kept by unions in order to limit entry, a policy which led to the sharp delimitation of skilled occupations from unskilled.

The first question we must resolve is how valuable the training received during an apprenticeship was, in terms of the genuine skill acquired by the apprentice. As we have seen, the dilution campaign revealed that engineering craftsmen were not easily replaced, and this is *prima facie* evidence that they possessed a considerable quantity of skill. And as we have also seen, there was a general perception by apprentices that they were reasonably well taught by journeymen. On the other hand, the evidence we have on the length of apprenticeships suggests that these did not bear any particular relationship to the amount of skill acquired: different firms, even within the same industry, took apprentices for different lengths of time; while in many cases firms were willing to vary the length of apprenticeship according to the age at which the trainee started.

In attempting to assess the period of time a worker actually needed to learn his job, or in modern training language 'reach experienced worker standard', as opposed to the length of time his apprenticeship lasted, we must penetrate behind the façade of apprenticeship to the realities of training. Let us start with the jobs which were easiest to learn.

Training and Skill in Apprenticed Trades

Ship-riveting was learnt very quickly. It is true that the apprentice might act as a rivet-heater or catcher for some length of time, and during this period he would be getting acquainted with the basic principles of the job, but since these were fairly simple it is likely that this process would not have taken long if there had been no apprenticeship. Once started on riveting proper, an apprentice was advanced to piecework within six months, implying that his training was virtually complete. It is also significant that riveting is neither rated nor paid as a skilled trade except in Britain.[1] Some of the other less important trades in shipyards which also recruited, at least partly, through apprenticeship, such as drillers or caulkers, probably also needed fairly limited amounts of skill.

Building presents a mixed picture. As we have seen, bricklayers and painters in particular were often recruited from labourers. But the fact that there was general agreement that in these trades the better quality work was very difficult to simply 'pick up' suggests that in their higher branches these trades were fairly skilled. Carpenters and joiners were undoubtedly more skilled than the general run of painters and bricklayers, so they will be discussed later.[2]

Cabinet-making is more difficult to classify. While much cabinet-making was learned by migration, or, as in the bulk of the High Wycombe furniture trade, there was regular service but little formal apprenticeship, it is not clear that the better quality branches could be properly learned without a fairly long apprenticeship. Cabinet-making is too small a trade for us to have a worthwhile biographical sample, so we will have to keep an open mind on this, but it is perhaps significant, for reasons which will become clear in a moment, that when cabinet-making was learned by apprenticeship it was common to have a spell of improvership afterwards.[3]

It may seem rather surprising to put printing next, as on the face of it this is a highly skilled craft. The basis of hand composing, however, is a series of fairly simple operations, although it requires considerable practice to perform them quickly:

> The typographer's work was from the beginning characterised by four operations: 1) taking the type pieces letter by letter from a typecase; 2) arranging them side by side in a composing 'stick', a strip of wood with corners, held in the hand; 3) justifying the line, that is to say, spacing the letters in each line out to a uniform length by using little black pieces of lead between words.[4]

(The fourth is distributing the type back after printing.) While a printer has to acquire a substantial amount of knowledge, of typefaces, layout and so on, beside the manual skill of composing, the main task in hand composing itself is to work up a satisfactory speed. At this period machine composing might well add to the skill needed because a printer would need to learn both hand and machine work, but there was still very little machine composing so this was not an important factor. It should also be noted that compositors rarely learnt press-work, which often did not involve apprenticeship at all, or to which apprentices were bound separately.[5] Nevertheless, it is probably true that a really thorough all-round knowledge of composing and all its ramifications required a genuinely long apprenticeship, although not the seven years usually served. But different sources put the time needed to learn the more limited skills which most journeymen acquired at as low as two years, and it is worth noting that one FLW respondent became a compositor without any apprenticeship at all, picking the trade up in a small provincial shop.[6] There was, of course, one thing which did distinguish printers from most manual occupations, and that was the high degree of literacy they had to possess.

In the growing industries which still kept apprenticeship, and of the trades which comprised those industries, it was carpentry and joinery on the one hand, and the numerous engineering trades on the other, which were the significant occupations requiring a lengthy period of training.

There is widespread testimony that the skill required by wood-workers in general was fairly considerable, although in the furniture trade with its scope for subdivision it could be more limited. The two other main branches of woodworking are carpentry and joinery, which are found on a large scale in building and shipbuilding, and in practically every industry in connection with maintenance work. The division between the two is, or was, most strict in building, in which carpenters perform the work of fixing the wood to the carcase of the building, that is fixing floors, roof trusses, window frames and so on: their work thus requires, besides mastery of the techniques themselves, some structural knowledge and an ability to work independently. Joiners' work is mainly in the workshop, making stairs, doors, cupboards, panelling and so on: it is finer and more detailed than carpenters' work, but capable of more subdivision and increasingly mechanised from the mid-century on.[7] Mechanisation, however, did not significantly affect the skill involved, for two reasons: first because the more complicated parts of the work were least affected by machinery; and second because the machines themselves required in many cases 'a very high degree of skill'.[8] Even so, many firms taught apprentices both hand and machine work. But the growth of a new class of woodworking machinists, who

also catered to an increasing extent for the furniture trade, and who were often apprenticed themselves, was a feature of the period.[9]

According to the 1925 Report, there was a growing tendency for apprentices to be trained as both carpenters and joiners, and this was noted also by the 1915 Report. It is worth describing in some detail one such apprenticeship because it gives some idea of how much had to be learned:

> For the first three months, the apprentice is engaged on squaring up pieces of wood, in 'trueing' and in planing. During the next two years, i.e. up to the end of his second year, he learns to make joints, and to joint articles together, to cut mitres and to make small articles, such as ledge doors and door frames. In his third year, he learns to cut rafters, to fix skirtings, to lay floors and generally to do inside fixing work on a contract job. [The fourth year − it was a five-year apprenticeship − is not described, but presumably he continued this sort of work.] In his last year of apprenticeship, he returns to the bench and learns to make door panels, sash frames and to do staircase work, which is considered to be an advanced stage of joinery. During his improvership period, he works more or less as a journeyman, but until he has served five years he is supervised all the time by a journeyman or by the foreman.[10]

The apprentice in this firm, therefore, was not reckoned a fully efficient worker until the very end of his apprenticeship. Obviously it would take less time to learn either carpentry or joinery separately, but since much of the work was common to both trades, and had to be learnt even if only one of them was taken up, it seems reasonable to say that three years or so was the minimum required to become a reasonably efficient worker.

Much the same is true of engineering. While it would be far too time-consuming to discuss in detail all the many trades in this industry, a brief account of the work which a turner might experience during his apprenticeship shows that there were a considerable number of techniques which he would have to master.

Training of an Apprentice Turner[11]

1. Drawing office and machine tool store.
2. Small slotting machine, helps at marking-off table.
3. Small planing machine.

4. Larger planing machine.
5. Lathe for turning shop tools.
6. Lathe for turning belts, pillars, hand wheels etc.
7. Small centre lathe   )
8. Larger centre lathe   ) In all these
9. Chuck lathe.   ) turning a number
10. Larger chuck lathe.   ) of different
11. Screw-cutting lathe.   ) objects.

Turners were generally reckoned to be, as engineering workers went, of average skill level — similar to fitters, but probably less skilled than patternmakers and toolmakers; and as already noted, a not inconsiderable number of engineering workers were trained at two different trades.[12]

Not surprisingly, therefore, it took some time before the apprentice was able to make a significant contribution to production. The Managing Director of Hawthorn Leslie, J.M. Allen, said:

> In any of the many trades embraced in the term 'Engineering', the first two years of apprenticeship are of little value to any but the apprentice himself ... By the end of the third year he is becoming of some use to his employer, and it is during the fourth and fifth year that the benefit of his help is felt and some return obtained for the earlier years of apprenticeship.[13]

As with carpentry and joinery, we can conclude that if adequate training was to be given, three years or so was needed before the engineering apprentice became even moderately productive.

The widespread practice of improvership, however, for which there is plentiful evidence in engineering and woodworking but much less in the other industries we have surveyed, suggests that even at the end of apprenticeship the apprentice was not necessarily a fully effficient worker. If woodworking and engineering workers had been actually worth full wages on finishing their apprenticeship, the normal workings of competition in the labour market would have earned that, by and large, they got them, since improvers were not bound legally or in any other way, and there were no seniority rules to prevent management promoting the ablest men. Undoubtedly improvership existed to some extent because the skills learned during apprenticeship were fairly specific, and especially if apprentices moved to a different firm when their apprenticeship ended they were able to broaden their knowledge. But this does not imply that training during apprenticeship was necessarily inadequate: specific skills were learnt simply because the actual amount of knowledge and skill needed was, as we have just seen, very high, even for one trade. Remarks from FLW respondents also suggest that improvership was not merely a customary institution, but fulfilled a genuine need: 'an employer wanted you to get off and get some exercise somewhere else then [i.e. at the end of apprenticeship] and then come back to him' (toolmaker): 'he [the improver] gradually got better and better because of course some of the technical parts of joinery are very complicated'.[14]

Finally we should note that in shipbuilding, although we do not have any particular evidence as to the length of time it took to learn the platers' and the shipwrights' trade, the considerable number of techniques which workers in both these occupations had to master suggests that they were considerably more difficult to learn than, for instance, riveting. Platers' work has already been discussed; shipwrights' work involved relatively simple tasks, such as the laying of decks and making of bulkheads, and also some much more complex ones, such as erecting the steel frames and beams of the ship, making sure that its construction was true, and making moulds and templates for various kinds of work performed by other operatives.[15] These trades should probably be ranked with others in engineering and woodworking, rather than in shipbuilding; indeed because of the necessity for a shipwright to work in wood and metal, his was perhaps one of the most skilled occupations.

The main purpose of this appraisal has been to give some idea of the time needed to reach Experienced Worker Standard in the growing industries in which apprenticeship still flourished, namely printing, building, woodworking, engineering and shipbuilding. We have not attempted to cover old trades where apprenticeship lingered on in bespoke sections, like tailoring, or trades which were dominated by artisan workshops, like the saddlers and wheelwrights, because to do so would not further the argument significantly.

How does the skill required in apprenticed trades compare with the skill required in other occupations? It might be argued that it is difficult to compare training times in apprenticed and non-apprenticed occupations, because in the former the apprentice had the advantage of direct instruction from the journeyman, and apprentice wages were adjusted to take account of this, while in the latter, the learner had to pick up his knowledge as best he could. But in fact, if we look at the actual method of learning in apprenticeship what we notice above all is that the apprentice spent most of his time working; as was shown by the biographical evidence, and other evidence such as the schematic outline of a turner's training shown above, after an initial period on errand-boy work, perhaps if he was lucky in the toolroom or the drawing office, the apprentice was set to productive work; the journeyman's and foreman's role was to start him off and supervise him. This was not because apprentice education was necessarily inadequate, but simply because to acquire a high degree of manual skill it is necessary to practise, while much of the knowledge required was, as Sir Benjamin Browne said, the knowledge of what was good work and what was bad — and for this, too, the only practical method of learning was to be there in the workshop.

Training and Skill in Non-apprenticed Trades

It is clear, then, that both apprentices and non-apprentices learned in essentially the same way, by working. And if this was the case, then it does not seem unreasonable to compare the learning times of the two groups. Even more than apprentices, however, non-apprenticed trainees were constrained from progressing upwards at the pace their abilities might dictate either by formal seniority rules or, in occupations where these did not apply, by the availability of vacancies in the ranks above them, and therefore in most cases it is not enough to use the time it actually took to be promoted, even if we knew this, as a proxy for the time needed to learn the job. The only exceptions to this rule are occupations which were learned by migration from firm to firm, but since this was a practice used mainly in the more subdivided branches of trades which also had apprenticeship, such as cabinet-making and moulding, it seems likely that in most cases the skill acquired was less than in the apprenticed branches.

The opinions of experienced observers do, however, give us a rough guide to the relationship between learning times and skill in some non-apprenticed and apprenticed trades. Reynolds, for instance, puts the time needed to become a competent engine-driver at five years — roughly comparable with an apprenticeship in engineering and woodworking, in which workers became productive after three years or so, but took considerably longer to become fully efficient. A papermill manager, who of course had experience of apprenticed maintenance workers as well as process workers, put the most skilled of the latter at a level comparable with the former. We do not have such a direct comparison for iron and steel workers, but given the considerable evidence which shows that the leading hands were highly skilled, it seems reasonable to put them on a similar level; the same probably applies to other workers in metal trades, such as heavy forge workers, workers in rolling mills, and tinplate workers. Even the machine-made boot and shoe industry, although subdivided, had workers in the upper echelons who earned wages similar to those of workers in apprenticed trades — wages in this industry, which had no strict seniority rules, being a better guide to skill than in most occupations.

On the face of it, then, there is nothing to separate non-apprenticed trades from apprenticed trades in terms of skill, some of the former demanding as much skill from their more senior workers as the more highly skilled apprenticed trades. In some cases work in apprenticed trades took less time to learn than work in non-apprenticed trades — notably so in the case of riveting, and perhaps in some of the other shipyard trades, but also so in printing; it is certainly arguable that in the case of the latter the managers of rotary presses, who were often not apprenticed, were just as if not more skilled than compositors, who usually were. So far, although the evidence suggests that Turner's hypothesis has something in it, it does not fully bear it out, because in most cases the wage levels of the non-apprenticed workers we have been considering were not dissimilar to those in apprenticed occupations, suggesting that wage levels in apprenticed trades were not artificially high;[16] but this could be at least partially explained by the existence of seniority rules, which as Turner showed in the case of cotton had a similar effect to apprenticeship in delimiting wages. What seems to lend even stronger support to his theory, however, is that only in apprenticed trades do we have the gulf between apprenticed and non-apprenticed worker; in every other occupation there is a hierarchy of different grades up which the learner progressed, either working a series of machines each of which was more advanced than the next, or advancing from third to second to first hand in a gang, or combining the two methods. This seems to be the strongest argument for saying that apprenticeship is an artificial institution: in most apprenticed trades, even the most skilled like engineering, there *were* workers who learnt their trade by the same gradual upward progression; why could not other workers in these trades have learned the same way?

Supposing we turned the question round. Why did not all industries have apprenticeship? It might be argued, after all, that apprenticeship was an historic method of teaching young workers, and that if it imparted valuable knowledge it was not a method of socially constructing skill, but of passing on genuine skill. I do not intend to argue in favour of this proposition as so baldly stated, but it is worth putting forward because it forces us to look at Turner's proposition in a new way. Should we, instead of seeing apprenticeship as an archaic survival foisted by the unions on management, see it as fulfilling a very real purpose? The next few pages are devoted to elaborating this point of view, first by criticising some aspects of Turner's argument, and then by advancing some counter-arguments.

Trades Unions and Apprenticeship

The first criticism we can make is of Turner's implied contention that unions enforced apprenticeship on management, at least in the growing industries with which we are primarily concerned. Turner's account of apprenticeship has it surviving in eighteenth-century handicraft trades through joint employer/employee regulation, the former supporting limitation as much as the latter because both classes were recruited from apprentices; he suggests that certain trades like printing were left aside by the Factory Revolution, and in these apprenticeship 'suffered no direct attack by employers, and survived naturally' – a comment implying that employer interest in apprenticeship was now declining, but that employers were not actually hostile; elsewhere, however, he implies that it was predominantly the journeymen who kept apprenticeship, commenting that

> The large-scale employers of the Industrial Revolution . . . found the apprenticeship system an obstacle to the spread (and hence cheapening) of skills, and neither they, nor the State in which they had become influential, were at all concerned to maintain it. So the journeymen were driven to assume the burden of its enforcement alone: and in the process their societies emerged as the modern craft unions, to which the preservation of apprenticeship was, and continued to be, the essential aim.[17]

Finally, he sees it imported into the engineering industry by the woodworkers, via the millwrights, who were primarily workers in wood; and it was also through the medium of skilled workers in wood that it gained a foothold in other industries such as ship and vehicle building.[18]

We are not concerned here with the early history of apprenticeship: Turner's explanation of its survival in the eighteenth century seems very plausible; equally there is no doubt that before the repeal of 1814 an attack was launched on it by numerous employers, although it is worth noting that there were some employers who supported it, and also that one of the freedoms which repeal gave was the right of anyone to become a master — in other words the repeal movement was not concerned solely with the right of employers to hire who they liked, but also with their right to carry on what business they liked.[19]

Where Turner's interpretation is more doubtful is his stress on the role of the woodworkers in engineering, and, more generally, the suggestion, implicit in his account, that unions were strong enough to force apprenticeship on employers who were at best indifferent to it. The early engineering industry was composed of a heterogeneous collection of workers from a whole variety of trades, and although millwrights worked in it, as did other woodworkers such as carpenters and joiners, they were not the only class of workers by any means. Other trades, no doubt, had their own apprenticeship regulations, or would have liked to, but Turner explicitly accords to the millwrights the main role in early engineering trade unionism, when he says that the journeymen-millwrights societies were the first of the New Model ASE's progenitors.[20] This is, quite simply, not the case. McClaine's detailed study of the early engineering trade unions traces the Journeymen Steam Engine and Machine Makers Friendly Society, the direct ancestor of the ASE, back to the Mechanics Friendly Institute of 1824, which provided for, *inter alia*, the admittance of Model Makers, Smiths, Joiners, and Wood and Iron Turners — a whole host of trades. And there is no direct link between that society and the various millwrights organisations which were active in the late eighteenth and early nineteenth centuries; on the contrary, the rapid expansion of engineering in the second decade of the nineteenth century broke the power of the millwrights' unions. It is also of considerable significance that several societies, such as the United Order of Smiths, Machinists and Engineers, did not insist upon apprenticeship as a qualification for membership, but were willing to admit those who were able to command the average wage for their employment.[21]

It is not a matter of mere antiquarian curiosity that there was no real connection between the millwrights' societies and the beginnings of engineering trade unionism. If we are willing to accept that engineering grew up gradually on the basis of the woodworkers' skill, then it is not difficult to see how apprenticeship survived, accepted as a customary institution by employers, although as we shall see even this account does not fully accord with the social construction hypothesis we are examining. But if the millwrights' influence had broken down at an early date, then the survival of apprenticeship in the engineering industry assumes a different significance. If we are to accept that it was a product of unilateral regulation by unions, then we have to believe that it was imposed upon employers by these unions from the 1820s onwards, when they began to emerge. And imposing an artificial method of training is likely to be much more difficult than merely ensuring that this method survives.

There is no evidence, however, that the engineering unions were strong enough to impose apprenticeship on their employers even by the mid-century, let alone in the 1820s or 1830s. While we have few hard and fast figures about the density of trade union membership in the mid-century, J.F. Clarke's study of the engineering industry in the North-East shows that unions were very weak: in 1852, for instance, there were 128 ASE members out of at least 2,000 engine and machine makers in the area; even allowing for other unions in the industry, total density was unlikely to have been more than 10 per cent. By 1861 density had increased in this area, although it was still low; and the Jeffreys' survey of the entire ASE membership at this date suggests that it covered a maximum of 40 per cent of all skilled workers – a figure that is almost certainly too high because it is a percentage of workers in engineering proper, and does not cover maintenance workers; taking all skilled unions into account, union density was a maximum of 50 per cent of all workers. The Carpenters and Joiners were even weaker: as late as 1888 they only covered about 13 per cent of the total skilled workforce.[22]

The prevalence of a particular strike tactic in the mid-nineteenth century, the 'strike in detail', reinforces our argument that the retention of apprenticeship cannot be put down to the influence of unions alone. The strike in detail involved the removal of unionised workers from a shop that did not meet union conditions.[23] In the social construction model with which we are concerned, technology and therefore skill are almost infinitely variable; but if this was really the case in the nineteenth century, then strikes in detail could not have been effective. Employers might not have been able to import unskilled labour immediately, because their machines would be adapted for the use of skilled workers, but they would soon learn to avoid such strikes altogether by using machinery which was simpler to operate. That they did not is obvious from the evidence that we have put forward on the continuing importance of skilled workers before the First World War. Strikes in detail could only have been effective where skill was genuine; therefore skill could not have been constructed by strikes in detail; and likewise the retention of apprenticeship as the route to skill could not have been enforced by such strikes.

So far, we have simply shown that an account of apprenticeship which put its survival down to unilateral regulation by unions must be inadequate. This limited conclusion is borne out by a study of other industries where apprenticeship did not survive. In papermaking the decline of apprenticeship is particularly striking. The old handpaper unions were amongst the strongest of all in the late eighteenth and early nineteenth centuries.[24] Machine papermaking brought with it in the 1820s a revolution in technique, but the industry carried on for the most part in the same locations, and still required considerable skill; yet apprenticeship survived only in an attenuated and almost unrecognisable form. Later in the century, exactly the same thing happened in the boot and shoe industry.[25] Whatever the reasons for the fact that apprenticeship virtually died out in these industries — these will be discussed later — it seems clear that if employers did not want apprenticeship, they did not have to have it. The argument that apprenticeship survived in engineering and woodworking because skills in these industries were transformed much more slowly is not acceptable within the framework of the particular social construction hypothesis we are examining, because as we have noted this assumes that technology, and therefore skill, is almost infinitely variable; it might, of course, be a salient argument if used outside this framework.

Since apprenticeship did survive, and since unions were not strong enough to enforce it themselves, there can be only one conclusion: that management was concerned to keep apprenticeship as well. At this point, it might be rightly objected that 'apprenticeship' could mean two very different things. It could mean the employment of juvenile workers who, bound to their employers through necessity, or misrepresentation of the nature of the apprenticeship offered, were forced to work as if they were ordinary workers, but were paid less than a full wage, and at the end of their time possessed no skill, whether genuine or socially constructed, worth having. As we have seen, this type of apprenticeship was familiar in the first half of the nineteenth century; we called such workers 'exploited apprentices'. Naturally enough, employers were keen to take this sort of apprentice, since they acquired the product of a worker at the wage of a learner.

'Apprentice' could also mean someone who learned something, or who had acquired at the end of his time the right to enter a restricted trade, and it was this sort of apprenticeship, it might be pointed out, that unions were concerned to keep. But the objections we have already raised to the strength of unions apply just as much here: in order to render this sort of apprenticeship effective, assuming — as in the social construction hypothesis — that it was not necessary to actually acquire skill, the unions had to be strong enough to both limit apprentices and also to refuse to work with 'journeymen' who had not been apprenticed. Now it is true by the end of the century unions and employers had many local agreements, often unofficial, over apprentice limitation. Thus in the building industry, firms in 70 out of 85 towns reported limitation, in one or more trades; in engineering there was little formal evidence of limitation in the 1890s, but the 1915 Report found that the number of apprentices was limited by custom and practice in many areas, in spite of the explicit disclaimer on limitation in the national agreement following the 1897-8 lockout; in iron-moulding and electrical engineering there were, similarly, local agreements on limitation in a number of areas.[26]

So the unions' contribution to the effectiveness of apprenticeship cannot be ignored, and will be returned to later; but it must be put in perspective. First of all, the very low density of union membership must be taken into account; because of this there were large numbers of firms exempt from union influence. The weakness of unions was most apparent in the building trades (see note 22, this chapter), but in the mid-century no industries were highly unionised: the resulting weakness made apprenticeship limitation impossible among foundry workers in the mid-century, while as late as the 1880s a two year-long engineers strike in Sunderland, over the same issue, failed.[27] And even where union density was fairly high, as in engineering by the beginning of the twentieth century, and there were local agreements on limitation, the proportion of apprentices allowed was quite generous: one apprentice to three journeymen was usual, and only occasionally one to four.[28]

It seems that we must accept that employers in certain industries were not only willing to keep apprenticeship but also provided a genuine training, since the persistence of skill differentials cannot be accounted for on the grounds of social construction. The willingness of employers to keep exploitive apprenticeship does not need explaining; what does need to be explained is the mechanism by which employers were encouraged to provide a proper training.

Employers and Apprenticeship

Let us first construct a model of how apprenticeship collapses: in some industry, be it lace-making, pottery, or one of the Birmingham trades, the profit to be made by employing juvenile labour encourages employers to take children offered to them by the parish; and custom, some residual skill left in the industry, or simply the lack of alternative child employment, may also lead parents to bind their children as apprentices, since they are likely to receive some wages, albeit low ones. When the child has served his time, he finds that he can earn no more at his trade than an adult coming to it with no experience, since there is little or no skill attached: indeed there may not be a job for him in it at all, if it is stocked entirely by cheap child labour. As time goes by, a number of things might happen. If the industry does require adult labour with some, but not very much, skill, the apprentice will be tempted to break his engagement as soon as he has acquired this skill and go where he can earn a wage reflecting his current productivity: this seems to have happened in the pottery industry. Or the supply of cheap skilled labour will be restricted through legislation, or through the rising incomes of parents which free them from the necessity of selling their children's labour at distress prices.[29] While the influence of legislation might be of considerable importance, therefore, the role of the market should also be considered as a factor.

We can use this as a foundation for our model of how apprenticeship survives: it must first and foremost offer something to the apprentice, and what it must offer is a genuine training or an effective limitation of the labour market. Where there was a choice of occupation, we can only believe that the exploited apprentice survived if we believe that parents and apprentices were either ignorant or stupid. So long as we take a reasonably optimistic view of humanity, we are unlikely to believe the latter; while some families may have suffered from their ignorance, it is unlikely to have been a high proportion because as we have seen a large number of apprentices entered the firm their father or a close relative was in; even when this was not the case, apprentices and parents would usually possess some connection with the firm, or have some knowledge of it where it was a large local employer. Even when they started work, apprentices were not completely at the mercy of employers: they had their sanctions, of complaining and making a nuisance of themselves, and as we have seen in some cases these worked.

To accept that parents and apprentices were an autonomous group with a measure of power and judgement, has important implications: given that unions were not strong enough to socially construct skill, employers had to offer a genuine training, which enabled the boy to compete effectively on the labour market. If they did not, and their apprentices found themselves unable to command a decent wage on completing their time, firms would soon find that apprentices would not come to them. What we now have to explain is why it was worth the employers' while to offer this genuine training: it is perfectly explicable why employers wanted apprentices whom they could exploit; but given that they could not exploit them to any significant degree, that apprentices were free to leave at the end of their apprenticeship, and that employers were not in general altruists who wished to train up workers for their rivals at their own expense, we have the apparent paradox that employers had to offer a genuine training and yet also make a profit on it.

One way of resolving this paradox was to train workers who were expected to stay with the firm; in this case firms did not need to cover their full costs of training until after the apprenticeship had ended. So long as they paid decent wages, employers might expect a fair number of workers to stay anyway, while quite often, no doubt, workers were trained to specific machines or processes. When workers achieved the standard rate of wages at the end of their apprenticeship – and the firm would have to pay that or it would find it difficult in the long run to attract apprentices – a specialised training was not necessarily to the workers' disadvantage, although they might encounter problems if the firm closed. One example of this sort of apprenticeship is given by de Rousiers, who noted that Platt Brothers, the huge Oldham textile machinery manufacturer, provided a seven-year apprenticeship to work of an 'extremely delicate and technical kind', which in de Rousier's opinion did not have much market value outside Platts.[30]

Plenty of apprentices did leave their firms when their time was up, however, and some firms seem to have expected this. In this case, the mechanism by which the employer could reconcile training with profit is explained by Sir Benjamin Browne:

> An easy compromise between the interests of the lad and those of his employer is aimed at by working on the following principles:
> – It is to the interest of the lad to learn to do whatever he takes in hand thoroughly well. It is not to his interest to continue at one class of work after he had learned all that is to be learned at it. But again, it is to the employer's interest to employ him on different and costly (or what is known in the shops as 'good' work) rather than on inferior work.

In other words, it was in both parties' interest for the apprentice to progress to more difficult work. That this was not simply the opinion of one enlightened employer is confirmed by Dearle, who says almost exactly the same thing: if boys are kept to simple processes, their work would never be worth more than a certain sum; those who learned more would make a greater contribution to the employer's overheads. He pointed out one other constraint: if a boy did work which could be done by an unskilled man, he would not produce as much, but would occupy valuable bench space.[31]

Training, then, had an economic rationale for the employer. As J.M. Allen of Hawthorn Leslie said, he lost money on the first two years of apprenticeship, at least in engineering, but he could expect to break even in the third, and make a profit in the fourth and fifth. Different employers, no doubt, found the point at which extra training became unremunerative occurred at different times: but in this all were constrained by the necessity of attracting apprentices, and no one could get away with out-and-out exploitation for too long.

We have finally to explain how over-stocking of the labour market was prevented. One reason was simply that if a genuine training was provided, a firm was practically limited in the number of apprentices it took; nevertheless, firms could in most cases have trained as many apprentices as there were journeymen, which would have over-stocked most occupations. More important, probably, was the fact that because apprenticeship was not an easy way of making money for employers, it did not suit many firms to take apprentices as all. If all the work called for a high degree of skill, of if the competition of other employment forced apprentice wages up to a higher level than was usual, then apprentices might not be worth the firm's while; for these reasons, and because of high overheads, London had few apprentices — and provided a market for many from outside. Taking apprentices, too, presented problems of communication and discipline which were, perhaps, better handled in small firms. At any rate, the discrepancy between large and small firms in their apprentice/journeyman ratio is very striking in 1925, and although union influence might be a factor in some cases, it could not explain the very low ratio in the largest firms.[32]

Union influence obviously had some overall effect on the number of apprentices trained, for as we have seen there were a large number of local agreements on limitation by the end of the century. But as we have also seen, unions were not strong enough to have had a major influence (although a partial exception should be made for printing and shipbuilding, considered later in this chapter). And while the large, high-class firms such as those Sir Benjamin Browne spoke for would not employ excessive numbers of apprentices because this would be incompatible with the high-quality training they found it expedient to give, the small and medium-sized firms which did employ large numbers of apprentices would be less likely to be unionised; the sanction which prevented them becoming a serious problem was, as we have already shown, the sanction of the market. To that could be added the unofficial restriction which must have obtained where journeymen covertly refused to train excessive numbers of apprentices property: there is little evidence for this in the biographical material, although Tom Bell refers to it; but where over-stocking of apprentices did exist, such refusal to train must have taken place. This would have resulted in apprentices receiving inadequate training, and consequently to a decline in the attractiveness of the firm to the apprentice.

We can perhaps sum up the influence of unions on apprenticeship in the bulk of woodworking, engineering and building trades by saying that they performed a useful role on the margin. They kept some firms up to the mark who would otherwise have been tempted to exploit apprentices: while in the long run apprentices would be discouraged from joining such firms, information about training standards would take time to circulate and there were always some people whom it would not reach.[33] Dearle pays a tribute to the role of unions in improving the standard of training by attacking abuses, although he was referring to the printing industry where, in London, unions were fairly strong.[34] Over the long run, however, we cannot accord unions an important position in the regulation of apprenticeship: they were far too weak, especially earlier in the nineteenth century, for any action they took to have more than a local and partial effect.

We must also reiterate that parents were not likely to be wholly ignorant of market conditions. It seems probable, for instance, that the failure of declining trades to become grossly over-stocked with workers was largely due to parents' perception of their decline, although in some old trades such as the London hatters there were effective union restraints. In general, the industries we are concerned with were growing throughout this period, and they could support a relatively high apprentice/journeyman ratio. But it is interesting to note that Wal Hannington's father, a bricklayer, was determined in the 1900s when building was depressed that his sons should not follow him into the trade.

The Rationale of Different Training Methods: Technology and the Labour Market

While we have explained why firms were willing both to take apprentices and, having taken them, to train them properly, we have not yet explained why firms chose to train their labour force by taking apprentices rather than by some other means. Since we must abandon the idea that apprenticeship was a 'social' institution, we must seek to explain it by looking at economic and technological realities.

First of all apprenticeship survived because of a combination of technological and product market constraints. The two are intertwined, because the nature of the market helps to shape technology. As Saul has shown, the nature of the market for British engineering products before the First World War was such as to encourage diversified rather than standardised output; the result of this was that the technology of the industry demanded the skilled, all-round worker, and the all-purpose lathe which could be switched about to different types of production. In some cases, however, such as building, the technology is essentially the same whether the product is supplied in large or small quantities, because only a limited amount of routinisation of work is feasible even in the former instance.[35]

Let us first examine the industries and occupations where apprenticeship both survived, and was a route to genuine and considerable skill. In the engineering trades and carpentry and joinery, the proportion of skilled workers was very high: in engineering in the 1900s it was probably around 50 per cent, and this was lower than the mid-century; in carpentry and joinery it was even higher, because there were no 'carpenters and joiners labourers' in building.[36] Furthermore, in carpentry and joinery there was no easy route for an unskilled man to acquire skill. In some departments of engineering this was possible: in turning, for instance, an apprentice would acquire skill by moving from the simple to the more complex machines, and therefore it was feasible, if difficult, for an unskilled man to acquire skill in the same way.

Since the skilled portion of the labour force in these occupations was so high, it was simply not possible to recruit it from less skilled men, even if, as in engineering, they were sometimes able to pick up their skill by progression. It must be remembered there that by no means all the less skilled workers in either engineering or building were either labourers or machine-operators; many of them had specialised positions of their own, such as scaffolding or crane-driving, which did not provide opportunities to learn 'skilled' occupations. Furthermore, it is doubtful if progression provided adequate training for any but the exceptional few, if they were able to command a fully skilled man's wages. As McClaine said of engineering,

> From 1824 [the foundation of the Steam Engine Makers Society and other engineering trade unions] the more exacting requirements of machine production made it clear to the employers that while many of the operations previously done by hand could be done by machines, the machines must be operated by skilled men, since an unskilled operator would spoil more work on a machine than he would if engaged in handwork. And so, apprenticeship, which seemed doomed when the Elizabethan Act was repealed, became as much a passport to a job as it has ever been.[37]

The nature of tasks in engineering, and also in the woodworking trades, explains this. Even at the end of the nineteenth century, although manual skill levels were perhaps declining, the work needed a very high degree of such skill. This skill could only be acquired by practice, the cost of which in terms of time and spoiled work was returned to the employer, in the case of apprenticeship, through the lower wages he paid the apprentices; but this cost could not be made up in the same way by an adult worker, or even by a young migratory worker who would expect to earn higher wages than an apprentice.

Before examining the role of the labour market, we should contrast engineering and woodworking with the industries where apprenticeship did not exist. In any one of these where considerable skill was required there were two features of employment. The first was that the work, because of its nature, was subdivided, either by breaking it down between a number of machines or by subdividing one particular task into a number of parts, as in process work. The second was that because of the nature of technology the work could be graded in difficulty, and the proportion of less difficult tasks was high. In engineering, work was also subdivided, but because of its highly variegated nature it was not economic to allocate all the less difficult work to specialised semi-skilled workers, and hence a high proportion of skilled workers was needed; in other apprenticed trades, such as carpentry, it was impossible to effectively subdivide the work at all. In trades learned by migration, the degree of subdivision and the proportion of less skilled tasks was higher, but as migration was often an alternative to apprenticeship it should not be seen as radically different to it, although leading in general to a lower degree of skill acquired over a rather longer period, in exchange for higher wages. In following-up, subdivision might be less, but the proportion of less skilled work was much higher: typically only the worker at the head of the gang needed to be very highly skilled, and as a result the less skilled workers had much longer to acquire the skill which would eventually enable them to take their position at the top. One other, not unimportant, characteristic of work learned by following-up, and process work in particular, was that it needed a high degree of knowledge, but a lesser degree of manual skill, compared with the apprenticed jobs we have surveyed above; even process workers who did need considerable manual skill, such as the teemers in crucible steel making, needed it only for one task rather than a whole host of them, as in engineering or woodworking. Because of this, process work could be learned by adults or juveniles who were also carrying on with their own tasks, because the absorption of knowledge does not need practice so much as time. Finally, we should note that one constraint upon apprenticeship in some industries was the necessity to use only adult labour: it would hardly have been practical (and certainly not economic) to have apprentice engine-drivers for this reason, and the same constraint applies to the iron and steel industry; but the fact that in many industries without apprenticeship, such as tinplate, crucible steel manufacture and papermaking, boys were used, shows that this was not a major factor.

Some trades which highlight the contrast between apprenticeship and other ways of learning are those where apprenticeship was adopted even though the trade was completely new, and those where apprenticeship had been very strong but was almost completely abandoned. Of the latter, papermaking by machine and the machine-made boot and shoe industry are particularly interesting; since both used boy labour, it would have been technically feasible to have retained apprenticeship and used it to maintain a gulf between skilled and less skilled workers, which the latter could not bridge. But because the tasks in both industries were subdivided and demanded a variety of grades of skill, progression, either from machine to machine or up the hierarchy of a gang, was equally feasible and in general a better and more practical method of training workers, who under this system mastered a wider range of tasks and became more flexible; it also gave the employer the opportunity to choose his skilled men from a much wider range.

One other point which should be noted about these and most other occupations learned by migration and following-up is that, just as with apprenticeship, decisions about which method of training to adopt were not solely the employers' prerogative. In such trades knowledge and manual skill could be acquired gradually and large numbers of workers with an intermediate degree of skill were required; therefore it would have been very difficult in practice to maintain a gulf between apprenticed workers and others because it was so easy for non-apprenticed workers to learn the trade. In these circumstances the long-term prospects of apprenticed workers were little better than those of any other workers, and, as in the pottery industry, if employers had tried to keep apprenticeship they would have failed because the institution did not furnish any advantages for young workers. Only in industries with certain exceptional features, such as printing and ship-building, could apprenticeship survive in these conditions.

On the other hand, woodworking by machine and electrical contracting provide instances of completely new occupations which adopted apprenticeship. The former, as we have already seen, required a high degree of skill; where it was pursued on a large scale or to less exact standards, as in machine sawying, it was learnt by progression; but where the product was diversified and had to be made to very exact standards, as in cabinet-making and joinery, it made sense to train woodworking machinists by apprenticeship. Electrical contracting is analogous to carpentry, in that it requires a high degree of skill, and like all building work cannot be reduced to routine.[38]

We can summarise the influence of technology and the product market on training as follows. Industries which kept apprenticeship were not by their nature able to *economically* use mass production techniques. This limitation might arise because the product, although not necessarily utilising very complex technology, was always changing and thus required a wide knowledge of techniques among the work-force; this factor would particularly apply to the building and wood-working industries. Or the limitation on mass production techniques might arise because the product's role in the market − as a producer good rather than a consumer good, for instance − was such that only limited numbers of a complex product were required, thus making the adoption of skill-maximising and capital-minimising techniques the only sensible course; this factor would particularly apply to the engineering industry. Industries where training was carried out by means of migration or following-up were characterised by a wide variety of jobs requiring varying degrees of skill; this skill, which often had a high knowledge element in it, was transferable from one job to another, thus facilitating learning by progression.

The impossibility of routinising, or as Stinchcombe has put it 'bureaucratising' building work is an illustration of the second important reason for the survival of apprenticeship, the nature of the labour market — although like technology, this is difficult to distinguish from the product market which sets the parameters for it. Stinchcombe was concerned with Weber's suggestion that a hierarchical and bureaucratised labour force, subject to rules and supervision, was the only rational method of organising work under modern conditions. He pointed out that in building the intense seasonality of the work makes it uneconomic to incur a high oncost by employing the numerous clerical and supervisory workers necessary to such an organisation, since for various reasons such workers have to be permanently employed. Furthermore, there are very real practical constraints on the amount of supervision possible on a building site. As a result, what Stinchcombe called 'craft control' of work was rational: workers were 'professionalised', a word he uses to mean that they were recognised by an independent authority as capable of performing certain tasks; in Britain, at any rate, such an authority would be apprenticeship lines/the union. Such workers could then be left to get on with the job.[39]

While Stinchcombe's theory undoubtedly does have particular applicability to building work, it is worth considering its relevance to apprenticeship in general. It is particularly notable that some of the industries in which apprenticeship flourished — especially heavy engineering and ship-building, as well as building itself — were subject to violent fluctuations of output, caused by trade cycles in the two former, seasonality and trade cycles in the latter, and the fluctuating order books of individual firms in all three. Craft control, with the reduction of oncost it allowed, was therefore a rational method of organising work for all of them.

One other point which is worth mentioning here is that trade unions' concern with apprenticeship limitation may not have been entirely due to a desire to socially construct skill, but is partly explicable as a practical response to the fluctuations of the labour market. In other words, in interesting themselves in apprenticeship, unions were concerned with what they said they were concerned with, namely preventing over-stocking of the labour market; they were not excessively worried about labourers acquiring their skill, because it was genuinely difficult to acquire; but they were worried because there was too much skill around at certain times, for instance depressions.[40]

We should not, however, overstate the influence of the labour market *per se* on apprenticeship. The latter survived in, for instance, large firms which were more subject to routinisation, such as Platts of Oldham; and it survived in occupations like joinery, or among maintenance workers, whose employment was much more stable.

Similarly, unions in engineering and building, as we have seen, could not have succeeded by themselves in limiting apprentices to any considerable extent because they were not strong enough. What we must explain, however was the role of unions in printing and shipbuilding.

Apprenticeship in Printing and Shipbuilding

Turner saw printing as an example of an old trade where apprenticeship had survived naturally, because the tasks did not change. This is no doubt true, but it masks a change in the relationship between printing and other skilled trades. It is arguable that the actual manual skill and knowledge required in printing was no greater, and possibly less, than in most engineering and woodworking trades, but in the early part of the century printers had to possess what at that time was a rare and precious commodity, namely literacy. The printers' seven-year apprenticeship, therefore, while not strictly necessary from the point of view of learning the trade, was effectively sanctioned by the fact that few interlopers could learn it. As time went by, however, literacy became a common possession, and the seven-year apprenticeship became more and more a means of socially constructing skill. As with all such attempts at unilateral regulation in the nineteenth century, it was subject to considerable attack; the unions had some hold through their strict limitation of the number of apprentices in large printing establishments, where they were likely to be stronger, but they had little control over apprentice ratios in small jobbing printers, while according to Musson there were large numbers of 'turnovers' — apprentices who had not served their full time; printing could be 'picked up' on occasion without apprenticeship at all.[41]

In spite of this, apprenticeship did survive, and after the First World War the unions launched a strong attack, which even succeeded in making machine-managing, formerly an open occupation, into a closed one.[42] The survival of apprenticeship in printing, and its continued strength, can be explained as a product of the desire of many employers, as well as the unions, to keep it; in other words, it survived as a result of joint regulation. Employers wanted to keep, and regulate, apprenticeship for two reasons. First, because the trade was learned relatively quickly and therefore employers could make a very good profit out of apprentices if they served the full seven years. Second, and more important, because of the peculiar market situation of printing. It was not an industry subject to international competition in any but a minority of branches; employers were not, therefore, necessarily interested in minimising costs, so long as they could control competition in their own country. Competition could be controlled by cutting off the supply of cheap labour to undercutting employers, and enforcing apprentice limitation to prevent apprentices being used as cheap labour to excess. It is noteworthy in this connection that in Holland a nationwide closed shop has been operated in printing for many years for precisely this reason.[43]

Shipbuilding provides an even more interesting instance than printing of an industry in which skill was socially constructed to some extent; it is particularly interesting because several different trades were involved, which were learned in different ways. Riveting was a trade which required only limited amounts of genuine skill; but a five-year apprenticeship was the rule, semi-skilled and unskilled workers such as holders-up and rivet-catchers who might well have 'picked up' the trade were prevented from doing so, and in theory there was strict apprenticeship limitation, although whether the Boilermakers' Union was as successful in enforcing this as it was sometimes thought to be is dubious.[44] In fact, riveting is a good example of how social construction has to have some genuine skill basis to be effective in the long term. By the 1900s the high wages which riveters obtained encouraged the employers to attack them in two directions: first by introducing machines on to some types of riveting; and secondly by using apprentices as low-paid 'dilutees'. The result of this latter policy was that apprentice riveters did not stay with one firm, but were subject to rapid turnover, while there was also a high ratio of apprentices to riveters.[45]

Platers, on the other hand, did exercise some very considerable skills; in their case the peculiarity was that they were at the head of a gang, and in most cases such work was learned by following-up. While there may have been technological reasons for apprenticeship in the case of platers, it seems unlikely that the work was impossible to learn by progression, since work of the highest skill in, say, iron and steel manufacture was learned in this way. In the case of platers, therefore, the skill was genuine, but the delimitation between skilled and unskilled by means of apprenticeship was artificial. Finally we might mention shipwrights, who needed genuine and considerable skills which it was probably appropriate to acquire by apprenticeship, but who had gained the right to exercise some of these skills, notably those connected with metalwork, only by tenacious defence, against the claims of the platers, of the shipwrights' historic right to play a part in the construction of the whole ship, and not just one part of it.

The question we must answer is why each of these groups had one common denominator, the learning of their trade by apprenticeship, when in the case of the first two groups it was not a particularly appropriate method. Before attempting a tentative answer, it would be helpful to examine one other peculiarity of the work of both riveters and platers, which is that like many other leading hands in gang work, they were subcontractors; that is, at least up to the nineteenth century and probably after that, they directly employed the workers under them. Subcontract was exceedingly common in the mid-nineteenth century, and there is evidence of its widespread survival outside shipbuilding until the first decades of this century.[46] Since it is a managerial device to delegate authority and risk, rather than skill, it does not really come within our ambit, although it is interesting if only because seniority rules were probably instituted at first in order to prevent subcontractors from undercutting each other, and also to legitimate the subcontractors' authority over their underlings, who could be sure that, in time, they would themselves become top dogs. Certainly seniority rules seem to have been established at an early date in the cotton industry.[47] How far subcontractors in others industries won their way up by sheer merit, or whether their success was due more to pertinacity or capacity for exploiting others, is not clear, and insofar as the means by which subcontractors acquired skills are uncertain, our earlier account of its acquisition in industries subject to subcontract is rendered somewhat problematic. Nevertheless, it seems probable that a subcontractor would have had to serve as an underhand or otherwise he would not have been able to do the job, and therefore in most cases underhands could presumably hope to be subcontractors in time.[48] In the light of this probability, the existence of apprenticeship in plating and riveting, inappropriate in itself as a method of training, seems even more out of place because it prevented the cohesion possible in gang work in other industries where everyone knew that their turn would eventually come. An interesting parallel could be drawn with hand glassmaking, which also had apprenticeship even though it was gang work; but it was actually learned by following up, and since it combined apprenticeship with strict seniority rules every member of the gang did get a chance to move up the scale.

It seems to me probable that apprenticeship became an institution in the iron trades — the black squad — in shipbuilding for the following reasons. In the days of wooden shipbuilding, the shipwrights were extremely powerful. At the same time shipbuilding required little capital, because much of the work could be subcontracted out, so that even ordinary shipwrights could become master shipbuilders. Apprenticeship was therefore accepted as the norm by both men and masters, many of the latter in the mid-century having served an apprenticeship themselves.[49] When iron shipbuilding started, there was an intermediate period during which the demarcation of work was uncertain. Some shipyards at first favoured the shipwrights' claims to work on iron; in addition, a number of ships in this transitional period were composites, that is built of wood and iron, as shown in Table 7.1.[50]

Table 7.1: Ships Built on the Wear, 1869

	No.	Tonnage
Wood	57	21,258
Composite	15	9,383
Iron	50	41,774

My conjecture is that apprenticeship became established in the iron trades during this confused period. Adopting apprenticeship rather than following-up was both natural in an environment where apprenticeship flourished, and also sound policy on the part of the unions because yard managers and owners, who might well have been shipwrights in their youth, were more likely to recognise claims to skill and high wages based on apprenticeship. Once apprenticeship was established, it was very hard to uproot it, because of the strength of the main shipbuilding union, the Boilermakers. The causes of their great strength and influence in the late nineteenth century have not been properly analysed, but it seems probable that it can be put down to two main factors: the large size and geographical contiguity of the yards, which made them easy to organise; and the role of the union as a supplier of labour and at times as an adjunct to management. Employers had mixed views about the Boilermakers because of their power and the fact that to fill vacancies the employers had to turn to the union, but Clarke thinks that 'the Society and its District Delegates played a considerable part in the establishment of labour discipline within the shipyard'; and certainly the union both issued frequent homilies against absenteeism and drunkenness, and took practical action by upholding contracts with employers, as when men had been overpaid and refused to return the money.[51] Control of the labour supply by the union in an industry with fluctuating employment also had its advantages for employers, since it spared them the trouble of recruiting. At any rate, given the Boilermakers' powers the employers were unlikely to quarrel about the relatively minor issue of training, so long as the total amount they had to pay out in wages to a gang was not excessive: in the case of platers, the wage bill was kept down by the low wages of platers' helpers;[52] in the case of riveters, as we have seen, the employers were constrained in the 1900s to reduce the total wage bill by various methods, of which the use of apprentices as low-paid dilutees was one. In this case, therefore, what started as a union-inspired attempt to socially construct skill ended with the employers using apprentice-ship as a weapon against the union.

The shipwrights are interesting as a rare example of a group who did follow the 'route to skill' shown in Figure 1.2. It would have been technically feasible, and also logical, to divide the shipwrights' work, which involved both wood and iron, and give it to other workers who specialised in these materials; but, presumably for the same sort of reasons as the Boilermakers, the shipwrights remained strong enough to assert their right to a wide variety of work. We can also conjecture that the employers accepted this situation not simply because they were weak, but because they had no desire to give even more power to the Boilermakers.

The case of shipbuilding reinforces our contention that the social construction of skill by unions was not the norm; it was exceptional, and where it existed there had to be acceptance, if not active com-pliance, from employers. Bearing this in mind, we can now conclude this chapter by briefly discussing the relevance of its findings to the three theories of skill considered in Chapter 1.

Conclusion

As we showed in Chapter 1, Turner postulates two separate 'routes to skill'. To us the second, as shown in Figure 1.2, is the more interest-ing; in this genuine skill arises out of the social construction of skill, the latter being a result, in particular, of apprenticeship.

It seems to me that this cannot be accepted as an overall explanation either of the survival of apprenticeship, or of the delimitation of skill. Turner's mistake is to conflate the role of apprenticeship and skill construction in certain minor occupations with its role in major ones. The Webbs pertinently note that the strength of apprenticeship among certain numerically small groups of workers in cotton mills can be explained partly by the fact that their wages formed such a tiny fraction of total expenses that the employers were relatively indifferent to their demands; and it is significant that Turner used another small group in cotton, the Strippers and Grinders, as an illustration of how hitherto unskilled trade can be made 'skilled' by entry limitation.[53] But the fact is that in the nineteenth century apprenticeship was the dominant mode of entry to very large trades such as engineering and woodworking; employers could not in these circumstances be indifferent to wage costs, and we must conclude that the wages they paid reflected useful qualities or genuine skill possessed by the workers. This, of course, is allowed for in Turner's theory, since the hypothesises that employers would meet the cost of paying 'skilled' wages by insisting that the men really were skilled; this hypothesis, however, starts from the untenable supposition that it was the workers, or their unions, which originally insisted upon apprenticeship. As we have seen, apprenticeship was in fact an institution which suited employers; but most important, it was an institution which, by and large, existed to serve a genuine requirement for skilled labour.

'Skill', as J. T. Dunlop said in a review of Turner's book, stems from strategic position and technology rather than from apprenticeship.[54] The instances which the Webbs give of apprenticed occupations in cotton are an illustration of how strategic position can aid skill construction: although the employers may have been relatively indifferent to their wage costs, no employer who is doing his job is totally indifferent even to the smallest unnecessary expense; but in certain circumstances a small number of workers, who possess enough useful qualities — not necessarily a very large amount — to make them temporarily irreplaceable, can 'construct' skill, and hence obtain high wages, through their strategic position. The whole rationale behind this sort of skill construction, however, is that the number of workers is small enough to prevent their wage costs becoming a major irritant to the employer: they have to be few enough to ensure that it will be cheaper to pay out excessively high wages (that is wages above marginal productivity) than to have a stoppage of work.[55] If the number of workers who try to claim these privileges becomes at all numerous, then it will not be possible to sustain them; the employer will either refuse to pay, or will pay and, except in certain special circumstances, go bankrupt. These special circumstances are when the industry is protected both from international and domestic competition, and they can only be fulfilled if the product is difficult to make in other countries (like houses and newspapers) and if the unions manage to obtain control over the labour supply to prevent undercutting. In this century only printing, in the market sector of the economy, fulfils both criteria, and in the nineteenth it did not fulfil the second. In the nineteenth century, therefore, apprenticeship survived in expanding industries partly because it fulfilled a genuine need, and partly because for various reasons it suited employers, as well as workers, that it should survive.

The other route to skill postulated by Turner, as shown in the right-hand path of Figure 1.1, is more straightforward and much less problematic. In work which is relatively simple but requires some degree of skill and a certain amount of supervision, the distribution of labels stating who is skilled and who is not is fairly flexible; so long as the total wage bill is not excessive, it does not worry employers much whether they pay some workers as 'skilled' and others as 'unskilled' or all as 'semi-skilled'. Thus in the case of the spinners, their relatively high wages were matched by the relatively low wages of the piecers, and furthermore the employers could help to cover their wage costs by giving the spinners supervisory functions which had to be performed by separate overlookers elsewhere.

This flexibility over labelling extends to some industries where the organisation of work is not itself flexible; as in spinning, this is work performed in gangs, where the allocation of wages among workers does not necessarily affect the total wage bill. Riveting could be seen as an example of this, but the riveters, exercising no very considerable skill, tried to claim excessive wages and were checked. But in work performed in pairs, as by engine-drivers and firemen, and plumbers and their mates, there were fairly sharp differentials which were legitimated for the assistants by the fact that, as with piecers, they could eventually hope to become 'skilled' workers.[56] Engine-driving is particularly interesting: as with piecers, an experienced fireman was effectively as skilled as a driver, since his promotion to the latter position would not entail any further training and even as a fireman he would perform many 'driving' duties. But firemen's wages were on average less than two-thirds those of drivers, suggesting a degree of social construction in drivers' wages approaching that of the spinners, although different in the sense that drivers and firemen possessed more genuine skill and correspondingly earned more than spinners and piecers. This social construction was nothing to do with unions, which had little influence on the railways up to the 1900s, and can only be accounted for by custom, which itself could probably be traced back to the earliest days of the railways when the driver's skill *was* sharply delineated from that of the fireman. We must modify Turner's simple model of social construction, therefore, by adding to the influence of unions on skill differentials and skill labels, the influence of custom.

The applicability of our findings to Marx's theory of skill under a capitalist system of production seems to be as follows. First of all, it does not need much analysis to see that Marx's simple demarcation between semi-skilled machine-tending occupations subject to extreme division of labour, and skilled maintenance and technical jobs, is unsatisfactory as a description of work at this period. The reasons for the inadequacy of Marx's theory need more attention. There is certainly no logical fault in his analysis: there might well be industries in which the most economical methods of production necessitate a minimisation of training costs by training each worker for just one machine. Such industries would be those in which the products are made in large quantities and are not highly differentiated, so that the need for flexibility in machinery and workforce is greatly reduced. There was one such industry in the nineteenth century — the textile industry, in particular the cotton sector, and it was obviously this that Marx took as his examplar of a deskilled industry. His mistake was to assume that its development was typical; in fact the textile industry actually declined in relative importance during the later part of the century.[57] Other industries which adopted 'machino-facture' had completely different types of product; we have seen how this affected the engineering industry, but the difference extended to consumer goods like footwear where the product was much more differentiated and the machinery generally took more skill to operate than in textiles.

Because these industries had different types of product which imposed different skill requirements, the training in them was also different to the limited and limiting training postulated by Marx. In the sense that the method of training chosen was usually that which minimised costs, the pattern followed Marx's prediction: but cost was not necessarily minimised by limiting training. It might be more economic to have all-round workers, as in engineering and wood-working. Or, as in the numerous industries learned by migration and following-up, the most economic method was to let workers acquire their skill by moving from machine to machine, process to process, or task to task, because some of the machines and processes were very complex and to train workers separately for them would have wasted the skill and experience required by others in the industry.

It should be noted, however, that whatever the method of training in use it was not a unilateral decision by the employer, as in Braverman's model, that was the deciding factor. Apprenticeship only survived where it could earn the apprentice a decent return on his initial investment, which he made by forgoing the higher wages earnable as a juvenile in other trades. In progression industries, on the other hand, any attempt by employers to delimit skill by confining certain work to one class of worker would have called into play competition from those employers who chose the more rational course of promoting semi-skilled workers. Only in those industries where *workers* were concerned to artificially delimit skill, and employers were neutral or even favourable, were such efforts successful. And if it was the case in the later nineteenth century that management had little overall control over skill levels, surely it must be even more the case in this century when the countervailing force of labour is so much stronger?

Notes

1. A. Milward, *War, Economy and Society, 1939-45* (Berkeley, Calif., 1977), p. 232; and note that in London riveting was not learned by apprenticeship (Chapter 6, note 71).

2. Masons have not been discussed, because the persistence of patrimony puts them in rather a different class to other trades; except in Scotland, they did not form a major part of the building industry (in 1901 masons and their labourers accounted for about 9 per cent of the total building labour force in England and Wales − Census). Plastering was somewhat similar to painting in regard to skill and recruitment, although there was probably a higher proportion of apprentices (1915 Report, p. 18). Plumbers have been discussed in Chapter 6.

3. For High Wycombe there is no direct evidence, but the impression given in L.J. Mayes, *The History of Chairmaking in High Wycombe* (1960), and also by various recorded reminiscences of High Wycombe workers that I have listened to, is that there was some apprenticeship, but not much. (I would like to thank Mr Sparkes of High Wycombe library for the opportunity to listen to these recordings.) Charles Booth *et al.*, *Life and Labour of the People of London*, 2nd series, *Industry* (5 vols., 1903), vol. 1, p. 185, and the 1925 Report both suggest a considerable use of improvership in cabinet-making. See Table 5.5.

4. *Encyclopaedia Britannica*, 15th edn.

5. A.E. Musson, *The Typographical Association* (1954), p. 181; Chapter 6, notes 41-2; Booth, *Industry*, vol. 2, pp. 215-16. According to the 1911 Census, the number of machine compositors was 3,711 against 37,281 hand compositors.

6. P. de Rousiers, *The Labour Question in Britain* (1896), p. 64, thought that two years was sometimes, and five years always, adequate to produce an efficient workman; Booth, *Industry*, vol. 2, p. 202, says two to three years to become an efficient typesetter, although to obtain a really thorough knowledge of the industry would take longer; K. Liepmann, *Apprenticeship* (1960), pp. 101-2, says that five years would be necessary for compositing, but this includes the learning of both hand and machine work. For presswork the sources suggest that two to four years were necessary. Note also Musson's reference to 'turnovers' who broke their apprenticeship after two or three years to earn higher wages (see Chapter 5, note 36). FLW respondent no. 34 was the respondent alluded to.

7. G.T. Jones, *Increasing Return* (1933), p. 94.

8. 1915 Report, p. 13.

9. Ibid., p. 15.

10. 1925 Report, vol. II, p. 95; 1915 Report, p. 14.

11. Ibid., p. 127.

12. J.W.F. Rowe, *Wages in Practice and Theory* (1928), Ch. V, for skill levels; see Chapter 5 of the present book for a discussion of the amount of 'all-round' training in engineering.

13. 1915 Report, p. 130.

14. FLW respondents nos. 219 and 41.

15. 1925 Report, vol. VI, pp. 68-9.

16. Apprenticed trades: fitters 34s 9d per week; turners 35s 1d per week. Non-apprenticed trades: spinners 38s 5d to 45s 11d per week; beatermen (paper-mills) about 35-40s per week; engine-drivers 45s 11d per week. All national average figures from the 1906 Wages Census.

17. H.A. Turner, *Trade Union Growth, Structure and Policy* (1962), p. 195.

18. Ibid.

19. T.K. Derry, 'The Repeal of the Apprenticeship Clauses of the Statute of Apprentices', *EcHR*, vol. III (1931-2), esp. p. 80; see also H.J. Fyrth and H.J. Collins, *The Foundry Workers* (Manchester, 1959), p. 20.

20. Turner, *Trade Union Growth*, p. 196, and see Chapter 9, Appendix 1, for a discussion of the division of labour in the early engineering industry.

21. W. McClaine, 'The Engineers Union', unpublished PhD thesis, University of London, 1939, pp. 92, 109ff., 142; there is no fundamental contradiction between this and the account in J.B. Jefferys, *The Story of the Engineers* (1946), Ch. 1.

22. J.F. Clarke, 'Labour Relations in Engineering and Shipbuilding on the North-East Coast in the Second Half of the Nineteenth Century', unpublished MA thesis, University of Newcastle, 1966, pp 57 and 66; M. and J.B. Jefferys, 'The Wages, Hours and Trade Customs of the Skilled Engineer in 1861', *EcHR*, vol. XVII (1947), p. 30; H.A. Clegg *et al.*, *A History of British Trade Unions since 1889* (Oxford, 1964), p. 468, Table 6 (carpenters' density: the authors point out that this understates the true figure because the union returns do not include labourers whereas the figures for the actual number in the trade do; but since there were few labourers in carpentry and joinery, this would not seriously affect the conclusion that unions were very weak among woodworkers. Burgess confirms this for all building trades: membership of unions was confined to 10-20 per cent of adult tradesmen as late as the 1890s; K. Burgess, *The Origin of British Industrial Relations* (1975), p. 99).

23. Clegg, *et al.*, *British Trade Unions*, pp. 8-9. The strike in detail was a tactic which minimised the public's awareness of the union's role.

24. D.C. Coleman, *The British Paper Industry 1495-1860* (Oxford, 1958), Ch. X.

25. A. Fox, *History of the National Union of Boot and Shoe Workers* (Oxford, 1958), Ch. 1.

26. Clegg *et al.*, *British Trade Unions*, p. 157 (building); it should be noted that firms in 170 towns were circularised and only 85 replied. Ibid., p. 140 (engineering, 1890s); 1915 Report, pp. 59, 60, 77 (engineering, iron-moulding, electrical engineering).

27. Fyrth and Collins, *Foundry Workers*, pp. 59-60; Jefferys, *The Engineers*, pp. 102-3.

28. 1915 Report, pp. 59, 60, 77.

29. See Chapter 3.

30. de Rousiers, *Labour Question*, pp. 254-6, 275-6.

31. 1915 Report, p. 127; N.B. Dearle, *Industrial Training* (1914), pp. 276-7.

32. See Table 5.8. Liepmann thought that the discrepancy between large and

small firms in 1925 may have been illusory (see Chapter 5, note 84), but it seems unlikely because the discrepancy was so large. Another possible explanation for the large/small firm discrepancy was the increasing routinisation of work in large firms, although the recent reversal of the trend (see Liepmann) poses some problems for this hypothesis and suggests that the one advanced in the text may be more appropriate. The basic point, however, is simply that it did not always suit employers to take apprentices: 'if an employer believed in apprenticeship and found that it suited the organisation of his works, he took apprentices. If he did not, then he did not take any.' W. McClaine, *New Views on Apprenticeship* (1948), pp. 66-7.

33. I think that the wretched, exploited apprentice in *The Ragged Trousered Philanthropist* should be seen in this light: his mother was a widow, and he lived in a town (Hastings) where employment opportunities were relatively poor; unfortunately in such towns unions were less likely to have influence.

34. Dearle, *Training*, p. 179.

35. S.B. Saul, 'The Market and the Development of the Mechanical Engineering Industrial in Britain 1860-1914', *EcHR*, vol. XX (1967), pp. 111-30; A. Stinchcombe, 'Bureaucratic and Craft Administration of Production', *Administrative Science Quarterly* (1959), vol. 4, pp. 168-87.

36. The definition of skill adopted here is that the worker either attracted a label used for a skilled trade (e.g. turner, pattern-maker), or earned a rate of wages equivalent to that earned by 'labelled' skilled workers; to embark on a discussion of whether such workers were really skilled will not, I hope, now be necessary; for the estimate of 50 per cent, see Chapter 9.

37. McClaine, 'The Engineers', p. 134.

38. There is a pre-First World War reference to apprenticeship in electrical contracting in the Board of Trade's *Handbook on Bristol Trades*, (HMSO, 1914), p. 29.

39. Stinchcombe, 'Administration of Production', pp. 168-87.

40. This point is emphasised in relation to unions' concern with apprenticeship limitation in the post-Second World War period by D.J. Lee 'Craft Unions and the Force of Tradition: the Case of Apprenticeship', *British Journal of Industrial Relations*, vol. XVII, no. 1 (March 1979).

41. Musson, *The Typographical Association*, p. 211; FLW respondent no. 34.

42. Musson, *The Typographical Association*, Ch. XVI for the post-First World War strength of the unions in printing.

43. Child refers to the favourable view that some employers took of the unions' activities in controlling wages and hours in the mid-nineteenth century, although employers were never very happy about apprenticeship limitation; and the Federation of Master Printers, founded in 1901, was much more concerned to institute standard costing procedures in order to prevent undercutting, than to confront the unions; J. Child, *Industrial Relations in the Printing Industry* (1967), pp. 91 and 100.

Printing may be contrasted with building, where a not dissimilar market structure (lack of international competition) obtains; unlike printing, however, the unions have had little success in enforcing apprenticeship in the post-Second World War period; Liepmann, *Apprenticeship*, pp. 168-70. (For a short period after the First World War they were more successful – see Chapter 6, note 86.) See G. Williams, *Apprenticeship in Europe* (1963), p. 61, for Holland.

44. Price found that in the 1890s, in spite of restrictionist agreement between employers and Boilermakers, the apprentice/journeyman ratio in riveting in Clyde shipyards averaged more than 40 per cent, rising to 50 per cent between 1901 and 1906, after the agreeement ended; Sylvia Price, 'Clyde Riveters Earnings 1889-1913', unpublished paper, p. 23. See also the account in S. and B. Webb, *Industrial Democracy* (1920 edn), pp. 456-7.

45. Price, 'Clyde Riveters', pp. 22-4.

46. A. Pugh, *Men of Steel* (1951), pp. 155-6; PP 1911, LXXXVIII, pp. xxii, xxv.

47. Turner, *Trade Union Growth*, pp. 127-8.

48. Various references in Pugh, *Men of Steel*, imply that promotion up the ladder proceeded in the same sort of way under subcontracting systems as it did elsewhere: thus on p. 96 he describes how John Hodge entered Parkhead as an underhand puddler, with the promise that he would be next in line for forehand (but the contractor broke his promise); on p. 158 he described how in a sheet mill those who wanted to get promotion had to 'kow-tow' to the contractor. Clearly subcontracting was often accompanied by favouritism, rather than by a strict seniority ladder, but the point is that promotion was basically from the lower ranks to the higher, and skilled work was not delimited by apprenticeship.

49. For the strength of shipwrights' trade unions see P.H. Rathbone, 'Account of Shipwrights' Trades Societies' in National Association for the Promotion of Social Science, *Report on Trade Societies and Strikes* (1860), pp. 479-520; for the recruitment of master builders from working shipwrights, Clarke, 'Labour Relations' p. 84, who emphasises that the employers had served 'genuine apprenticeships'.

50. Clarke, 'Labour Relations', pp. 128-9.

51. *11th Special Report of the U.S. Commissioner of Labour* (1904), pp. 804-5 and 812-13; Clarke, 'Labour Relations', pp. 202 and 203-6. Unfortunately the two histories of the Boilermakers' Union are not helpful for our purposes: D.C. Cummings, *A Historical Survey of the Boiler Makers and Iron and Steel Shipbuilding Society* (Newcastle, 1905); J.E. Mortimer, *History of the Boilermakers Society*, vol. 1 (1973).

52. Platers on piecework (the majority) earned 64s 7d per week on average; their helpers earned 24s 4d per week; 1906 Wages Survey (PP 1911, LXXXVIII).

53. Webbs, *Industrial Democracy*, pp. 478-9; Turner, *Trade Union Growth*, pp. 163-5.

54. Review in *British Journal of Industrial Relations*, vol. 11 (1964), pp. 287-92.

55. For the concept of strategic position, see also J.T. Dunlop, 'Labor Relations and the Development of Labor Organisation' in R.A. Lester and J. Shister (eds.), *Insights into Labor Issues* (New York, 1948), pp. 180-3.

56. Average wages per week and differentials expressed by index numbers (lower wage = 100):

Occupation	Wage	Index no.
Fireman	27s 5d	100
Plumber's mate	23s 8d	100
Piecer (adult)	18s 4d	100
Smith's striker	24s 1d	100
Engine-driver	45s 11d	168
Plumber	36s 2d	153
Spinner	41s 0d	224
Smith	37s 0d	154

It is noteworthy that the differentials between smiths' strikers, who could not always expect to gain promotion, and smiths, were lower than in the other groups except for plumbers (and differentials in building were traditionally low).

All wages are averaged from time and piece earnings, and are taken from the 1906 Wages Census.

57. 10.1 per cent of all employed males worked in the textile industry in 1851, 4. 8 per cent in 1901.

SKILL AND INDUSTRIAL STRUCTURE

We should conclude our analysis of skill by some attempt at an international comparison. While the existence of a high proportion of skilled workers in British manufacturing industry is explicable in terms of technology, which in turn is determined, at least in the case of engineering, largely by the market, it seems worth enquiring what actually makes this market. For it is certainly noteworthy that the British market, not just for engineering products but also for consumption goods, and production goods such as locomotives and wagons, was highly variegated and very different from the American market with its large demand for standardised items.[1]

In his pathbreaking article on this subject, S.B. Saul explained why individual sections of the market were more fragmented in Britain: railway companies built their own locomotives, for instance, thus splitting the industry into many relatively small parts. He also points out that Britain specialised much more in heavy engineering goods, and this in itself limited the amount of mass production which took place because such goods are not demanded in large numbers.[2] The rigidity of tastes, both for consumer goods and producer goods, in a country with a well-established middle class and old-established industries could also be put forward as a factor which encouraged heterogeneity. Nevertheless, there is one important theoretical drawback to a series of particularistic explanations, which is that there is no real reason to expect that a number of unconnected factors should all have the same result; when they do, our suspicions of *post hoc* reasoning should be aroused.

One suggestion that has been put forward by several commentators is that immigration to the United States cheapened the price of unskilled labour relative to skilled, and thus encouraged a concentration on technology which maximised the input of unskilled labour.[3] While the actual ratio of skilled to unskilled workers in the two countries does not seem to have been much studied, there is evidence which suggests that the United States had a significantly higher proportion of unskilled workers at the end of the nineteenth century. Thus P.R. Shergold found the following ratios in Pittsburgh, America, and Birmingham and Sheffield in England, and he also noted the widespread contemporary impression that America had a higher proportion of unskilled workers.[4]

Table 8.1: Proportion of Unskilled Workers in the Labour Force[5]

	Pittsburgh	Birmingham	Sheffield
Building (labourers)	48%	36%	42%
Steel	50%*		30%

Dates: building 1911; steel 1906 and 1907.
*Comprising 42% common labour, and 8% paid but not classed as common labour.

So far as skill differentials have been studied, we have varying conclusions for the different periods. Rosenberg has pointed out that according to one source in the 1820s most skilled labour in the United States was little more expensive, relative to unskilled, than in Britain, and in the case of highly skilled engineering workers the differential in Britain was wider.[6] As Rosenberg says, however, there is only one set of data to rely on, and the figures for individual groups might not be representative;[7] it might be added that abnormal conditions of labour demand at a time when the English machine-building industry was expanding very rapidly may have played a part in heightening English differentials in engineering.

What is striking is that skill differentials in America by the late nineteenth and early twentieth centuries were considerably higher than in England. This is indicated by Phelps-Brown and Browne, where it is stated that unskilled wages in the United States in the early twentieth century were less than 50 per cent of skilled, both in building and in factory work in general; in Britain unskilled wages ranged from 53 per cent in shipbuilding to 59 per cent in engineering and 66 per cent in building.[8] These figures are confirmed by Shergold's detailed comparison between Pittsburgh, and Birmingham and Sheffield. Some extracts from Shergold's findings are shown in Table 8.2: it should be noted that although he found some narrowing of skill differentials in the United States between 1899 and 1913, these do not significantly alter the general picture.[9] As Shergold brings out clearly in his discussion of the figures, the differential widens as the skill ladder is climbed — although at the top end of the scale it might be truer to say that, taking into account seasonal declines in building wages, the skilled British workers' wage in engineering and building was virtually identical, but the American builders won a further substantial differential.[10]

Table 8.2: Hourly Wages of Various Occupations Expressed as a Percentage Superiority over the Wage Paid to the Engineering Labourer

		Pittsburgh	Birmingham	Sheffield
Engineering labourer	1905	—	—	—
Building labourer	1906	89.2	48.9	21.9
Machinist	1906	100.0	79.3	89.6
Compositor*	1906	107.0	76.1	74.0
Boilermaker	1906	111.4	90.2	87.5
Patternmaker	1906	129.7	90.2	87.5
Carpenter	1906	177.2	109.8	90.6
Bricklayer	1906	299.4	109.8	101.0

*Comparable work.

We now have to account for these wide differentials. Shergold, taking into account Rosenberg's evidence which suggests much narrower skill differentials in the United States at the beginning of the century than at the end, advances a number of reasons to account for the widening. He points out that whereas the American unskilled labour force in the early part of the century was of a relatively high quality because of public education, by the end of the century the opposite was the case. Much of it consisted of functionally illiterate immigrants, and it is significant that unskilled workers speaking English earned an extra 2c per hour. At the same time the language barrier effectively segmented the labour market, not so much because of immobility between unskilled jobs — in fact there was high mobility — but because it made it impossible for immigrants to enter jobs which required any length of training. He also suggests that in England the organisation of the unskilled in unions improved their bargaining position, whereas again the unskilled in America were at a serious disadvantage in unionising; but in view of the relative stability of English skill differentials over a long period, and the weakness of 'new unionism' in England, this cannot have been an important factor.[11] One further point that might be added is that the American skilled worker may have been more skilled than his British namesake because of, for instance, better technical education. This is highly conjectural, however, and certainly the differentials even for workers with exactly the same job description — patternmaker, carpenter, bricklayer — were much wider in America.

Can we link the evidence on wage differentials with Saul's picture of the variegated demand for the products of British industry, by hypothesising that the skilled/unskilled wage differential provides at least a partial explanation of how British, as well as American, industry developed in the later nineteenth century. Put very simply, just as the expense of skilled labour in America encouraged the development of mass production, so the cheapness of skilled labour in England meant that small-scale production did not impose any significant cost penalties, while producing a more tailor-made, and thus more desirable, product.

One problem with adopting such an approach is Rosenberg's evidence for the 1820s, which suggests a high wage differential in the crucial engineering industry. It is arguable, however, that developments in technology were so inchoate before the mid-century that wage differentials would not have had much effect. By the time America was developing mass production techniques, a shortage of skill was seen as a serious problem which the system of interchangeable parts could solve: Whitney described the leading object of this system as 'to substitute correct and effective operations of machinery for that skill of the artists which is acquired only by long practice and experience; a species of skill which is not possessed in this country to any considerable extent'.[12]

If Shergold is correct, then the higher rewards to skill in the United States as compared with Britain could be partly accounted for by the relatively poor quality of American unskilled labour; this would not in itself lead to any bias for or against the use of skilled workers, because the high relative wage of unskilled labour in Britain would be matched by its higher value to the employer, and thus there would be no incentive to maximise the use of skill.[13] But he also suggests that the labour market in America may have been more segmented insofar as entry to skilled trades was concerned. If there was any link between wage differentials and technology, it must be connected with this factor.

Let us build on Shergold's suggestion by first examining, not why it was difficult to acquire skill in America, but why it was easy in Britain. The answer to this will be clear enough to the reader: skilled labour was abundant and cheap in Britain because, given the initial existence of skill, it cost little or nothing to train skilled workers. In the case of apprenticeship, the relatively small cost in terms of forgone wages was borne by the worker, while in other industries learned by migration or following-up there was little or no penalty in terms of learning costs at all.

We have already examined at length why the situation outlined above obtained. It will now be helpful to give a concrete illustration of why America could not produce its skilled workers as cheaply as Britain, even leaving aside the very real problems of language and culture involved in teaching immigrants skilled work. George Barnes the ASE General Secretary, who visited America in the early 1900s, noted that in a large locomotive works the employees were organised in gangs, with one skilled man in each gang. The work itself was not performed to such a high standard as in a British engineering works.[14] Given this situation, which the evidence suggests was standard in American factories of all kinds, it was extremely difficult for an American worker to acquire the highest degree of skill. Semi-skilled workers who progressed from machine to machine would lack examplars, since such skilled workers as there were would not be able to give them individual attention; and as we have seen in Britain, although varieties of skilled work were learned by migration, it was not usually work which required the highest skill, because only practice and the contiguity of many other skilled craftsmen could teach this. Furthermore, the method of migration took longer than apprenticeship, since the skill was acquired more gradually, and in itself imposed the requirement that a higher proportion of the work be subdivided, and consequently less skilled.

This argument has important implications outside the question of Anglo/American differences in technology. It was suggested in Chapter 4 that it was in practice impossible to estimate investment in on-the-job training. Strictly speaking, however, the investment can be estimated: it is the difference between the wages of a trainee and a non-trainee, on the assumption that the machinery of the factory, and its skilled labour, would have been necessary to production anyway. But although we might be able to measure the actual cost of training, we cannot measure the value of it because this is imparted not just by its duration or intensity or other factors which affect cost, but by the quality of the skill which is acquired by the trainee; and this, as we have seen, depends on how skilled those he works with are − how skilled as workers, that is, and not primarily on how skilled as teachers. It seems to me that this makes the whole concept of investment in on-the-job training problematic. It is not so much that we cannot measure such investment, because in cash terms we probably could, in theory (it might be difficult in practice), but that to do so yields us a meaningless figure because it does not tell us what quality the skill acquired is. Neither can we 'capture' the value of a skilled worker's skill by estimating the excess of his wages over those of an unskilled worker; the excess might reflect lower quality among the unskilled rather than higher among the skilled; it might reflect an element of social construction in the skill − not, we have argued in Chapter 7, that this is likely to be very considerable, but it might well have been more considerable in the United States because of cultural and language barriers to the promotion of immigrants; and finally it will reflect differences in the cost of acquiring skill. Skill was cheap to acquire in England, expensive in America; because of this Anglo/American skill differential and, if my suggestion is correct, differences in technology, reflect a paradoxical conclusion: in a way, Britain was more efficient than America because it trained skilled workers more cheaply.

At this stage it must be pointed out that a detailed study of individual industries would be needed to validate the suggestion that differences in Anglo/American technology depended on variations in skill differentials. And one obvious criticism of the suggestion is that skill differentials cannot by themselves provide a universal explanation. This is because the initial skill which provides the basis for lower skill differentials in future has to be acquired, and it is presumably acquired in response to market demands. It might be useful to try to develop a theory in which Rosenberg's technological convergence hypothesis, which suggests that greater American knowledge of mass production light engineering led to increased American concentration on this sort of engineering, and the extension of its principles to other branches of engineering and other industries, is integrated with my suggestion which also focuses on the possession of knowledge of techniques, and the difficulty of diffusing such knowledge; in Rosenberg's hypothesis, of course, it is American management which possesses the knowledge, while in my suggestion it is the British labour force.[15]

In a final development of the argument advanced in this chapter, we will turn the suggestion advanced earlier about the 'route to skill' on its head. In Chapter 1 we presented in diagrammatic form the theories of skill advanced by various thinkers: among them were Turner's and Braverman's, both of which held that 'skill' was essentially a construct of workers/management. In Chapter 7 we argued that skill was in reality a product of technology, although strategic position might play a part. But the implications of the present chapter are that technology is partly a product of skill. It is the prior existence of skilled workers that determines the price of skill; technology adapts itself to the skill on offer; and the product market adjusts itself to the relative price of the commodities it is offered, and demands more of those made by the more skilled workers, because they are cheaper or better. As we have already noted, the initial skill has to be acquired, and since we must bring the prior existence of a market in at this point we cannot make skill into a universal explanation. Nevertheless, it seems worth bringing out into the open the intimate links between technology, the market and the skilled workers, because all too often in economic history the latter is taken as a static not a dynamic element, a mere segment of a homogeneous factor of production which economists, with their misleading simplicity, call labour.

Notes

1. Mass production of wagons in America is recorded in the Royal Commission on Technical Instruction, PP 1884, XXXI, vol. ii, where it was stated that some towns virtually specialised in them (Qu. 2261). For other examples of mass production in America see note 14 below.

2. S.B. Saul, 'The Market and the Development of the Mechanical Engineering Industries in Britain, 1840-1914', *EcHR*, 2nd series, vol. XX (1967).

3. H.J. Habakkuk, *American and British Technology in the Nineteenth Century* (Cambridge, 1967), p. 131; Brinley Thomas, *Migration and Economic Growth*, 2nd edn. (Cambridge 1973), pp. 163-74. Habakkuk's general thesis about the expense of *all* American labour leading to the substitution of machinery for labour has been criticised by, e.g., D. Whitehead, 'Review of Habakkuk', *Business Archives and History* III (1963); and P. Temin, 'Labor Scarcity and the Problem of American Industrial Efficiency in the 1850's', *Journal of Economic History*, XXVI (1966).

4. P.R. Shergold, 'The Standard of Life of Manual Workers in the First Decade of the Twentieth Century', unpublished PhD thesis, University of London, 1976, p. 149. Also note the evidence of George Barnes, *Mosely Industrial Commission to the United States* (1903), p. 55: 'In America [specialists who were rated at 20% less than skilled workers] are far more numerous than in Great Britain'; and contrast it with de Rousiers talking of Platts, which produced standardised textile machinery on a large scale, 'Except the porters, who are superseded as far as possible by lifts and locomotives, almost every indiviudal employed by the firm is a skilled workman' (P. de Rousiers, *The Labour Question in Britain* (1896), p. 255).

5. Shergold, 'Manual Workers', p. 149.

6. N. Rosenberg, 'Anglo-American Wage Differences in the 1820s', *Journal of Economic History*, XXVII, 2 (1967), pp. 221-9.

7. Ibid., pp. 228-9; Adams confirms that, over a longer period, there was little difference in skilled/unskilled differentials in the two countries; if anything, the skilled differential was higher in America, averaged over all occupations: D.R. Adams, 'Some Evidence on British and American Wage Rates 1790-1830', *Journal of Economic History* XXX, (1970), pp. 499-520.

8. E.H. Phelps-Brown and M. Browne, *A Century of Pay* (1968), p. 47; English figures are from 1904, American from 1909.

9. Shergold, 'Manual Workers', p. 129.

10. Ibid., Graphs 3.2 and 3.3 and discussion.

11. Ibid., pp. 142-8; see J.W.F. Rowe, *Wages in Practice and Theory* (1928), pp. 42 and 44, for the stability of skilled/unskilled differentials at a time when unskilled workers' unions were growing rapidly (1886-1913).

12. Habakkuk, *Technology*, p. 22.
13. This point might be rather obscure. It can be illustrated by considering the American situation: although American unskilled labour was relatively badly paid, its cost to the employer may have been no less than in England because its low quality (illiteracy etc.) increased costs in other ways, e.g. the cost of supervision.

My argument goes on to suggest, however, that although this may have been a factor, there were also differences in the relative price of different types of labour that were unrelated to differences in quality.

14. Barnes in *Mosely Commission*, pp. 62-3. Barnes was almost certainly referring to the Baldwin works; from his account the latter carried subdivision to an extreme, and the standard of work in America was by no means always so low but the important point about the number of specialised workers was generally true, while apprenticeship of any kind was a rarity; ibid., pp. 55 and 67.

The comments about woodworking are equally striking: 'the great majority [of American workmen] never serve their apprenticeship, and only get one particular part of the work to perform. If given the drawing and lumber, they would be entirely lost and could not do the job; at their own particular part they become experts'; evidence of H. Crawford, *Mosely Commission*, p. 201.

It should be noted that the comments of both these trade union leaders were by no means marked by unreasoning hostility to American methods; they were impressed by many things about American factories, and said so.

15. N. Rosenberg, 'Technological Change in the Machine Tool Industry, 1840-1910', *Journal of Economic History* (1963). The suggestion I have put forward bears a close analogy to, and was indeed partly stimulated by, that put forward by J.R. Harris, 'Skills, Coal and British Industry in the Eighteenth Century', *History* vol. 61 (1976); Harris argues that knowledge of metalworking techniques in the late eighteenth and early nineteenth centuries largely resided in the skilled workforce, who were neither very mobile nor very articulate; such knowledge was therefore difficult to diffuse. To simplify my argument considerably, one might say that in the later nineteenth century there were two types of machine technology – the American and the British – and neither could easily be diffused because both depended heavily on the knowledge and skills of individuals.

Part IV

CHANGES IN SKILL

Introduction

It is now time to turn from the static analysis of skill, around which the discussion has centred up to now, to a more dynamic analysis focusing on changes in skill levels. While some account of changes in skill was given in Chapter 2, it was confined to the engineering industry and was only intended to provide a preliminary introduction. This chapter will discuss changes in skill requirements in general, and changes in the engineering industry in detail; it will also consider changes in the kind of skill required.

General Trends

It has already been made apparent in Chapter 3 that there was a slow decline in apprenticeship to many old crafts, perhaps more in the cities than in the small towns and countryside. To quantify these changes would be impossible without a major study, because it is very difficult to judge which crafts at any particular time were highly subdivided and effectively deskilled, making apprenticeship in them, if it existed, virtually meaningless. If Mayhew is correct, for instance, tailoring, shoe-making and cabinet-making were subject to intense subdivision in London by the mid-century, and it has already been noted that Booth's account suggests that some reskilling had taken place in the latter industry by the 1890s. On a smaller scale, the High Wycombe furniture industry seems to have followed a similar trend, developing from a subdivided mass-production industry with a very limited range in the mid-century to an industry with a wider range of products, some of them of high quality, by the end.[1]

We can certainly say, however, that in industries like footwear, tailoring, milling and papermaking there was a steady trend towards large-scale mechanised production, in which, characteristically, work was learned by migration or following-up in the ways already described. Mechanisation in these industries had, it should be noted, become established by the mid-century or soon after — earlier in the case of papermaking — and therefore the late nineteenth and early twentieth centuries should be seen as periods which continued existing trends, rather than as being radically innovatory. Indeed in one major industry, textiles, the revolution was virtually completed by the mid-century. Concurrently with the new trends noted above, there was decline or stagnation in old crafts like hatting, basketmaking and coopering, and a growth of completely new, or formerly minuscule, industries, like chemicals, light engineering and floor cloth and linoleum manufacture, whose workers were mainly trained, as in other growing occupations, by migration or following-up.

Whether there was an increase or decrease in skill as a result of these developments is, it should be clear, highly problematic. As has been said, a major study would be needed before any firm opinion on this should be expressed, because of our lack of knowledge of how much really skilled work there was in the mid-century or earlier, but some general comments can be made. The first is that, quite apart from the existence of a considerable degree of subdivision in the mid-century, some so-called 'crafts' did not really involve very much skill. It seems likely, for instance, that much tailoring and shoemaking work comes into this category, although high-class bespoke workers in these trades should be excepted. Thus, except for a short period during the Napoleonic Wars when, according to Francis Place, the London tailors were organised in a strong and effective combination and possessed at least a 'socially constructed' skill, and its concomitant high wages, the majority of them seem to have ranked as semi-skilled workers at best.[2]

> The next class [after the foremen] is the mere working Taylor; not one in ten of them know how to cut out a Pair of Breeches: They are employed only to sew the seam, to cast the Buttonholes, and prepare the work for the Finisher ... They are as numerous as locusts, are out of Business about three or four months in the Year, and generally as poor as Rats.

This was written of London tailors in 1747.[3]

Similarly, the amount of skill involved in hand shoemaking should not be exaggerated: of three FLW respondents who learned the trade, one, in Scotland, had a five-year apprenticeship. But another, one of a family of leatherworkers, was taught shoemaking in six months by his brother and went on to do high-quality work, making the shoe throughout; that this was not the result of some special talent is suggested by the fact that the son of a carman, who was apprenticed to hand shoemaking, learned the trade in a year and set up on his own account.[4] Another old craft, cornmilling in a small combined steam and wind mill, was also not that difficult to acquire, according to a respondent: his father, who owned the mill, fixed the term of his apprenticeship at two years, because learning it was 'just a question of putting the corn in ... at the top of the mill and ... doing the sacks and winding up ... there was no trade attached to it'.[5]

We can therefore say two things about skill levels in the host of trades which gradually underwent mechanisation during the nineteenth century. The first is that the skill attached to the original trade was often not very considerable, either because the trade was subdivided or because it involved only simple tasks. Because of this, mechanisation of the trade, which might or might not involve further subdivision, contains no *necessary* implication that skill levels declined. Mechanisation might be used to increase the quality or variety of the product: shoemaking, papermaking and milling are all examples here. Or machines would take over the more simple and laborious parts of a task, but need complex setting up, in which case overall skill levels might well increase: machine woodworking is an example of this. And very commonly, machines would take over tasks which, although they required considerable manual skill, were repetitive and involved little judgement: sawying and some tasks in shoemaking would come into this category; and an excellent example is provided by wallpaper manufacture, where the machine branch involved considerable skill in judging the tension of the rollers and operating the machines, while the hand branch involved manual skill but constant repetition of one action.[6] There are also numerous instances where mechanisation replaced unskilled or semi-skilled labour, as with the adoption of steam hoists and overhead cranes, but these are outside our immediate concern here which is with 'skilled' work.

We must certainly accept that much of the work in mechanised industries was not very skilled: in many cases mechanisation did involve merely speeding up and simplification. But we must also recognise that there were important differences between industries. In that exemplar of mass production, textile manufacture, the scale of the industry meant that the standard practice was for large numbers of identical machines to be placed together in one department: the result of this was that there was little progression from machine to machine, at least in the spinning and weaving departments.[7] But as we have seen, in most industries the complete opposite applied. Machines had different functions and were of different complexity, or, in process industries, there were a variety of different processes. As a result, many workers in the mechanised industries were not confined to one machine or process: they gradually worked their way up, and at the top, in industries like shoemaking or papermaking, ranked as fully skilled workers.

This should not be seen as a description of the situation of all workers in these industries. In grainmilling and other process industries large numbers of labourers were needed, some of whom probably never progressed upwards; while in industries like footwear the number of workers needed on the very simple machines probably exceeded the number on the more complex, and led to the problem of excessive boy labour. Nevertheless, very large numbers of workers had the opportunity to benefit from upward progression. We can make two comments about this: on the one hand, the fact that workers were able to acquire skill by methods other than apprenticeship has implications for the nature of the relationship between skilled and other workers; these implications will be explored in the last chapter. On the other hand, it enables us to make our second point about skill levels in mechanised industries, which is that although the average skill level in them might have been lower than in the craft trade which they replaced (a statement subject to the caveats we entered in the last paragraph but one), a high proportion of the workforce had the chance of becoming fully skilled workers *at some time*, even if the process took longer than before.

While as we have said it would be unwise to make any general comments about changes in the average level of skill during the nineteenth century, there does seem a *prima facie* case for saying that the evidence does not support a thesis of unilateral decline. To investigate the subject properly, a thorough study would have to be made of pre-mechanised craft work, as well as of work in modern industries. Without such a study, arguments which have been put forward as to a decline in the average level of skill in the late nineteenth century remain unsubstantiated.[8]

Skill Levels in Engineering[9]

As an industry central to the process of continuing industrialisation in the late nineteenth century, and one which employed a growing proportion of the labour force, engineering is a suitable candidate for a detailed study of skill levels; and as we have seen in Chapter 2, it was also an industry subject to allegations of deskilling. Although it was argued in that chapter that skill was still needed in the industry, the exact amount, and the extent to which it might have changed before the war, were not considered in detail.

We can best investigate the problem by dividing it into two: first, we will look at changes in the amount of manual skill and knowledge needed by workers in the engineering industry; and second, at changes in the extent to which the craftsman took decisions about the planning and execution of his work. Change was said to have occurred in the amount of manual skill and knowledge needed, as a result of the introduction in the 1880s and 1890s of more specialised machine tools, such as grinding and milling machines, and of semi-automatic and automatic lathes; and in the extent to which the craftsman took decisions, as a result of the routinisation of work, exemplified by the introduction of 'feed and speed' men, and the growth of piecework and premium bonus schemes. The two problems are best separated, because up to now we have been mainly concerned with skill in the sense of manual skill and knowledge; but as was shown in Chapter 1, an important part of the Marxist argument on deskilling concerned the increasing separation of conception from execution, or the hiving-off of decision-making powers from the manual workers.

The first problem can be divided into two parts: what was the actual proportion of skilled workers before the First World War, and how far had this proportion changed in the later nineteenth and early twentieth centuries; and did the changes in work *within* each engineering department lead to deskilling, reskilling or to changes in the type of skill required but no overall movement upwards or downwards?[10]

Unfortunately there are not, so far as I know, any national figures available before the 1880s which would help us to answer the first question; but since the beginning of the 'machine revolution' is usually dated to that decade, it is as good a time as any to start.[11] The 1886 and 1906 Wages Censuses give a fairly detailed breakdown of occupations, the first survey covering some 54,000 engineering workers, and the latter no less than 60 per cent of all workers in the industry. The figures for the two dates are given in Table 9.1.[12]

These figures are extremely interesting, for they indicate that if skill is adequately defined either by labels − turner, fitter etc. − or in the case of some unlabelled groups by pay, then the decline between the 1880s and the 1900s was extremely slow. Some confirmation that by the later part of the period there was no dramatic shift in the proportion of skilled workers required is provided by the Jackson

Table 9.1: Engineering, Broad Skill Categories

	1886	1906
Skilled	53.0%	49.5%
Semi-skilled	23.0%	28.0%
Unskilled	24.0%	22.5%

See note 12 for the basis of the computation.
Source: PP 1893-4, LXXXIII, pt. ii; 1906 Wages Census, PP 1911, LXXXVIII.

Report, published in 1909, which questioned 28 firms in engineering and allied trades in London, and 66 outside. It found that there was little, if any, tendency for the substitution either of boy labour for adult labour or of unskilled labour for skilled. It did note – something borne out by the figures given in Table 9.1 – that there seemed to be a tendency for labourers to become semi-skilled machine-operators.[13]

It might be argued, of course, that if some groups had become deskilled these figures are not reliable. In order to test this argument, we must now turn to a consideration of the work performed by the various groups within engineering.

The first point to note is that a number of important departments in engineering had experienced little change in the amount of skill needed: these departments included the smithy and the boiler shop; and there may have been some *increase* in the amount of skill needed in the foundry and the pattern shop – slight in the case of the former, rather greater in the case of the latter. Patternmaking is a woodworking craft, and as with joinery the introduction of machinery relieved the pattern-maker of the more arduous and unskilled, rather than the finer and more delicate, work; furthermore, patterns themselves were becoming steadily more complicated.[14]

The crucial areas of change were the turning and fitting departments. Even here it is arguable that the changes involved not so much a decline in skill as a requirement for a different type of skill; less manual skill was needed, but more of the quality which we have loosely described as 'knowledge'. This particularly applied to the turner: he had to work more complicated designs than his predecessor, using more detailed blueprints; in addition, the new machines were much more compli-cated and the turner needed to possess more knowledge in order to set them up correctly.[15] In the case of the fitter, knowledge was needed which had not been in the nineteenth century, as of micrometers and other measuring instruments; but while some fitters still needed considerable manual skill, others had become specialised in one type of assembly work.[16]

J.W.F. Rowe suggested that while there may have been some absolute decline in the skill level of fitters and turners, it was not considerable; but that there was an element of social construction in their position in the wages hierarchy because their skill declined relative to other groups, such as patternmakers, while their wages did not.[17] This social construction, it should be noted, was not at the expense of unskilled and semi-skilled workers, but of other skilled grades; it does not therefore vitiate the argument developed in Chapter 7 to the effect that it was impossible to maintain socially constructed skill, and the concomitant differentials, for *all* craftsmen in any large industry over a long period.

To return to the question of skill levels. While there was undoubtedly a steady erosion of the manual skill needed by some groups of workers, there would seem to be a case for saying that the amount of knowledge and intelligence needed by most groups was increasing. While an overall estimate of skill levels in engineering is very hard to make, it might be a help to set out the percentage of workers in the main departments of engineering, together with movements in skill levels so far as they can be assessed on the evidence.

If Table 9.2 is a fair outline of the changes which were occurring, then it would seem that two tendencies can be distinguished. First, the departments where skill was, if anything, increasing, were themselves experiencing a relative decline, and vice versa; in that sense the average skill level was probably declining slightly, assuming that the initial skill requirements in these departments were roughly equal, which is suggested by their similar levels of pay. And second, the departments where skill may have been decreasing were larger numerically than those where it may have been increasing, that is if we except machinemen. The latter most probably experienced some increase in skill, because while the manual skill requirements of their machines were never very high, the knowledge necessary to work them would increase as the machines became more complex; Dearle was certainly of the opinion that the overall skill level of semi-skilled work was increasing.[18] On balance the overall tendency in engineering was probably downwards, but at a slow rate, and mitigated by a number of countervailing factors such as the increased knowledge requirement of most jobs and the generally increased skill required by some groups such as patternmakers; furthermore, no account has been taken of probable increases in skilled work 'off the job', as for instance among draughtsmen, ratefixers and feed and speed men.

Table 9.2: Skill Requirements in Engineering[19]

	1886	1906	Manual skill requirement 1886-1906	Knowledge requirement 1886-1906	Overall skill level 1886-1906
	% of total engineering workforce				
Fitters	12.4	16.4	↓	↑ ?	↓
Turners	6.2	6.7	↓	↑	↓ ?
Smiths and hammermen*	8.6	5.0	–	–	–
Foundry	9.4	6.4	–	↑ ?	↑ ?
Boiler shop**	5.2	4.2	–	–	–
Patternmakers	2.9	1.8	–	↑	↑
Machinemen*	7.2	10.6	–	↑	↑

Key: * Semi-skilled   ↑ = Increase   ? = Change probably small
     ** Some semi-skilled   ↓ = Decrease
                          – = No change
Source: PP 1893-4, LXXXIII, pt. ii; PP 1911, LXXXVIII.

The connection between this survey and our study of dilution in Chapter 2 is obvious. The dilution study, while it did not examine the work of specific grades of craftsmen, showed that it was not possible to replace skilled workers in most occupations without incurring a cost penalty, unless the scale of production was greatly enlarged. The study of individual grades of worker has shown that in all cases they continued, in the period under consideration, to exercise a considerable degree of skill; in some cases rather less, relative to other workers than previously, in some cases rather more. Can we leave the last word on this with the Managing Director of the large engineering firm of Hawthorn Leslie?

Without a plentiful supply of skilled artisans, engineering, as practised at the present day, would quickly decline, because the standard of workmanship is constantly being raised and the men to meet this required standard are an essential to the modern business.[20]

Discretion in Manual Work

We must now consider the second problem which we posed earlier, that is whether there were changes in the amount of discretion exercised by craftsmen. We identified two particular developments which might be indications of a decrease in discretion, namely the increase in piecework and the increasing use of specialists such as feed and speed men in the machine shop.

Piecework and bonus schemes do not by themselves imply increasing control by management: most payment schemes are a form of disguised piecework, because for most wage payments, whether nominally by piece or by time, an expected output is required to be produced;[21] piecework schemes do, however, imply that work is more routinised, because daywork tends to be used where the output is difficult to measure very precisely. But an increase in piecework does not mean an increase in routinisation in every case, because there are other constraints on methods of wage payments such as union strength, union preference, managerial knowledge and custom. It seems likely that at least some of the increase in piecework payment in engineering at this period, as shown in Table 9.3, owed itself to the weakness of the ASE, which was hostile to piecework, after the 1897 lockout; and another part to the increasing knowledge by employers of the advantages of new methods, which eroded the hold of custom on wage payment schemes.[22]

Table 9.3: Payment Schemes

		1886 %	1906 %
Turners	Time	94.0	61.5
	Piece	6.0	29.0
	Bonus		9.5
Fitters	Time	93.5	70.0
	Piece	6.5	22.0
	Bonus		8.0

Source: PP 1893-4, LXXXIII, pt. ii; PP 1911, LXXXVIII.

The role of the feed and speed men was to work out for each job the depth of cut and cutting speed, tasks which previously had been the prerogative of the turner himself, using his own judgement; the evolution of a separate class of specialist supervisors can be dated to the 1890s.[23] We should be cautious, however, both in assessing the speed with which such developments were introduced, and also in predicting unilateral tendencies in them towards the removal of control from the craftsmen. W.F. Watson put his finger on the limitations of management power in this respect, in his account of the wholesale introduction of feed and speed men and bonus schemes at Thorneycrofts in the 1900s. The feed and speed instructions were very crude: a combination of worker resistance, and their own inaccuracy, effectively put a stop to the introduction of the instructions in their original form, and much more responsibility had to be given back to the workers in order to make the scheme operate satisfactorily.[24] Elsewhere, Watson in his description of life as an engineering worker in London before, during and after the First World War gives numerous examples of the survival of small and medium-sized jobbing shops, where such methods were not so much unknown as inappropriate because of the diversity of the work.[25]

A final point that should be made in this connection is that to postulate a decrease in discretion simply because of specialisation is unacceptable. The analogy of medical specialisation used in Chapter 1 is pertinent here: the skill and discretion content of a doctor's or surgeon's work might well increase as a result of his specialisation. Therefore the fact that certain parts of the turner's work which were hitherto his responsibility were taken over by specialists does not necessarily imply that the turner exercised less discretion: if other facets of his work became more complex and needed more planning, he might need to exercise so much more discretion in some directions as to outweigh the loss in others. Rowe implies that this might be the case:

> The modern turner's skill lies in the stages preparatory to the actual operation of cutting. He must think out the quickest and simplest order in which the various operations can be done; he must organise his work as the management do theirs, and even this simple organisation demands a longer view, and a more trained mind, than were required forty years ago. He must fix his work in the light of these reflections, and here there is great scope for individual skill.[26]

Whether or not the particular exemplar we have used, the turner, needed to exercise more discretion or not overall is a moot point, but the general principle remains valid: except perhaps to a strict follower of Marx's views on the subject, specialisation *per se* need not involve loss of discretion, or in Marxian terms the separation of conception from execution.

It is worth pursuing the question of discretion in work a little further. To commentators on the subject, 'craft' work tends to be imbued with an almost mystic value; the ideal type of craftsman pursues his work independently, using his own skill and judgement, and unfettered by authority. It seems to me questionable, however, as to how far craftsmen in old crafts such as thatching and wheelwrighting actually had control over their work. While it is no doubt the case that,

even when employed by someone else, the craftsman worked independently, the actual work he did was strictly prescribed, as a reading
of George Sturt's book *The Wheelwright's Shop* shows. It was prescribed because the products were made unvaryingly in accordance with
local custom; not merely the designs, but the methods of working,
were programmed into the craftsman from his apprenticeship.[27]

In this there is a considerable contrast to modern work where
apprenticed craftsmen are employed. Building provides a link between
the two — a building worker, even when working with unvarying local
designs and materials, has to exercise some discretion because of the
vagaries of the site. A skilled engineering worker, or a shipwright, or
a printer, will constantly be faced with new types of work, or old
types of work combined in a new way; is not the discretion he must
use to complete the work as expeditiously as possible greater than
that of the old-fashioned craftsman, who in spite of his 'independence'
never dreamed of working in anything but the time-honoured fashion
of his youth?

As we saw in Chapter 1, Alan Fox, who elaborated the concept of
discretion in work which we have used in this chapter, thought that
the late nineteenth and early twentieth centuries saw a quickening
pace of rationalisation of work, and may have been a key period for
loss of discretion. While it is tempting to comment further on this,
our self-imposed limitation on our field of study prevents us from
doing so *in extenso*. The evidence put forward in this chapter does
suggest, however, that so long as we consider (as Fox does) that loss
of discretion is not necessarily coterminous with increasing specialisation, then we must be doubtful about his hypothesis; specialisation
undoubtedly did increase in some trades, such as engineering; but there
is also evidence that in some ways discretion increased as well. Furthermore, the mechanisation of former hand crafts like papermaking and
shoemaking may have made it possible for many workers to exercise
more discretion at some period of their working lives — that is when
they had progressed upward to fully skilled work — than previously.
Finally, we might question whether a high level of discretion really
was a feature of much old-fashioned craft work.

Marx would assert that any increase in specialisation represented
a further stunting of the worker's potential. Since no one would dis-
pute that specialisation has increased with the development of capitalist
organisation, there is no point in considering this argument other than
on the philosophical level; but my study is of relevance to Marx's
predictions insofar as he also believed that machinofacture necessarily

led to a reduction in the skill of the worker, when skill is expressed as a function of training time. It was suggested in Chapter 7 that the desire of employers to minimise costs did not necessarily lead them to minimise training costs; different technologies and markets demanded differing proportions of skilled labour, and although the textile industry, which Marx perhaps took as his exemplar, did use large numbers of specialised semi-skilled workers, this was by no means always the case elsewhere.

Braverman takes Marx's arguments further. He appears to suggest that skill in modern industry, so far as it exists, is an artefact of management, a view that few would share. Within this version of the social construction argument, however, he accepts Marx's basic de-skilling thesis. It is not our task here to investigate Braverman's empirical findings, which relate to the recent past. But it is relevant to his thesis to point out that it is curiously similar to that advanced by commentators like Hobson and Tawney 75 years or more ago. While the existence of such similar opinions relating to such widely separated periods is not necessarily incompatible — for instance there may have been reskilling and then further deskilling between 1900 and today — it must make us doubt the soundness of one view of the other (or both). Perhaps it is cynical to suggest that Braverman is merely the latest in a long line of 'deteriorationists' which started with Mr Escot in Peacock's *Headlong Hall*, and has included both Marxists and conservative rural romantics like H.J. Massingham.

Notes

1. L.J. Mayes, *History of Chairmaking in High Wycombe* (1960), pp. 33-4, 76-7.
2. E.P. Thompson, *The Making of the English Working Class* (Pelican edn, 1968), pp. 282-3.
3. R. Campbell, *The London Tradesman*, 1st edn 1747 (reprint Newton Abbott, 1969), pp. 192-3.
4. FLW respondent nos. 166, 257, 369.
5. FLW respondent no. 276.
6. P. Thompson, *The Work of William Morris* (1967), p. 85.
7. It is worth noting that the relative importance of this industry, where skill levels were generally low, fell steadily from the mid-century on: 10.1 per cent of all employed males worked in it in 1851, and 4.8 per cent in 1901.
8. This interpretation is different from that put forward by A.L. Levine, 'Industrial Change and its Effect upon Labour, 1900-1914', unpublished PhD thesis, University of London, 1954; see also his book, *Industrial Retardation in Britain 1880-1914* (1967), pp. 86-9. Levine advances a deskilling thesis, although he does not substantiate it by any close investigation of apprenticeship

and training in the period prior to the late nineteenth century. This thesis, which echoes the opinions of commentators like Hobson and Tawney, is familiar to students of this period: in relation to engineering it is implicit in Hinton's book (see Chapter 2), and is mentioned in K. Burgess, *The Origin of British Industrial Relations* (1975), pp. 49 and 64.

9. In the Appendix to this chapter the origins of the types of skill needed in the engineering industry are discussed.

10. For details of changes in engineering technology and techniques see J.W.F. Rowe, *Wages in Practice and Theory* (1928), Ch. V and Appendix III, and Chapter 2 of the present book; see also Levine, 'Industrial Change', pp. 122ff., 156ff., 362ff., 372ff., 433ff.

11. Rowe, *Wages*, pp. 90-1.

12. The allocation of workers to the categories of 'skilled', 'semi-skilled' and 'unskilled' was made on the following basis: labourers and platers' helpers were counted as unskilled; smith's strikers, machinemen and holders-up were counted as semi-skilled (and in 1906 slingers and riggers, and enginemen and cranemen, were also included in this category); the totals of unskilled and semi-skilled men were then subtracted from the grand total to give the number of skilled. There were large numbers of workers (about 15 per cent at both dates) who were not classed, however; in 1886 it was possible to identify a proportion of these as unskilled, on the basis of wages, and the same proportion was taken for 1906; in both years it seemed, again on the basis of wages, as if about one-third of the rest should be taken as skilled, and two-thirds as semi-skilled, and this was done.

13. Jackson Report, p. 133. The reader's attention is also drawn to the discussion in Chapter 2, notes 29 and 31, where it was suggested that the overall decline in the proportion of skilled workers which became noticeable during and after the First World War was due more to the growth of new, lighter branches of engineering, than to the actual (as opposed to relative) decline of older sections; in the older sections, the proportion of skilled workers continued to be high.

14. Rowe, *Wages*, pp. 93-7.

15. Ibid., pp. 99-100. The reader is also referred to the present book, Chapter 4, note 15 and the related discussion: *already skilled* workers needed a further 15-18 months of on-the-job training, or 15 weeks of specialised training, to learn how to set up and maintain *one group* of specialised machines.

16. Ibid., pp. 101-3.

17. Ibid., pp. 109-11; he attributes the stability of their differentials to the strong position of turners and fitters within the ASE, and also to the influence of custom.

18. N.B. Dearle, *Industrial Training* (1914), pp. 157-8; Sir Benjamin Browne thought that 'the semi-skilled of today is in many cases as good as the skilled man was a quarter of a century ago' (albeit in a more limited sphere); Evidence to the Royal Commission on the Poor Laws, PP 1910, XLVIII, Qu. 86333.

19. At both dates millwrights are included with fitters.

20. 1915 Report, p. 130.

21. D.F. Schloss, *Methods of Industrial Remuneration*, 3rd edn (1898), p. 14.

22. The ASE's hostility to piecework can of course be attributed to the difficulty, under piecework conditions of payment, of maintaining the standard rate when there were large varieties of different work; S. and B. Webb, *Industrial Democracy* (1920 edn), pp. 291-7.

Knowledge of new methods of wage payment, and of other managerial innovations, was increasingly disseminated in periodicals and books from the mid-

1890s on; L.H. Jenks, 'Early Phases of the Management Movement', *Administrative Science Quarterly*, vol. 5, no. 3 (Dec. 1960), pp. 428-35.

23.   Levine, 'Industrial Change', p. 364. I would like to thank my father for his assistance with this section.

24.   W.F. Watson, *Machines and Men* (1935), pp. 89-92.

25.   Ibid., e.g. pp. 67, 70 and 184-6. The application of 'Scientific Management' principles has not been discussed here because such applications, so far as they can be distinguished from the introduction of bonus schemes etc., were very limited in England before the First World War; see Craig R. Littler, 'Understanding Taylorism', *British Journal of Sociology*, vol. XXIX, no. 2 (June 1978), p. 187. (Taylor was the first and most famous exponent of Scientific Management.) Littler makes the point that Taylorism was as much an attack on internal subcontract, that is systems of labour subcontracting within a firm or unit of work, as on 'craft control' of work; ibid., pp. 144-5. But there is very little evidence by our period of subcontracting in engineering, or for that matter in any of the apprenticed trades except plating and riveting. (The Jefferys consider that it had almost totally died out in engineering by this period; M. and J.B. Jefferys, 'The Wages Hours and Trade Customs of the Skilled Engineer in 1861', *EcHR*, vol. XVII (1947), p. 44.) It flourished in the iron and steel industry, in some of the Birmingham trades and in an emasculated form in cotton-spinning. Littler's additional point that Taylorism was also an attack on the power of the foreman is more relevant to us, as is his general point that subcontracting or powerful foremen had already reduced craft control of work. While his comments deserve further investigation, we must place a question mark against them at the moment because Littler does not give a detailed account of the 'craft control' which allegedly existed before the development of subcontracting etc.

26.   Rowe, *Wages*, pp. 99-100.

27.   George Sturt, *The Wheelwright's Shop* (Cambridge, 1934). Change did occur slowly, but, Sturt's book suggests, as a result of outside influences, such as the development of mass produced iron castings, rather than as a result of internal innovations.

Appendix: Early Engineering Workers

There is a pervasive myth about the origins of the engineering industry which is repeated by a number of historians. The myth is that the ancestor of the engineering worker was the millwright, the constructor of wind and water mills, who in the words of William Fairbairn, 'knew something of geometry, levelling and mensuration . . . could calculate the velocities, strength, and power of machines . . . [and] could draw in plan and section'.[1] The result of the adoption of this myth is that the engineering worker of the later nineteenth century is portrayed as a lesser figure than his alleged ancestor, as a detail worker pursuing only one part of a trade, however skilfully, rather than as an all-round worker.[2] We have already suggested that Turner's contention that the origin of engineering trade unionism lay in the millwrights' trade societies had no real foundation.[3] The origins of the engineering worker himself are worth a brief enquiry.

Apart from the foundry workers, who were obviously descended from ironworkers and not millwrights, one of the larger departments in any engineering shop in the nineteenth or early twentieth century was the blacksmiths'. Smithing, like foundry work, was a trade which had its own very long history, but the early smiths were not merely the ancestors of their namesakes in a modern engineering shop. Where their trade was on a large scale, as in London, it became subdivided even in pre-engineering days. As R. Campbell described it in 1747:

> In all Smith's Shops they are divided into three classes; the Fire-Man, or he who forges the work; the Vice-Man, or he who files and finishes it; and the Hammer-Man . . . the Vice-Man requires the nicest hand and the most mechanic Head, especially if concerned in Movements.[4]

Since filing metal forged by a blacksmith or shaped by a lathe are not essentially different, the viceman is the true ancestor of the fitter, the largest single occupational class in engineering, who likewise 'files and finishes' the work of the smith or turner.[5] In 1818 we read of the foundation of the Friendly and Benevolent Society of Viceman and Turners, and as late as the 1840s engineering employers referred to their apprentices to fitting as 'filers'.[6] The records of Boulton and Watt

195

also suggest that the smiths, with their long tradition of metalworking, played just as important a part in the early engineering industry as the millwrights. At the original Soho Engine Manufactory there was little subdivision of labour, although most workers were not described as millwrights but, significantly, as engineers and smiths; but at the newer Soho Foundry set up in 1795 there was considerable subdivision, which was carried so far as to assign different fitters to different assembly tasks, although this was not always followed strictly in practice. Whether or not fitting was minutely subdivided, it is clear that the fitters were seen as distinct from the turners.[7]

E.P. Thompson's comments are illustrative of the view that until a certain date there was one class of engineering worker, the millwright or machinist, whose demise Thompson dates to the repeal of the Statute of Artificers in 1814. He goes on to suggest that the introduction of the slide-rest on the lathe led to an 'influx of youths and unskilled' and a breaking down of the engineers' craft followed by the establishment of a new hierarchy.[8] The new hierarchy seems to have been established remarkably quickly, for by 1824 William Galloway, a leading engineering employer in London, whose workers included millwrights, smiths, vicemen and filers, and turners, reported paying wages of up to two guineas a week for skilled workers.[9]

The reality was that all these groups had existed long before the repeal of the Statute of Artificers: engineering was not, as shoemaking later in the century *was*, one trade which mechanisation broke down into numerous different tasks; it was a synthetic industry, drawing from its inception on a host of occupations in both metalworking and woodworking. Galloway's comments suggest that he saw the 'engineer's economy' as quite separate from the millwright's trade, not growing out of it:

> We make our machines so much better, and so much cheaper, that [the millwright's] trade, that used to scoff and spurn at the name of an engineer, are obliged to take up the name of an engineer, and conduct their business by the engineer's economy.[10]

Notes

1. W. Fairbairn, *Treatise on Mills and Millwork* (1861), part I, pp. v-vi.
2. See, e.g. W. McClaine, 'The Engineers Union', unpublished PhD thesis, University of London, 1939, p. 9; in many ways this is a very well-informed thesis (not least because the author had been an engineering worker); an example

of the curious doublethinking about the engineering trade is that before asserting that the engineers' 'true line of descent' was from the millwrights, McClaine points out that in the eighteenth century blacksmiths were called in to execute repairs to the Newcomen engine.

H.A. Turner, *Trade Union Growth, Structure and Policy* (1962), pp. 195-6, traces the engineers' origin to woodworkers in general, and the millwrights in particular.

E.P. Thompson, *The Making of the English Working Class* (Pelican edn, 1968), p. 271, likewise sees the millwrights as the engineers' ancestors.

Perhaps Plato could have sorted the whole thing out, and told us what formed the essence of an engineering worker.

3. See Chapter 7.

4. R. Campbell, *The London Tradesman*, 1st edn 1747 (reprinted Newton Abbott, 1969), p. 180.

5. By the 1900s fitters formed some 16 per cent of the engineering work-force and almost a third of the skilled workforce; smiths and hammermen formed some 5 per cent of the total workforce: see Table 9.2.

6. Thompson, *English Working Class*, p. 271; Royal Commission on Children, PP 1843, XIV, p. 510.

7. E. Roll, *An Early Experiment in Industrial Organisation* (1930), pp. 155, 178ff., 185ff.

8. Thompson, *English Working Class*, pp. 270-2.

9. Select Committee on Artisans and Machinery, PP 1824, V, pp. 27-8.

10. Ibid., p. 28. Professor Musson lends his authority to the interpretation I have put forward here: engineering workers 'were not some new elite emerging in the mid nineteenth century. They had been recruited into the industry from a medley of other metal- and woodworking crafts in the second half of the eighteenth and early nineteenth centuries'; A.E. Musson, 'Class Struggle and the Labour Aristocracy', *Social History*, no. 3 (1976), pp. 352-3.

10 THE RESPONSE TO CHANGE: TECHNICAL EDUCATION

Introduction

There is a considerable amount of information available, both in published works and in unpublished theses, on the institutional development of technical education;[1] this chapter will therefore concentrate on its practical effects, and its relationship with other forms of manual training, giving only enough details of the growth and development of technical education as are necessary for an understanding of the main themes of the chapter. The outline of this growth and development will constitute the first and second parts. The third part will consider the attitude of employers to technical education, and the fourth part the attitude of employees. Finally, an attempt will be made to relate technical education to other forms of training, and to explain its pattern of growth.

Definition of Technical Education

It is unfortunate that even the published works on this subject tend to be rather careless about defining technical education; as a basis for our discussion we will distinguish five different types. First, there was higher technical education in both scientific and technological subjects, that is the level of education nowadays found in universities and polytechnics. Second, there was technical education which aimed to teach pure science at a more elementary level; the reason for calling this technical education is that in the period before full-time secondary education became widespread, science teaching was only available to many people in evening classes, and as such was often referred to under the generic heading of technical education. Third, there was technical education which aimed to give an elementary theoretical background to technological subjects such as machine and building construction. Fourth, there was technical education which aimed to impart the practical knowledge needed in a specific occupation, such as shoemaking or lathe work in engineering; and fifth, there was technical education which aimed to impart actual manual skill in these same subjects; these last two were often referred to as 'trade training'. Somewhere between the third and fourth types is drawing, especially mechanical drawing, which was by no means unimportant.

We will primarily be concerned in our discussion with types three, four and five, in line with the fact that the second type, which was really an extension of elementary education, falls outside our scope, while in relation to skill our interest is in its acquisition by manual workers, not by scientific and technical workers who would make use of technical education of the first type. It would be carrying classification to an absurd extent to look at each type of technical education separately; but in the ensuing discussion it will be important to make clear which type is being referred to. In order to facilitate this, they will be distinguished as follows: the second type (science teaching at pre-university level) as elementary scientific; the third type (theoretical instruction in technological subjects) as technological; the fourth type (the teaching of the knowledge content of specific occupations) as theoretical trade training; and the fifth type (the teaching of manual skills) as manual trade training.

Part One: Up to 1890

It would be fair to say that up to about 1890 technical education of any form except elementary scientific, whose value to industry was dubious, was little developed in Britain. What impact it did have on industry came from the examination of the Science and Art Department, and the work carried out in preparing for them. Commentators on technical education rightly point out the theoretical nature of these examinations, and their lack of relevance to trade training, both theoretical and manual.[2] Nevertheless, it was an unfair comment by the Bryce Commission on Secondary Education to say that all the Science and Art Department did was to foster a peculiar and limited form of secondary education.[3] It is true that examinations in magnetism and electricity, and inorganic chemistry, would be classified as elementary scientific and as such would not nowadays be regarded as technical education at all, although these particular subjects did have some relevance to industry; but there were also examinations in building construction and drawing, and machine construction and drawing, which would be classified as technological and have obvious relevance to occupations in these fields.

What is clear is that theoretical and manual trade training were not catered for to any significant extent until the end of this period (see Part Two for their early development). What is also clear, and is more important, is that the facilities which existed were seen as being largely for the benefit of managerial and technical staff, or those who hoped to become such. The replies to the circular sent out by the Royal Commission on Technical Instruction bring out this fact, as shown in Table 10.1.

Table 10.1: Facilities for Technical Education, 1884

	Engineering	Chemicals	Porcelain and glass	Textiles	Total	Replies by individual firms to question-naire on the effect on their work-men of exis-ting Science and Art classes in their locality
a	2	1	—	4	7	
b	2	—	—	—	2	
c	—	1	1	3	5	
d	5	2	3	7	17	
e	4	—	1	2	7	
Total	13	4	5	16	38	

Key
a   Technical education encouraged for those intending to become managers, clerks, draughtsmen and technical staff.
b   As a, plus foremen.
c   Technical education facilities used by all grades of worker.
d   No significant facilities for technical education in the locality.
e   No clear answer.
Note: It should be noted how in several cases draughtsmen and technical workers, but not foreman, were mentioned; in several cases foremen were specifically excluded, as not being liable to benefit. Where, as in several instances, the lack of technical classes in the vicinity was mentioned, their potential use to design staff rather than to foremen or workmen was put forward as a reason for developing them.
Source: Royal Commission on Technical Instruction, PP 1884, XXXI, pt. ii, Appendix G.

The impression given by Table 10.1, that manual workers were not expected to benefit much from instruction, is in keeping with the general attitude towards its uses held by both employers and experts on technical education at this time; this attitude will be discussed in Part Three of this chapter. More conclusive proof of the relative unimportance of technical education to the majority of workers at this time comes from the figures showing the numbers taking technical examinations. Table 10.2 below shows the number taking Science and Art Department examinations in two key technological subjects, compared with the numbers in the relevant industries.

We now have to consider whether these figures bear out my contention that manual workers were little affected by technical instruction until the 1890s. To do this we first have to estimate what proportion of workers would need to be technically trained to satisfy the requirement for trained supervisory and technical staff. We will first make the assumption that workers who had received technical training would be promoted in preference to those who had not; in view of the fact that, even in the 1880s, some firms expressed a desire for technically trained foremen, and a number for technically trained draughtsmen, this seems reasonable. We then have to estimate what the proportion of supervisory and technical staff was: a figure of 5 per cent seems reasonable.[5] If we then take 30 years as the working life of an adult, the proportion who would have to receive technical training each year would be, assuming a numerically stable labour force (5 per cent divided by 30) i.e. 0.17 per cent of the total labour force.[6]

Table 10.2: Technical Education and the Workforce, 1863-93[4]

		A	B	C	D
1863	a	194	373,000	0.05%	0.03%
	b	107	356,000	0.03%	0.02%
1873	a	1,969	434,000	0.45%	0.22%
	b	663	427,000	0.14%	0.07%
1883	a	5,251	488,000	1.08%	0.54%
	b	2,401	525,000	0.46%	0.23%
1893	a	10,232	575,000	1.78%	0.89%
	b	3,800	539,000	0.70%	0.35%

Column A   Number taking examinations.
Column B   Number in relevant occupations.
Column C   Column A as a percentage of Column B.
Column D   Column C adjusted for examination pass rate.
   a   Examinees in machine construction and drawing; number of males in metals, engineering etc.
   b   Examinees in building construction and drawing; number of males in building construction.
See Note 4 for further details of sources and methods used in estimating numbers.

There were, however, two factors which must have increased this proportion: first, the labour force was growing, and this would have increased the proportion of workers who at any given time needed to receive technical training to fit them for supervisory positions in the future; and second, the proportion given assumes that only new entrants were technically trained, whereas there were undoubtedly many post-apprenticeship workers who were training as well.[7] I would suggest, therefore, that to supply trained entrants to supervisory and technical positions, and to train some of those already in such positions, some 0.25 per cent of the labour force would have to experience technical training every year. If the proportion was higher than that, it can be concluded that there was some 'leakage' into the manual sector of the workforce; but to give technical training to a substantial proportion — say 30 per cent — of the skilled workforce, 1 per cent or more of the total workforce would have to experience technical instruction; furthermore, this proportion would only be reached after 30 years or so.

Taking the figures we have in Table 10.2, and making all due allowances for inaccuracies of one kind or another, it would seem, taking the figures in Column D as giving us the most accurate possible guide, that in engineering the figure of 0.25 per cent may have been reached in the late 1870s, and from thenceforth there may have been some impact from technical education on manual workers; but even by the 1890s this impact was relatively small, probably under 10 per cent of skilled workers being affected. In building and construction, only by the late 1880s were a substantial proportion of putative supervisory and technical staff being reached; many of the older ones would not have been affected, and the impact on manual workers, except perhaps in London (see Part Two) was probably minimal.

One point that is pertinent, however, is that the influence of technical training was unevenly spread, especially in engineering where the policy of the firm made an important difference. As Table 10.1 shows, some engineering firms showed little interest in technical education; but others such as Mather and Platt, in Salford, and Armstrongs in Newcastle, had their own technical schools closely attached to them.[8] In these cases some manual workers must have experienced technical education, and certainly foremen would have done — as was specifically stated by Armstrongs in their reply to the Royal Commission. But in many other firms there would have been no one with technical training except perhaps one or two of the managers and draughtsmen.

Part Two: 1890-1914

So far we have only discussed the provision of elementary scientific and technological education, because as noted there was in the earlier period significant provision only for these types. There were, however, a few people who felt that technical education should go further, and the origin of trade classes, at least on any scale, can be traced back to Regent Street Polytechnic founded in 1881 by one such person, the philanthropist Quintin Hogg.[9] Table 10.3 shows the stage at which technical education of various kinds, including trade training carried on by this and similar institutions, had reached in London by 1892.

Table 10.3: Technical Education in London, 1892

	A	B	C	D	E
Carpentry and joinery	39,489	98	0.25%)		
Bricklaying	23,591	51	0.22%)	2,520	3.33%
Plumbing	7,269	341	4.69%)		
Locksmiths	5,263	—	—)		
Engineering and metal	54,061	266	0.44%	2,924	5.41%

Column A Number engaged in trade in London.
Column B Number in attendance at special trade classes (theoretical and manual) (excluding those not engaged in the trade).
Column C % of those in trade in special trade classes.
Column D Number (including those not engaged in the trade) in attendance at *all* classes bearing on the trade.
Column E % of those in trade experiencing some form of technical education.
Note: The proportion in Column E is found by taking the numbers in Column D, against the numbers in Column A. This will overstate the proportion because not all in Column D were in the trade; furthermore, in building the total number of workers is understated by omitting, e.g., painters and plasterers.
Source: C.R. Millis's chapter in F.W. Galton (ed.), *Workers on their Industries* (1885), p. 11, citing H. Llewellyn-Smith's *Report to the L.C.C. Special Committee on Technical Education* (1892).

While an attempt is made, subject to the caveats entered in the note, to relate in Table 10.3 the numbers in classes to the total in the industry, the figures are just as or even more problematic than those available from the examination statistics: we have no measure of the quality of the teaching, although contemporary comment suggests that it was low in the trade classes;[10] furthermore, many of those in the classes may have stayed for two or more years, thus leading us to overestimate the numbers who actually completed a course. Allowing for this, we might guess that the proportion of workers undergoing technical instruction, as opposed to the proportion taking examinations, would have to reach at least 0.5 per cent of those employed in the industry before such training would have much impact on the manual workforce. Even so, the figures suggest that in trade training for the engineering and metal industries the breakthrough point was on the verge of being reached in the early 1890s, while in plumbing it was considerably exceeded. In the former industry it would, of course, take a number of years before the workers thus educated would form a significant proportion of the total labour force. The figures also suggest that, even discounting the outsiders taking technical subjects, and those in the industry studying more than one subject, technical education of all kinds was by now making a significant impact on the London labour force in both engineering and building.

The precocious development of trade classes in London probably owed a good deal to the capital's failure to provide much in the way of apprentice training, as has been discussed in Chapter 3. It is also worth noting that because a good proportion of the London workforce, at least in some woodworking trades and in engineering, came from outside London to work as improvers, some of the benefits of technical education may not have gone to the native London workers but to these migratory workers, who might or might not stay in London. George Barnes is an example of one such: he started his apprenticeship in London, but moved to Dundee; he then moved back to London, and in the 1880s went to classes in machine construction and drawing at Woolwich Arsenal.

In Part One it was established that by the 1890s, and in certain progressive engineering firms rather earlier, technological education was in a position at which, if carried on at the same rate or expanded further, it would affect a significant proportion of the manual workforce within a few years; so far in this part we have established that theoretical and manual trade training had only just reached this position by 1892 in London, and it had almost certainly not reached it in most other parts of the country. From the 1890s on, however, the pace accelerates considerably. This acceleration is associated with two developments: the application of the so-called 'whisky money' to the furtherance of technical education from 1890, and the growth of the City and Guilds examinations.[11]

Before presenting some figures which show the growth in numbers taking technical examinations, we might draw a parallel between the employers of the 1900s and those of the 1880s, using the results of a questionnaire sent out by Sadler and Beard. Although the classification used is rather different from that in Table 10.1, because the answers provided were much fuller, the results of the surveys make a startling contrast: for instance in Table 10.4, which tabulates the results of the later survey, there is no need for a column showing those firms which replied that there was no significant provision or need for technical education in their areas, because no firms replied that this was the case.

Table 10.4: Facilities for Technical Education, 1906

	Engineering, shipbuilding and metal	Chemicals, soap and dyeing	Textiles	Total	
					Replies by individual firms to questionnaire on the effect on their employees of existing technical classes in their locality.
a	2		2	4	
b	31	4	2	37	
c	1	3		4	
d	11	1	1	13	
e	24	7	1	32	
Total (a + b + c)	34	7	4	45	

Key: a Firms encouraging drawing office and premium apprentices only to attend technical classes.

b Firms encouraging all apprentices (and other young workers in non-engineering firms) to attend technical classes.

c Firms enforcing compulsory attendance on all young workers.

A to c are exclusive of each other. D and e, below, contain firms included in a to c, and in each other.

d Firms giving time off during the day for technical classes (or time off during the day in lieu of time spent in evening classes).

e Firms making a substantial contribution (possibly based on attendance or progress) to the fees of *ordinary* (i.e. not premium) apprentices or other young workers. Includes firms increasing wages in lieu of returning fees.

Source: M.E. Sadler and M.S. Beard, 'English Employers and the Education of their Workpeople' in M.E. Sadler (ed.), *Continuation Schools in England and Elsewhere* (Manchester, 1907), pp. 274-308.

It must be borne in mind that only about a third of firms who were circularised replied, and those which did were no doubt those with an above-average interest in technical education, for as we shall see there is plenty of evidence that not all employers were interested. Even taking this into account, however the impression given is that interest in technical education had now spread to a substantial number of really important firms: names like Vickers, Clayton and Shuttleworth (agricultural machinery), Swan Hunter and Siemens appear in engineering and shipbuilding; and Brunner Mond, Crosfields and Lever Brothers in soap and chemicals. Furthermore, in the majority of cases even ordinary apprentices were encouraged, and sometimes even compelled, to attend technical classes.

As technical education of all types developed, however, it becomes increasingly difficult to use the examination statistics of the Science and Art Department as a measure of growth. There are two reasons for this. On the one hand there was an increasing realisation by educationalists that examinations were not necessary if the teaching was good enough, and by their nature could lead to the acquisition of knowledge rather than understanding.[12] The results of this changing attitude are seen in the cessation of payments by results for technical examinations in 1898, followed by the making of elementary examinations in the science subjects of the old Science and Art Department syllabus optional; these measures were followed by a rapid drop in entries — from 8,510 in the elementary stage of Machine Construction to 4,846 in 1903, around which level the numbers stabilised; much the same pattern is evident in the Building Construction examinations.[13] On the other hand, statistics of the Science and Art Department examinations alone would also be misleading because of the rapid growth of the City and Guild examinations.

Table 10.5 shows the number of City and Guild students for certain years, the number of papers by candidates and the number of passes, with the combined figures for the two Science and Art Department examinations already discussed set alongside.

Table 10.5: City and Guild Students

	A	B	C	D	
1884	5,874	3,635	1,829	(1883)	7,652
1894	22,703	9,907	5,481	(1893)	14,032
1904	41,089	19,041	11,293	(1903)	8,181
1914	55,996	23,119	14,570	n.a. (not printed during war)	

Column A   Number of City and Guild students.
Column B   Number of City and Guild papers.
Column C   Number of City and Guild passes.
Column D   Elementary papers in Machine Construction and Building Construction (Science and Art Department examinations)
Sources: Columns A-C: F.E. Foden, 'A History of Technical Examinations in England in 1918', unpublished PhD thesis, University of Reading, 1961, Appendix C, p. xxii; Column D: relevant reports of the Science and Art Department.

The City and Guild examinations were of numerous types: there were highly theoretical examinations, such as that in Mechanical Engineering, which was strongly criticised for this; as a result it was not nearly as popular as the Science and Art Department examination in Machine Construction, attracting in the 1900s between 1,000 and 2,000 annual entries.[14] There were numerous trade examinations, though, and some of these included practical work — manual trade training.[15] Although in the early days even the trade class syllabuses were often too remote from the ordinary worker, by the 1890s advisory committees of manufacturers and educationalists were becoming established, and the syllabuses were much more in touch with industrial life.[16] Some of the subjects offered by the end of the period are shown in Table 10.6, with the number of candidates. Against these figures are shown the number of recruits needed to the various industries assuming a thirty-five year working life for an adult worker, and the proportion the number of examinees bears to this figure.

Table 10.6: Recruits to Certain Industries

	A	B	C
Boot and shoe (grades 2 and 3)	204	3,845	0.05
Cotton-spinning	1,657	1,175	1.41
Electric wireman's work			
Electrical engineering (grade 1)	1,519	2,333	0.65
Road carriage building	1,158	2,388	0.48
Typography (grade 1)	519	1,039	0.50
Boilermakers' work	122	477	0.26
Iron and steel shipbuilders' work	79	553	0.14
Brickwork	305	2,299	0.13
Cabinet-making	227	1,222	0.19

Column A Number of examinees.
Column B Number of recruits to industry per annum.[17]
Column C Column A as ratio of Column B.
Source of Column A: Foden, 'Technical Examinations', Appendix E, Table III.

These figures show clearly that technical education was starting to have a substantial impact on the manual workforce of certain industries, but that in traditional apprentice-taking trades (except printing) it was less important. We have to take into account, however, the fact that many technical institutions and continuation schools were placing less emphasis on examinations; there is plenty of evidence that there were numerous well-organised courses, especially in engineering and related trades, by the 1900s; almost certainly many who attended these courses did not take the final examinations.[18]

The experience of the FLW respondents is worth citing here (their comments on technical education will be referred to again in Part Four). We do not know if any respondents had technical training but did not refer to it, but the figures for those who did mention it are shown in Table 10.7. Of the respondents who definitely did have technical training, only two, one in engineering and one in woodworking, started at a slightly higher level than the ordinary apprentice: the woodworker, actually a boatbuilder, studied naval architecture after his apprenticeship ended; the engineering worker was originally an ordinary apprentice, and won a scholarship from his firm to enable him to attend day classes. All the others seem to have been ordinary trade apprentices.

Table 10.7: FLW Respondents and Technical Training

	A	B
Engineering	16	4
Metals	9	—
Carpentry and woodwork	9	1
Miscellaneous skilled	12	2
Total	46	7

Column A   Number of respondents in industry/occupation.
Column B   Number of respondents who stated that they had attended technical classes.

These figures in Table 10.7, and the other evidence we have, all suggest that technical training was having some influence on manual workers by this time. But they also suggest that the influence was limited; it was workers in larger firms which believed in technical education who particularly benefited. It is now time to examine the attitudes of employers more closely, in order to establish both why the attitudes of some employers changed and why the attitude of many others did not.

Part Three: The Attitude of Employers

There is little doubt that up to the 1880s there was little support for technical education from employers. There were a number of reasons for this attitude, the main ones probably being simple conservatism, and the practical fear that the facilities given to workers to meet together, and the dissemination of knowledge among them, would mean that trade secrets would quickly leak out to rivals.[19]

When support for technical education did grow, as we have seen that it did among a number of employers by the mid-1880s, the emphasis was still largely on technological education, that is the teaching of general theoretical knowledge which would be of use to present or future supervisory and technical staff. The reason for the prevalence of this attitude is clear: both manufacturers and educationalists believed that actual trade knowledge and practice could best be taught in a factory. As Philip Magnus, a member of the 1884 Royal Commission on Technical Instruction, put it:

> it would be impossible to introduce into an evening school the same facilities for instruction as exist in a factory itself. The whole of the plant of a factory, which forms an essential part of an apprentice's training, could not very well be introduced, except at enormous expense, into an evening school.[20]

Exactly the same points, and some others, were made by H.T. Wood, of the City and Guilds Institute, in 1877: artisans' skill was founded upon long practice, not theoretical knowledge; if it was attempted to teach it in a school, the machinery would always be on a small scale and out of date.[21]

As we shall see in Part Four, this view was not shared by some workers, and these dissidents were backed up by certain educationalists. But it was a view backed by the Royal Commission itself, which suggested that the main improvements needed in manual workers' education were at the elementary level and in drawing.[22] How was it that a number of employers came to change their attitude by the 1900s, and actively encourage technical education among their young workers, as we have seen from Table 10.4 that they did?

Three reasons can be identified as particularly important. The first was the realisation by employers that by making such education available to all apprentices, there were more potential recruits for higher positions. This can be related to the fact that the number of such positions was growing, both absolutely and relatively. The evidence of a Birmingham firm of engineers to Sadler and Beard puts the position very well:

> The evening continuation classes are . . . of very great use to young, intelligent and self-reliant artisans, and, moreover, give opportunities to youths of marked ability for fitting themselves for more responsible work. [The firm] hope, with the special technical classes on two afternoons a week for a selected few, and one scholarship at a University annually, to educate a useful class of assistant engineers.

Another firm put it more bluntly: 'Only those apprentices thus qualified [by attending technical classes] are admitted to the Drawing Office.'[23]

The second reason why employers encouraged technical education was its socialising value. It is difficult to separate this from the economic rationale of education, because undoubtedly the hope was that well-educated apprentices would become more responsible and self-reliant, and hence more efficient, workmen — in itself a striking contrast to the suspicious attitude endemic twenty or thirty years before. Thus Mather and Platt, who started technical education well before most firms, found that it 'has been of the utmost advantage in developing general intelligence, accuracy, and a desire to know more of the scientific foundations on which [the apprentices'] practical work is based'. Burroughs Wellcome, the drug firm, considered that classes as a whole were 'of undoubted benefit in tending to produce more intelligent and self-respecting workpeople'. And two probably exceptional examples of the merging of technical education with general welfare work were the schemes of Cadburys the chocolate firm, and of Crosfields of Warrington the large soap-manufacturers: in both cases the firms emphasised that they provided facilities like swimming baths, physical training classes and ambulance lectures, as well as technical training.[24]

Nevertheless, the 'welfare capitalism' side of technical education, with its connotation of buying loyalty on the cheap, should not be overemphasised. Burroughs Wellcome also stressed the practical value of technical education: to them, the classes were 'more directly useful when they have a bearing upon their particular business, and in a number of cases the usefulness of employees has been increased and their progress advanced as a result of the knowledge gained at the classes'. While the comments in most of the replies to Sadler and Beard's questionnaire were in favour of technical training, they do not usually make it so clear as to why the training was thought valuable. But it is worth noting that Mather and Platt, whose experience was unrivalled, and who like Burroughs Wellcome had noted the general educational value of technical instruction, also like them emphasised that the training was valuable because it was given to the apprentices 'in close connection with their practical work'. While Clayton and Shuttleworth, who had recently developed a carefully thought out scheme, listed the main aims of it as '(1) to supplement the shop work with courses of instruction directly bearing on the work in the shops, and (2) to give to all deserving apprentices a varied shop experience'.[25]

The third reason for the growth in interest in technical education, therefore, was its practical value to work in the shop. The firms cited above were moving away from wanting purely technological education:

but the emphasis, as is shown by, for instance, the numerous courses given by various technical colleges and listed by Creasey in 1905, was on the teaching of the knowledge content of jobs via theoretical trade training, rather than on the teaching of actual manual skills via manual trade training.[26] The early development of trade classes in London, noted in Part Two, must therefore be set in context. While some of these classes may have taught manual skills, the prime aim of such classes as they developed in engineering and textile centres in the 1890s and 1900s was to teach the knowledge content of manual work. The implications of this will be explored in the last part of the chapter.

We must resist the temptation to overemphasise the importance of technical education: there were still many employers in the 1900s who did not specifically encourage it, and some who even opposed it. Dearle found that although 'a very fair proportion' of employers in engineering and printing positively encouraged technical instruction, a large number of firms and foremen in the majority of trades gave it only 'passive acquiescence and support', although only a minority were actually hostile.[27] There is a striking memorandum written during the dilution campaign on the difficulties of introducing workers from technical colleges into factories, which noted that 'the traditional attitude [among employers] is one of apathy, if not of actual hostility, to men trained in the Technical Schools'.[28] In fairness to the employers, the workers referred to may have had their *only* training in technical colleges, and thus their employment may have been attended with very real drawbacks. But as late as 1923 an engineering industry survey found that opinion was evenly divided on whether technical instruction was of use to manual workers.[29] This last finding suggests that, numerous and important though the pro-technical education employers were, especially in engineering and science-based industries like soap, drugs and chemicals, a majority of employers before the First World War were still in all probability indifferent or even hostile to such education.

Part Four: The Attitude of Employees

We will divide our study of the attitude of employees to technical education into two parts: first, the attitudes of more or less organised groupings of employees will be discussed, and second the attitude of individual employees.

The attitude of trade unions to technical education was fairly neutral. In more recent years the attitude of unions has been cautious, although by no means so negative as is sometimes made out.[30] The reason for this caution is, of course, that technical education offers a facility which is not under union control for learning a trade. Anyone who has read so far might well point out that since few unions had much control in our period over apprenticeship or any sort of entry to a trade, their attitude to technical education is more or less irrelevant; and broadly speaking I would agree with this.

It is worth noting, nevertheless, that the ASE had accepted by the 1900s that a four year technical college course entitled an apprentice to two years off the usual apprenticeship period of five years; while the Typographical Association allowed one or two years off the usual seven-year apprenticeship so long as the intervening period was spent at school.[31] On the other hand, at a more local level it is recorded that trade class entrants at the Regent Street Polytechnic refused to let unskilled workers enter the classes, at least in the early days.[32] Since there are later references to the facilities which technical education gave to migratory workers to learn the finer points of their trade, it seems unlikely that this sort of restriction had much effect.[33] But is it interesting to note that the memorandum on dilution already alluded to referred to the hostility of union foremen, as well as employers, to workers trained in technical colleges.[34] This suggests that opposition for sectional reasons to technical education from organised labour might have had some effect at local level, although probably only a sporadic one.

On the other hand, there was one strand of thinking among workers which advocated more technical education, and in particular more trade classes. It was a group of such workers, with the clergyman Henry Solly, who started the Artisans' Institute named after him, in the 1870s; this was later transferred to the Finsbury Technical College, founded at the same time, 1881, as the Regent Street Polytechnic; like the Polytechnic the Institute and its successors emphasised trade training. An educationalist who supported their aims was C.T. Millis, Principal of the Borough Polytechnic.[35] But as we have already noted, the development of trade classes in London should be put in context: most trade classes in Britain as they developed in the 1890s and 1900s stressed theory, albeit theory applied to individual industries and trades, rather than teaching actual manual skill; in other words they concentrated on theoretical rather than manual trade training. And the entries for the City and Guilds examinations show that engineering and electricity, and textiles, were far more important than instruction in the manual techniques of building and cabinet-making. Yet it was the latter occupations and skills which the early exponents of trade classes had stressed. This emphasis stemmed from conditions — the decay of apprenticeship — peculiar to London; but writers on the subject, then and now, have tended to generalise from London conditions to the wider world, and have fostered some misapprehensions about the relationship of apprenticeship and technical education which will be discussed in the last part.[36]

The impact of organised labour on specifically technical education, as opposed to adult and continuation education in general, was therefore small.[37] More important were the attitudes of individual apprentices and young workers to technical edcuation. In the FLW survey an apprenticed wood machinist stated that he did not go to technical classes through lack of time; he thought that few did. An apprenticed leather worker did go to classes: 'I was supposed to study things. I passed them but I never studied them.'[38] This comment, really the only comment as opposed to factual information which respondents offered on the subject, may be untypical, as may the wood machinist's experience. But the evidence suggests that the views of these two workers are representative of those of many others.

The fact that, for most workers, technical education had to take place in the evening was recognised by several commentators as a serious drawback. Creasey in particular drew attention to it, and noted that some firms, such as the London and South Western Railway, did not allow evening instruction at all;[39] other firms, as we have noted in Table 10.4, gave time off in lieu of evening instruction, but in several firms the 'time off' mounted to no more than half an hour or so; when many evening courses took up six hours per week in three sessions, added to the 54-hour week usual in the 1900s, the burden on young workers was considerable.

Not surprisingly, there was a high drop-out rate for most classes, and it is this above all which makes any statistics of attendance highly problematic. Sadler found that in both Liverpool and Birkenhead evening classes attendance had fallen by February to some 50 per cent of the figure registered at the beginning of the academic year. Creasey noted that, while only 14 hours' attendance was necessary per subject in continuation schools in order to claim a grant, only 60 per cent of students managed even this.[40]

These figures are replicated in the replies of firms to various surveys. One of the most striking features is the relatively low level of attendances which employers set as a target for exceeding which apprentices could reclaim fees or earn a bonus. Thus Barr and Stroud, Glasgow optical instrument makers, expected a minimum of 50 per cent of marks and 75 per cent of attendance in two classes before they gave a bonus; a higher level of attendance and achievement earned a higher bonus. In spite of these relatively lax conditions, many apprentices did not fulfil them.[41] Hawthorn Leslie returned fees to just 13 per cent of the apprentices in 1911; and Vickers' Sheffield works returned fees in 22 per cent of cases in 1903-4 and 47 per cent in 1904-5.[42] It is true that most firms replying to Sadler and Beard said that they were generally satisfied with the results of the technical education, but as we have seen firms' motives were usually mixed, and they might be satisfied even if the number of manual workers attending technical classes was low, because they had other aims for education such as training supervisors and technical staff; and several fims replying to the questionnaire specifically mentioned that only a small proportion of workers and apprentices actually utilised the facilities offered.

Table 10.8: Technical Training at Barr and Stroud

	A	B	C
1905-6	45	75%	13%
1906-7	72	74%	30%
1907-8	87	64%	30%
1908-9	96	65%	40%
1909-10	116	61%	29%
1910-11	136	56%	36%

Column A   Number of apprentices.
Column B   Percentage earning bonus.
Column C   Percentage earning higher-level bonus.

The picture we have, therefore, is that technical education, even when it was intended for manual workers as well as those aiming at higher positions, was limited both by the problems of access to it — primarily those problems caused by long hours of work, but also of course the problem of access for those living in small towns or the country — and also by the unwillingnesss of workers to follow it up systematically. To explore why workers, even when they received encouragement from their firms, were so unwilling is really beyond the scope of this thesis, although some suggestions will be offered in the conclusion. In many cases, however, what appeared to be unwillingness was probably more a recognition of their own inability to profit from the education offered. A remark by J.H. Reynolds, a leading expert on technical education in Lancashire, is indicative: he stated that he would like to see all technical schools closed for ten years if at the end of that time all pupils would enter them fully prepared.[43]

This remark highlights the difficulties of introducing mass technical education when the school-leaving age was 13 and when many children had dead-end jobs until they were 15 or so, in which period they forgot most of the little they ever learned. The 1915 Report noted that a large Scottish engineering firm had sent all its apprentices to technical school for three years, but had found the results unsatisfactory. It now had a preliminary examination in elementary arithmetic, and those who failed it were given continuation schooling, paid for by the firm, before they started technical education proper.[44] We have already noted that some firms insisted upon their entrants reaching a certain educational standard, but we have also noted that this was rare; where, as so often, there was a commitment to take the children of existing workers, and when elementary educational provision was so poor, only the best employers could set a high initial standard. The result of this was that many employees, even when they were encouraged to go to technical classes by their employers, could not benefit because the subject matter was beyond them; and short of employers taking upon themselves a much more paternalistic role, as a few firms like Cadburys and the unnamed Scottish engineering company did, employees would continue to be inadequately prepared until elementary education improved.

Part Five: Conclusions

The relevance of technical education to the manual workforce in British industry during our period may be summarised as follows.

The Impact

Technical education was primarily of importance, right up to the end of our period, for supervisory and technical staff rather than for ordinary manual workers. This statement should not be taken to mean that Britain lagged in the provision of technical education: contrary to what is sometimes said or implied by historians, Britain provided more technical education for more workers than most countries did.[45] In all major industrial countries, however, the focus was on technical education for those above the rank and file of the workforce; but within this broad emphasis there were important differences in direction. In Germany, the country with which Britain is most often compared, there was excellent provision for higher technical and scientific education; on the other hand, Britain excelled in the number and quality of her evening schools, which primarily offered an opportunity for young workers to become foremen, draughtsmen and suchlike – to 'rise from the mill'.[46]

This contrast, and the particular emphasis in Britain on the education of aspiring young men of working-class origins, are well brought out by Arthur Shadwell, who made a careful comparative study of conditions in Britain, America and Germany in the early 1900s. Although Shadwell was perhaps mistaken in writing off the impact of technical education on manual workers as completely as he did, his basic point is confirmed by the study we have already made of the motives of employers and employees:

> These young fellows [in evening classes] are the pick of the working-classes, the most intelligent, enterprising, and ambitious. They do not intend to be workmen; they are qualifying for superior positions. I have found the technical schools universally regarded by trade unionists and intelligent workmen as 'stepping stones out of the mill'.[47]

The system which provided these schools, already highly developed by the 1900s, was described by an American commentator in 1929 as 'A magnificent system of local technical institutions, devoted principally to part-time and evening instruction for industrial employees.'[48] This remark shows the naivety of uncritical attacks on British technical education at this time; the higher branches, of course, may have been less satisfactory, but that is not our concern here.

The Value

Shadwell was not entirely justified in writing off the value of technical education for ordinary manual workers: there was some realisation among larger firms in several industries that it could play a part. We have already noted how a few firms made evening classes compulsory for their apprentices and young workers – not all of whom could hope to rise beyond the skilled worker level. The rationale behind this is brought out in a statement by the Works Manager of Brunner Mond, the chemical firm, on the effect of systematic technical education on the engineering apprentices in the maintenance section:

> up to a few years ago very few mechanics understood a drawing, and still fewer could make a hand sketch to illustrate an idea. Many of our lads now show great ability in hand sketching with chalk or pencil, and can be employed in measuring up for alterations or repairs, placing their measurements in an understandable form on paper. They can all grasp the meaning of an engineering drawing.[49]

The statement goes on to outline other ways in which technical education had made the apprentices more effective workers.

Two comments might be made about this statement. The first is that it confirms the point made in Chapter 5 about the skill needed in maintenance work, and also the point made in Chapter 9 about the difficulty of detecting any universal tendency towards deskilling. Clearly the Works Manager preferred to have workers who exercised responsibility and judgement, because such workers were more efficient. Second, it would seem that one of the reasons for encouraging more formal education for manual workers was the growing complexity of work in some occupations — among them engineering. The use of complex blueprints was increasing, and greater accuracy was demanded. But to engineering might be added a number of other trades, some of which had already developed apprenticeship or formal training schemes even though they were of recent origin: among these were occupations connected with electricity and gas supply. The number of City and Guild examinees in electrical work has already been noted (see Table 10.6). As a further example, part of the training scheme of the Gas Light and Coke Company, a London gas company, could be cited. The four-year scheme — it does not seem to have involved an apprenticeship agreement — included instruction in arithmetic, English subjects and drawing, on a day release course in LCC Technical Institute: practical work in the shops and out with the fitters; and, most significantly, a whole year (six months in each of the first and second years) in which the mornings were devoted to direct instruction from experienced men in the shops. The syllabus for this instruction included a host of subjects: the nature and composition of gas; pressure and gauges; methods of laying and joining mains, and the tools used; meters and meter connections; screwing, bending and fitting of pipes; use of gas for fuel; and many others.[50]

The increasing amount of technical instruction — for the instruction detailed above, although it took place in the shops, was more akin to technical instruction than to old-fashioned apprentice training – can be related to the growing knowledge component of manual work. Trades like basket-making or thatching needed a sort of 'craft knowledge' which could be as well picked up on the job as anywhere else. Even a more sophisticated trade like cabinet-making, or mill-wrighting in its early days, did not require any knowledge which could not be acquired in the course of working alongside a journeyman. But occupations in electricity and gas supply, and increasingly in engineering, demanded considerable theoretical knowledge. Because of this, theoretical trade training, and even technological education providing a more general theoretical background, was increasingly relevant not just to aspiring supervisory and technical staff but also to ordinary manual workers in the above-mentioned occupations.

The Scope

If this was the case, it could be asked why more manual workers were not technically trained. As we have seen, even in 1923 a survey found that only 50 per cent of engineering employers thought that such training was of value to manual workers. The explanation which is put forward by Cotgrove finds echoes in a number of other writers. Cotgrove starts with the assumption that apprenticeship had to all intents and purposes collapsed. In view of this, it might seem that there would be a great demand for technical education. According to Cotgrove this did not happen because educationalists had become so imbued with the idea that technical education ought never to teach the practical details of work that it was very hard to swing it in a more practical direction; and such a change was resisted also by employers because they feared the dissemination of trade secrets.[51]

This hypothesis leads to the conclusion that a vacuum existed in education for manual workers in Britain, from the alleged collapse of apprenticeship in the mid-nineteenth century, until the large-scale development of practical technical education or trade training, which started under the aegis of the City and Guilds but had to wait for its full flowering until the post-1945 era.[52] It is not part of our task to examine why this peculiar view of apprenticeship has come to be held by so many historians. What is clear is that by accepting that apprenticeship was alive, well and making a real contribution to training, we can substitute a much simpler and more rational explanation of employers' *relative* lack of interest in technical education for manual workers.

The production of skilled workers was the desired result of training of any kind. There were two kinds of such training: apprenticeship

and other on-the-job methods such as migration and following-up (for
the sake of convenience apprenticeship only will be referred to); and
technical training (usually in practice associated with a more traditional
method, but again for the sake of convenience referred to as if it was
the only method). Apprenticeship was the method favoured by most
employers, for some very simple reasons: it provided a good training
in manual skills, and as long as many firms used technology that was
intensive in manual skills such training was good enough both for
them and for the apprentice, on whose willingness to submit to the
system of apprenticeship its success ultimately depended. Furthermore,
apprenticeship was cheap, both to the apprentice because he earned a
wage, albeit a low one, and to the employer because the value of the
apprentice's work in the later stages of his apprenticeship made up for
the expense of training him earlier. This fact alone explains why so many
employers were reluctant to pay for technical education: unless they
were paternalistic or highly specialised organisations which could
expect to keep the apprentices they trained – railway companies, firms
like Brunner Mond and so on – they had no guarantee of a payback
from their involvement in technical education, as it was unlikely that
they could amortise the cost over the period of apprenticeship, beyond
which they had no certainty that the trainee would be working for them.

Arguably the social returns to technical education were higher than
the private returns to the employer. The experience of Brunner Mond
suggests that, although apprenticeship was effective enough as a method
of training, technical education (allied with apprenticeship) was more
effective: it produced a better worker. But unless the employer could
expect to be recompensed for his expense, he was not going to finance
technical education. In these circumstances, it could have been financed
either by government or by private individuals. Government made a
substantial contribution, via the whisky money and Department of
Science and Art grants, but expected fees to be paid as well, not un-
reasonably since the benefits of technical education were partly private.
Given that a technically trained worker was a more efficient worker, and
could expect in the long run to earn more, why were relatively few young
workers willing to follow technical courses systematically?

The Difficulties

The physical difficulties for many workers of following such courses
have already been mentioned, and in cases where employers did not
pay fees young workers had to pay these as well. On the other hand,
taking up an apprenticeship implied some willingness to sacrifice

immediate income for future benefits, and this would suggest that apprentices were boys of rather above-average character and foresight. This suggests that there were other reasons for their reluctance to go to technical classes. One reason may have been that technical education was seen as a continuation of school — which in a sense it was — and disliked for the way in which it impinged on the adult world of work which the apprentice had now entered. A director of Brunner Mond referred to the disciplinary problems which arose at the inception of compulsory attendance by young workers from his firm: 'some of the unwilling ones threw things about to the subversion of discipline'.[53]

Perhaps the most fundamental reason why technical training lagged was that although it conferred some benefits, they were remote and they were not guaranteed. A time-served worker could be reasonably sure of employment at the full skilled man's wage; in a number of industries, a worker who learned by following-up could be sure of promotion because of seniority rules. A worker with additional technical training had first to pass his examinations, and then had no guarantee of promotion. This dichotomy highlights one of the most crucial points about apprenticeship, and other on-the-job methods of training; far from being inefficient, archaic systems of training, they were extremely cheap and efficient. Since employers did not have to employ time-served workers — they could always sack them — the fact that most of such workers obtained reasonably steady employment shows that their training must have been adequate. Technical training failed to overtake apprenticeship or other methods of training, not because employers and educationalists did not realise what their real requirements were, but because these requirements were met adequately and inexpensively by the older methods.

Notes

1. Michael Argles, *South Kensington to Robbins* (1964); S.F. Cotgrove, *Technical Education and Social Change* (1958); J. Blanchet, 'Science, Craft and the State', unpublished DPhil thesis, University of Oxford, 1953; P. Keane, 'Evolution of Technical Education in Nineteenth Century England', unpublished PhD thesis, University of Bath, 1970.
    2. Argles, *South Kensington*, p. 21.
    3. Cited in Cotgrove, *Technical Education*, p. 37. It is worth noting at this point that except for examinations in elementary scientific subjects, which were increasingly taken by schoolchildren, most of the technical education which is discussed from now on catered for continuation students, most of whom up to

the 1890s would go to evening classes. By the 1900s day release was becoming fairly well established among larger firms; see Table 10.4 and sources cited there.

4. The figures in the various columns have been arrived at as follows.

Column A: 1863, all entries to examinations in relevant subjects; 1873 on, entries to elementary-level examinations in relevant subjects (advanced-level entries have been omitted on the grounds that most candidates for them must have taken the elementary examinations, and therefore to include the advanced level would lead to double-counting). Sources: 1863, F.E. Foden, 'A History of Technical Examinations in England to 1918', unpublished PhD thesis, University of Reading, 1961, p. 215; 1873 on, relevant reports of Department of Science and Art.

Column B: Number in (a) engineering and metals, reduced to 50 per cent to reflect proportion of skilled workers only. Source: B.R. Mitchell and P. Deane, *Abstract of British Historical Statistics* (Cambridge, 1962), p. 60; see Chapter 9 for proportion of skilled workers. Consideration was given to including workers from engineering only, but due to constant changes in the Census it was very difficult to arrive at consistent figures; furthermore, many workers outside engineering and metals, e.g. in railways and maintenance work, would be interested in the subject; the exclusion of these helps make up for the inclusion of others, e.g. blast furnace workers, who would in general not be interested.

Number in (b) building and construction, reduced to 60 per cent to reflect proportion of skilled workers only. Source: Mitchell and Deane, *Abstract of Statistics*; proportion of skilled workers from 1906 Wages Census.

Column C: Column A as percentage of Column B.

Column D: See next paragraph.

There are various ways in which the percentage shown in Column C may overstate the proportion of workers experiencing *useful* technical education. There is overwhelming evidence that many of those attending technical classes were not in relevant occupations, but merely interested outsiders (see, e.g., Cotgrove, *Technical Education*, p. 57); it seems probable however, that many of these would have taken general interest subjects like chemistry, and so possibly their impact on our figures is not considerable. We also have to take into account the quality of the education. Foden suggests that the average pass rate was only about 40 per cent, although before 1893 it seems in the years given in Table 10.2 to have been rather higher; but even when it was higher, the low standard of the examinations must be taken into account, for when the second-class pass in the elementary examination was abolished in 1893 the pass rate fell to only 30 per cent, although it improved again later. The low pass rate was partly due to the necessity up to 1898 to earn a grant by presenting students for the examination, even if they had little hope of passing; Foden, 'Technical Examinations', p. 245.

Taking into account the fact that many students can have had little grasp of the subject, and also the fact that some students had no connection at all with the relevant industry, I would suggest that the proportion in Column C should be reduced by 50 per cent to arrive at a more meaningful figure, and this has been done in Column D.

5. There are various figures available to estimate this.

In some figures presented to the Royal Commission on the Depression of Trade and Industry, the proportion of foremen and draughtsmen to all workers, in the engineering section of Palmer's Shipbuilding Co., fluctuated between 2.3 and 2.7 per cent between 1865 and 1882 (PP 1886, XXIII, p. 298); this was a proportion of *all* workers, however, and as a proportion of skilled workers would be considerably higher, especially if managerial staff were added. In the 1906 Wages Census, foremen constituted 2.1 per cent of all workers – again higher as a proportion of skilled workers; furthermore, draughtsmen were not included in this total.

In building, the 1906 Wages Census gives foremen as some 6.5 per cent of all skilled workers, and in addition there were far more employers in this industry. Therefore using a 5 per cent ratio for technical and supervisory staff might result in overstating the effect of technical training on the manual section of the workforce.

6.   30 years is a 'guesstimate': in 1871-80, a male aged 20 years could expect to live for a further 39.4 years; the expectation of an urban working-class male must have been lower, while some workers would have retired or emigrated. For a later period (see note 17), the expected working life is taken as 35 years, since by 1901-10 a male aged 20 could expect to live for a further 43.01 years; *Registrar-General's Decennial Supplement* (HMSO, 1931).

7.   In 1908-9, for instance, 9.5 per cent of the 5,038 candidates for Elementary Machine Construction and Drawing were over 21; Education Statistics, PP 1910, LXXI. At all evening classes, and for both sexes, the percentage over 21 in the early 1900s was 25 per cent. Mining and building classes contained higher proportions of older workers than engineering; C.H. Creasey, *Technical Education in Evening Schools* (1905, p. 68). The proportion was probably higher in the early years, when very few existing workers were technically trained and there was more catching up to do.

8.   Royal Commission on Technical Instruction, PP 1884, XXXI, pt. ii, Appendix G, for the Elswick Technical College (Armstrong's); Mather and Platt's school was founded in 1873; Blanchet, 'Science, Craft and the State', p. 81.

9.   The Polytechnic had been founded earlier but was only established on any scale in 1881; it catered for other kinds of continuation education besides trade classes, of course; Cotgrove, *Technical Education*, p. 62. There were a few regional schools which may have given some trade training; Argles, *South Kensington*, pp. 23-4. There was also Solly's Artisan Institute, for which see below, Part Four.

10.   Cotgrove, *Technical Education*, p. 33. The standard improved as time went by.

11.   Argles, *South Kensington*, p. 35, for details of the whisky money, which was raised from increased licence fees for public houses. Many of the counties, which received the money, set up technical education committees to administer it, which then set up technical colleges and polytechnics; Blanchet, 'Science, Craft and the State', p. 211. These existed parallel to the Continuation schools administered by local School Boards, until they were merged in 1902. Both offered technical education, but because of the limitations on the finance of continuation schools, which depended on Department of Science and Art grants for technical instruction, the technical colleges could offer a wider choice. After the amalgamation, the two types of continuation education often overlapped, a feature criticised by M.E. Sadler, *Report on Secondary Education in Liverpool* (1904), p. 121.

Examinations in trade subjects were started by the Society of Arts in 1873, but were on a very small scale until the City and Guilds of London Institute took them over in 1880s; Argles, *South Kensington*, p. 22. The Institute was started in response to political pressure on the Guilds to spend their money more productively; in effect, however, it became an independent institution: see Foden, 'Technical Examinations', *passim*, for details.

12.   See G. Lowndes, *Silent Social Revolution* (1969 edn), pp. 15, 31-2, 35.

13.   Foden, 'Technical Examinations', p. 245; Creasey, *Technical Education in Schools*, p. 79, note 1; statistics from relevant reports of the Science and Art Department, and later the Educational Statistics Sections of the Annual Reports

of the Board of Education.

14. Foden, 'Technical Examinations', p. 646.

15. The amount of such education which went on should not be exaggerated. A brief resumé might be useful.

Manual training in schools: this largely consisted of light woodwork, and all sources agree that it was of no relevance to industrial training, whatever its educational value; N.B. Dearle, *Industrial Training* (1914), p. 305; A.P.M. Fleming and J.G. Pearce, *Principles of Apprentice Training* (1916), p. 37.

Secondary schools where technical education and trade training were stressed: these were developing only towards the end of our period. In 1912-13 there were 2,884 students of both sexes enrolled at these schools in London — of whom many were only attending particular classes or were learning non-technical subjects such as art or domestic economy (Dearle, *Training*, pp. 309-13); a slightly contradictory account gives 32 schools in the whole country in 1912, with only 2,813 students (1915 Report, p. xiii; possibly only full-time students were counted). Whatever the exact number of students, the effect in our period was clearly very limited. See M.E. Sadler and M.S. Beard, 'English Employers and the Education of their Workpeople' in M.E. Sadler (ed.), *Continuation Schools in England and Elsewhere* (Manchester, 1907), pp. 430ff., for further details.

Trade classes for continuation students: see below, and discussion in Part Four; basically it can be said that theoretical training was more important than manual.

16. Foden, 'Technical Examinations', pp. 412, 523-6.

17. Figures in Column B were compiled by taking the number of adult workers in the industry and dividing by 35; a longer working life was assumed (than in note 6) because of the later date. The following groups were used:

Boots and shoes: all male boot and shoe workers.

Cotton-spinning: all male cotton spinners and big piecers.

Electric wireman's work) Total in electrical section of metals etc.,

Electrical engineering   ) plus electricity supply.

Road carriage building: Motor-car mechanics, car body makers, coach and carriage makers and wheelwrights.

Typography: all male typographers (hand and machine)

Boilermakers' work: all platers and riveters in boilermaking.

Shipbuilding: all platers in shipbuilding and all shipwrights.

Bricklaying: all bricklayers.

Cabinet-making: all cabinet-makers.

Sources: 2, 7, 8, 9: Wages Census. Rest: 1911 Census. The number of recruits to growing industries like electrical engineering and road carriage building must be understated; even so, the proportion taking technical education was probably quite high.

18. See for instance the extensive details in Creasey, *Technical Education in Schools*, pp. 109-63.

19. Cotgrove, *Technical Education*, pp. 25-6.

20. PP 1884, XXXI, QU. 3884.

21. Cited in Blanchet, 'Science, Craft and the State', p. 111; of course the City and Guilds came to change its attitude.

22. Royal Commission on Technical Instruction, PP 1884, XXIX, pp. 517-25.

23. Sadler and Beard, 'English Employers', pp. 277 and 185.

24. Ibid., pp. 283, 293, 294-5.

25. Ibid., pp. 293, 283, 276-7.

26. Creasey, *Technical Education in Schools*, pp. 109-63.

27. Dearle, *Training*, p. 327.

28. PRO, Mun. 5, 76/325/1.

29. The Association for Education in Industry and Commerce, *Report on Training of Manual Workers in the Engineering Industry* (1930, based on survey made in 1923), p. 14.

30. K. Liepmann, *Apprenticeship* (1960), p. 154, for a negative assessment of trade unions' attitudes to training, whether by apprenticeship or other methods. D.J. Lee, 'Craft, Unions and the Force of Tradition: the case of Apprenticeship', *British Journal of Industrial Relations*, vol. XVII, no. 1 (March 1979), argues convincingly that unions' attitudes have not been so negative as Liepmann and others have suggested.

31. 1915 Report, pp. 63 and 87 (ASE); p. 262 (Typographical Association). It is worth noting that apart from one local agreement by the Sunderland plumbers to the effect that one year's study at a technical college could reduce the period of apprenticeship from six years to five, there are no other such agreements recorded in the Report, which has details of a large number of collective agreements in a variety of trades. Nevertheless, the ASE and the Typographical Association were two of the most important unions, and agreements with them cannot be ignored; but of course few trade apprentices would be able to afford to spend four years in technical college; while the Typographical Association's relaxation still left its apprenticeship period at five years.

32. Blanchet, 'Science, Craft and the State', p. 152.

33. See Chapter 6, notes 3 and 11, and text.

34. PRO, Mun. 5, 67/325/1.

35. Blanchet, 'Science, Craft and the State', p. 86; Argles, *South Kensington*, p. 23; C.T. Millis's chapter in F.W. Galton (ed.), *Workers on their Industries* (1895), p. 1.

36. See the discussion in Part Five, and note 51.

37. See B. Simon, *Education and the Labour Movement, 1870-1918* (1965), for information about trade unions and education.

38. FLW respondent no. 56.

39. This firm did, it should be noted, encourage attitudes at day classes; Creasey, *Technical Education in Schools*, p. 170. The railway companies were generally enlightened in this respect, and paid particular attention to their mechanical engineering apprentices; see also Sadler and Beard, 'English Employers', pp. 266-73.

40. Sadler, *Liverpool*, pp. 125, 127, 226-9; also M.E. Sadler, *Report on Secondary Education in Birkenhead* (1904), p. 79, and Creasey, *Technical Education in Schools*, p. 30.

41. 1915 Report, pp. 100-1; see also Sadler and Beard, 'English Employers', *passim*; a number of other companies returned fees if 75 per cent attendance was registered.

42. 1915 Report.

43. Cited in Blanchet, 'Science, Craft and the State', p. 249, note 1.

44. 1915 Report, pp. 62-3.

45. A not untypical passage comes in Corelli Barnett, *The Swordbearers* (1963), pp. 191-3, where the general deficiency of British industry is contrasted with the efficiency of German, and put down partly to lack of technical education; it is true that Barnet focuses on higher technical education, but he does not modify the severity of his judgement by referring to the success of other kinds. Lowndes, *Silent Revolution*, pp. 149-50, also suggests that technical education in Britain was weak, without explicitly comparing it to that in other countries.

Shadwell noted that in Germany and the United States the long working hours precluded attendance at evening classes for most manual workers; A. Shadwell, *Industrial Efficiency* (1906), vol. II, p. 101.

46. Williams noted that technical instruction for apprentices was still better in Britain than Germany in the 1960s; G. Williams, *Apprenticeship in Europe* (1963), p. 43.

47. Shadwell, *Industrial Efficiency*, pp. 432-3.

48. W.E. Winchenden, *A Comparative Study of Engineering Education in the United States and Europe* (Washington, 1929). Cited in R. Floud, 'Technical Education and Economic Performance: Engineering in the late Nineteenth Century', unpublished paper. I am grateful to Professor Floud for allowing me to look at this paper.

49. 1915 Report, p. 301.

50. Ibid., pp. 386-7; the South Metropolitan Gas Company had a similar scheme.

51. This is a summary of the argument developed by Cotgrove in his first four chapters. On the decline of apprenticeship, see Cotgrove, *Technical Education*, pp. 21-2; by taking the evidence of witnesses to the Royal Commission on Technical Instruction in trades like shoemaking and painting, Cotgrove gives a very misleading picture of the real state of apprenticeship in other industries and trades. On industrialists' attitudes, see ibid., p. 25. On educationalists' attitudes, see ibid., pp. 35-8.

52. Ibid., p. 67.

53. Sadler and Beard, 'English Employers', p. 191.

Williams, *Apprenticeship in Europe*, pp. 90-1, notes that young workers in France were thought to have a favourable attitude towards workshop training because they liked feeling part of an adult team.

THE ACQUISITION OF SKILL AND THEORIES
OF THE LABOUR ARISTOCRACY

Theories

A study of the acquisition of skill must be relevant to the concept of
the 'labour aristocracy'. Discussion of this by recent writers has focused
not so much on the labour aristocracy's alleged role in the segmentation
of the working class, but on whether there was a labour aristocracy, and
if there was what its distinctive features were.

Since commentators in the later nineteenth century used the phrase,
there is undoubtedly a phenomenon to be explained.[1] The most
detailed historical studies are those by Gray and Crossick, whose
findings may be roughly summarised as follows. There was a substantial
segment of the working class, which may be roughly identified with
those in apprenticed trades or in trades generally recognised as 'skilled',
and which was distinct in various ways from other segments of the
working class and from the middle class. The hallmarks of the labour
aristocracy's distinctiveness included: a low rate of marriage into the
families of other groups, both middle and working class; leisure-time
pursuits which, while they were not distinctively different from those
of certain middle-age groups, were nevertheless *sui generis* — were
parallel to, not identical with or emulating, middle-class pursuits; and
the holding of certain beliefs which marked the labour aristocracy off
from both the middle classes and the rest of the working classes,
notably beliefs in trade unionsim and also in voluntary co-operative
action in a wide field, as exemplified by membership of friendly
societies. Finally, Crossick and Gray both suggest that there was a
lessening of the labour aristocracy's isolation from the rest of the
working class by the end of the nineteenth century.[2]

While Gray's and Crossick's documentation is such that their picture
of the labour aristocracy as an identifiable group cannot be challenged,
there is one point where their thesis lacks definition. This is in relation
to that crucial area, the workplace. The question that they fail to
answer clearly is this: given that high wages and skill are necessary if
not sufficient to make an aristocrat, what gives each individual aristocrat his skill and high wages?[3] Their vagueness is the more surprising
because two other studies by Foster and Stedman-Jones, which are

concerned *inter alia* with the labour aristocracy, specifically focus on the actual process of creation of the aristocracy, which both identify with the workplace. And in both cases the 1850s is seen as a major divide, with Stedman-Jones emphasising the weakness of craft control in the workplace after this date — and by implication, the weakness of the labour aristocracy as a concept — and Foster emphasising the reconstitution of control on the basis of authority over other workers.[4]

One important feature which differentiates Gray's and Crossick's approach from Foster's is that the latter adopts a Braverman-type theory of the construction of skill, since he implies that management constructed skill and hence created the labour aristocracy.[5] (This is the route to skill mapped out by the dotted lines in Figure 1.2.) Gray and Crossick, although they are nowhere very explicit, would seem to accept that skill arose either out of worker initiative in constructing it, or out of a genuine demand for it. This difference in approach reflects the existence of an ambiguity in the whole concept of a labour aristocracy. Gray and Crossick view it in functional terms as a collectivity which helped solve the real problems of those who belonged to it. Foster views it in Marxist terms, following Lenin in emphasising the role it played in weakening working-class opposition to capitalism.[6] It is important to remember that in using the term 'labour aristocracy' we are not necessarily adopting a Marxist approach; we can merely use the term as a useful label for describing a group of workers with clearly identifiable common experiences both at work and outside it.

Whatever the validity or otherwise of their theoretical approach, both Foster and Stedman-Jones, it seems to me, greatly overemphasise the scope and nature of the change in the mid-century. Foster's emphasis on piecemastering as a distinctive feature of the 'new' aristocracy would seem to be overdone since piecemastering was endemic before the mid-century.[7] Furthermore, in adopting a Braverman-type approach to the construction of skill Foster ignores the fundamental constraints on methods of production which were imposed by technology. Jones may be criticised simply on the grounds that much work, as in textiles, had lost its craft nature by the mid-century, while in heavy industries like engineering there is no real evidence of any substantial change at that time.[8]

My purpose, however, is not so much to criticise these writers as to point out that, right or wrong, they do raise the question of how the aristocracy became delineated from other workers *at work*, a question nowhere satisfactorily answered by Gray and Crossick. A quotation from the latter illustrates this weakness:

> The complex factors that gave skilled workers their bargaining power . . . dovetailed, and it is hardly relevant to enquire whether it was the union that gave them their strength, or their strength that gave them their union. Both grew out of the craft culture, solidarity, and pride of so many skilled inudstrial workers in nineteenth century Britain.[9]

It seems to me highly relevant to enquire into this matter. For as our thesis so far has shown, we cannot satisfactorily explain the existence of skilled workers as a result of union control over apprenticeship. If skill was mutable, then most unions were certainly not strong enough in the nineteenth century to construct it, and the classic tactics of the period — the strike in detail — would have been ineffective because an employer would simply have imported unskilled labour. In fact, of course, skill in most cases was genuine, acquired by an apprenticeship or some other method of training, which for the most of its length gave real instruction and was not merely a restrictionist device. The answer to Crossick's unasked question, then, is that skilled workers' strength gave them their union.[10]

The Acquisition of Skill by Labour Aristocrats

This still does not answer the question of how skilled workers, and hence the labour aristocracy, were delineated from other workers. If we leave aside for the moment the acquisition of skill by following-up or migration, the answer is obvious: the serving of an apprenticeship. The crucial question, therefore, is the criteria by which apprenticeships were allocated; since all the evidence shows that there was strong intergenerational continuity among skilled workers, apprenticeships must have gone by and large to the sons of skilled workers; but how was this selection made?[11]

We have answered a large part of this question at the beginning of Chapter 5: many employers gave a strong preference to the sons of their own employees; but why this was done is less clear. Three tentative explanations can be put forward: first, employers wished to keep the goodwill of their employees, and could do so by exercising favouritism in the allocation of apprenticeships; second, employers believed that sons of employees were more likely to make good workmen,

either through the inheritance of talent or through the greater scope
they had for emulation; and third, a blend of paternalism and, in
smaller shops, an old-fashioned empathy between master and man
led employers to wish to favour their own employees for non-economic
reasons.

These cannot have been the only reasons for the strong continuity
among skilled workers, however, because there is ample testimony to
the fact that many employers would open their gates to any eligible
lad who wished to become an apprentice, and that the criteria for
eligibility were not very high. But there were a whole host of factors
which operated against the sons of less skilled workers. There was some
pecuniary sacrifice involved in an apprenticeship, even if it was usually
small; but to very poor families even a small sacrifice was too much.[12]
A poor family's child would have a smaller chance of reaching even the
relatively low level of educational achievement that many employers
demanded. And there were no doubt indefinable cultural factors that
led families to channel their ambitions in certain well-signposted
directions, and put their sons to the humble occupations which they
knew, rather than the slightly less humble ones which they did not.

While it is difficult to rank the importance of factors which led to
social segregation, another important one must have been geographical
position. The opportunities for entering an apprenticeship were
especially high in engineering and shipbuilding centres; they were
moderate in small towns where apprenticeship still flourished in
building and miscellaneous crafts; but they were low in London, non-
engineering industrial centres, specialised towns like seaside resorts,
and the country. London and many non-engineering industrial centres
offered other careers leading to upward progression such as clerical
work; but the country, seaside towns and semi-industrial towns like
Norwich and Reading were particularly badly placed. As a result — and
this, it must be added, is conjecture — it would seem likely that much
of the less skilled strata of large industrial areas was recruited afresh
each generation from those in even worse positions outside, while those
in the less skilled strata already in such centres had a rather better
chance of rising out of it.[13]

Finally, while we are on the subject of recruitment to the labour
aristocracy, we must make one fundamental point which is so obvious
that it can easily be forgotten. Women have not been considered
because it is not possible to fit women's work into the general hypothesis of skill and its acquisition advanced here. This is because women
were excluded by custom not merely from apprenticed trades, but

from practically every occupation which led to the acquisition of skill.
Excluded from these opportuntities, women formed a vast pool of
necessarily unskilled labour which was usually paid less than the minimum wage of an unskilled adult male.[14]

The Decline of the Labour Aristocracy

One of the most important suggestions advanced by both Gray and
Crossick is that the labour aristocracy was becoming a less isolated
part of the working class by the nineteenth century. Gray advances
some evidence from marriage registers which suggests that there was
increasing — although still not very considerable — intermarriage into
less skilled workers' families.[15] Futher evidence to support this interpretation is supplied by the FLW survey, in which only one family
among the 450 or so respondents was of an exclusive labour aristocratic type, although of course there were large numbers of individuals
who were labour aristocrats by the usual definitions of occupation and
wage.[16] And Pelling makes the point that, while surveys like Booth's
and Rowntree's found that a large proportion of the working class
were in poverty around the turn of the century, they also found that
around 50 per cent enjoyed a comfortable standard of living; by no
means all these would be labour aristocrats, unless the definition is
widened beyond the criteria usually adopted; yet economically
speaking these workers experienced conditions more similar to those
enjoyed by the labour aristocracy than suffered by the very poor.
Finally, Crossick suggests that the growth of a 'labour movement'
was another reflection of the decline of the labour aristocracy.[17]

Crossick attributes this decline to a variety of causes, among them
changes in the work situation; the latter he views in fairly orthodox
terms — 'speed-up', loss of status among craftsmen and so on.[18] Since
our study has been largely concerned with the end of the nineteenth
century and the beginning of the twentieth, the period when commentators see the labour aristocracy declining as an independent entity,
we should be able to add something to Crossick's interpretation. While
generalised allegations about the reduction of 'discretion' in work
were criticised earlier as being too simplistic, I would not want to
contradict Crossick, because my survey has not been closely concerned
with this aspect of work; his suggestion certainly merits further study.
But it would seem more worthwhile here to advance some more positive explanations for the increasing integration of the labour

aristocracy into the manual workforce as a whole.

A crucial point, it seems to me, is that the lines of demarcation between skilled and unskilled were becoming blurred in an increasing number of trades. This was not so much due to the increasing numbers of semi-skilled workers in industries like engineering and building which had previously been divided into skilled and unskilled: the evidence suggests that, in engineering at least, the skilled man's position was extremely strong up to the First World War, and it was still difficult to reach the fully skilled ranks other than by apprenticeship. The blurring of distinctions arose more because as old trades declined they were replaced by industries in which the customary method of acquiring skill was by migration or following-up. Among occupations where this had happened at some time in the nineteenth century, or where it was still happening in the period we are concerned with, were papermaking, milling, footwear, clothing and the precious metal trades. New industries with the same forms of training included bicycles and electrical and motor engineering; to these could be added formerly small but rapidly growing industries like food manufacture, chemicals and railways.[19]

These changes affected the distinctions between skilled and other workers in two different ways. First, the growth of skilled occupations which were not learned by apprenticeship reduced the importance of this method of training, previously one of the peculiar hallmarks of the labour aristocracy. This change, of course, was linked to another distinctive feature of new forms of work, which is that they tended to be more specific than the old. Whereas one of the characteristics of apprenticeship was that it conferred on the craftsman's skill, at least theoretically, a nationwide acceptability, new forms of skill were less easily interchangeable.[20] This distinction can be overdone: a time-served gold-beater or sailmaker could not be said to have had a very wide training while it is probable that a good papermill machineman or chemical foreman had a wide market for his skill; but in an increasing number of occupations seniority rules did restrict the inter-changeability of non-apprenticed skilled men. By itself, therefore, the growth of non-apprenticed skilled work diluted the labour aristocracy, and, if such skilled workers are to be counted as labour aristocrats, then the definition must be widened to include others beside 'craftsmen'.

This argument could be elaborated to take into account the different amount of discretion involved in the work of apprenticed craftsmen and non-apprenticed skilled men. Arguably the skill of the latter lay more in their knowledge of the machinery and details of the process, especially in process industries. According to this argument, one of the peculiar features of the labour aristocrat in his heyday would not be apprenticeship *per se*, but the control of the work process which time-served workers possessed. This argument will be recurred to, but it might be said at this point that, as we have already shown, many non-apprenticed workers did exercise a considerable amount of discretion in this period; in some cases, as in work learned by migration, because they were doing much the same jobs as apprenticed workers; and in many process industries because the lack of instrumentation made the skill of the worker a vital part of the production process.

The second way in which the growth of non-apprenticed skilled work affected the distinction between skilled and less skilled workers was perhaps the crucial one. Because such work did away with the 'closed' entry method of apprenticeship, and substituted training extending over a longer period, often well into adult life, it created a large class of workers who, although they might be classed and paid as semi-skilled, could expect with greater or lesser degrees of confidence to become skilled.

The existence of this class of worker, although it is obvious enough, seems to have gone largely unremarked by historians. One exception is Matsumura, who identified such a group among the flint glass workers, and who makes the valuable point, based on this observation, that membership of the labour aristocracy might depend on what period of his life-cycle a worker was in. But unfortunately the flint glass workers are a bad example from which to generalise, because very few, if any, other workers combined apprenticeship with seniority rules; it would be quite wrong to take the glassmakers' example to mean that most ex-apprentices had to continue as semi-skilled workers for a number of years after their apprenticeship, as the glass makers did; in many cases time-served workers earned the full rate immediately their apprenticeship ended, and in other cases they served for two or three years, not more, as improvers.[21]

There were, however, large numbers of aspirant labour aristocrats in many other industries. Apart from those in the industries we noted above such as milling, chemicals and railways, the skilled grades in spinning and in the iron, steel and tinplate industries were usually recruited by promotion of less skilled workers.[22] Obviously there were considerable differences in the chances of workers reaching the highest positions: in spinning promotion was virtually guaranteed, at least as long as the industry was still expanding; in milling it was said that large numbers of labourers were needed and not all could achieve promotion; in chemicals, probably only a minority rose above the semi-skilled ranks. It would be particularly interesting to ask how the probability or chance of promotion affected the attitudes of the less skilled workers; here, however, we are concerned with how the attitudes of the fully skilled workers, who had already achieved promotion, were affected.

Since this is a problem which has not really been identified before, we only possess rather sketchy evidence. On the face of it, the relationship between workers in these industries, and the groups below them to which they had originally belonged, was no different from that between time-served labour aristocrats and non-apprenticed groups below them; in other words, it was not particularly close. The high differentials between spinners and piecers, and engine-drivers and firemen, have already been noted, and spinners were particularly notorious for their efforts to keep the piecers firmly subordinate to them; wide differentials in these occupations could be explained, however, by the fact that less skilled workers were certain of promotion, and thus willing to accept a low wage because it was temporary.[23]

Against the evidence pointing to exclusiveness, there was one very important development which promoted a degree of cohesiveness among all grades, whether classed as 'skilled' or not. This was the growth of unions which reflected the fact that there were no hard and fast barriers between grades by recruiting workers at all levels of skill. Again, the Spinners seem to have done this as much to head off possible revolts among the piecers, as to show any real solidarity with them. But there is plenty of evidence to suggest that the motives of many in the 'all-grades' unions were to end sectionalism. The Steel-Smelters' policy, which included the institution of seniority rules, contrasted sharply with that of the 'aristocratic' Ironworkers, which was a union of piecemasters; the Railway Servants launched all-grades programmes in 1897 and 1906-7. Both the Steel-Smelters and the Railway Servants gained ground rapidly during our period, as did the Associated Society of Locomotive Engineers and Firemen; while significantly the National Union of Boot and Shoe Operatives, in one of the industries most strongly affected by the decline of apprenticeship, had never adopted anything but an all-grades policy.[24]

In spite of there being a strong tendency to exclusiveness even among workers promoted from the ranks, there were, therefore, tendencies in the opposite direction, which found expression in the growth of all-grades unions. With this in mind, the suggestion seems justified that the growth of skilled occupations which were not recruited by apprenticeship weakened the exclusiveness of the labour aristocracy, because skilled workers in these occupations identified more closely with those in the less skilled ranks beneath them. This leads to the conclusion that the growing identification between the labour aristocracy and the rest of the working class, insofar as this was caused by changes at work, was not due so much to a reduction of the aristocrats' skill as to changes in the methods of recruitment to skilled work which increased the number of semi-skilled workers.

One further influence which may have helped to promote greater homogeneity among the working class should be mentioned here, because although it does not rise directly from our study, it suggests a similar conclusion. This was the influence of better education, which combined with rising real wages among the lower paid must have strengthened the ability of the latter's children to enter, and to finance, apprenticeship training. As we have seen, the children of skilled workers still had a much greater chance of entering skilled occupations even at the end of the nineteenth century; but the degree of self-recruitment was very probably higher earlier in the century, when the less skilled were in a much weaker economic and educational position. This suggests, as does the growth of non-apprenticed skilled occupations discussed above, that the greater homogeneity of the working class may have been caused by a strengthening of the weak as much as by a weakening of the strong.

Our conclusions so far can be summaried as follows. It is generally accepted that by the end of the nineteenth and beginning of the twentieth centuries, the labour aristocracy was not sharply segmented from other groups among the working class. The evidence of this book suggests that, insofar as this represented a change from a previous period of isolation, one important cause of the change was the growth in numbers of skilled workers who were not recruited by apprenticeship, and who were more closely identified with lower grades of worker through membership of the same union.

The Status of the Labour Aristocracy

Having come so far, it may seem surprising, but it is necessary, to ask a more radical question: so far we have assumed that at some period there was a labour aristocracy; but is that assumption fully justified? Certainly we must accept that a grouping of skilled workers with clearly identifiable and distinct views and attitudes existed in areas with a substantial number of apprentice-taking trades: Edinburgh had such workers in the building, printing and engineering industries; Kentish London in the building, engineering, shipbuilding and miscellaneous metal industries.

There were numerous areas, however, without such sectors. Chief among these, of course, were the mining areas, whose workers had always formed a relatively homogeneous group, the majority earning high wages. The cotton areas were also anomalous, because spinners always lacked the hallmark of apprenticeship, although their behaviour seems to have closely approximated to the labour aristocratic type. First-hand iron and steel workers were another group who had always been in the position of earning skilled wages, even though they were recruited by promotion. And what are we to make of Birmingham, whose trades had long been relatively 'open'? Or for that matter Inner London, whose skilled 'legal' workers, if Mayhew is to be believed, were in a very small minority in the middle of the century, compared to those who had gained entry to the trade by some back-entrance?[25]

We must therefore accept that there were considerable regional differences in the size and composition of the labour aristocracy; if there was a sizeable labour aristocracy in the areas mentioned above, then it must have been different from that which Gray and Crossick have identified. That is not my concern here, however; instead I would like to finish by taking a little further Stedman-Jones's criticism of the whole concept of a labour aristocracy, which he makes on the grounds that craft control in the workshop was eroded after the mid-century.

I pointed out earlier that there was no real evidence that the nature of engineering had changed sharply in the mid-century, and that other industries like textiles had also moved on to a factory basis well before this date. The fact remains, however, that although one might argue about the date of the transition, there was a distinct difference between work in a 'modern' factory, whether in engineering or textiles, and work in an old-fashioned handicraft 'shop', whether in wheelwrighting, hatting or a hundred other trades. This difference did not, I would suggest, lie either in the skill of the worker, defined as it was at the beginning of this book, or even in the discretion he exercised. I argued earlier that the discretion of workers in old crafts was severely circumscribed by the necessity for them to perform a limited range of custom-based tasks, in which failure would soon be found out and punished by dismissal.[26] Similarly, the knowledge needed by most workers was very limited, certainly as compared with modern skilled occupations like engineering (not perhaps spinning), even if the manual skill needed was high.

In spite of all these counter-arguments, there is an important sense in which Stedman-Jones's criticism remains valid. Although engineers and other 'modern' groups of workers exercised both skill and discretion, their actual control over the life of the workshop was very circumscribed. Thomas Wright's description of an engineering workshop in the 1860s shows that while the men managed to keep alive customs like drinking and smoking at work in spite of management proscription, these habits could not be openly flaunted.[27] Furthermore, employers in large factories kept checks on attendance and enforced regular hours, since their heavy overheads meant that there was no room for those not producing enough.[28] In contrast to this was the hatting shop in which Frederick Willis worked in the early twentieth century, where practically everything — times of attendance, output (paid by the piece) and the ordering of the 'inner life' of the workshop — was in the hands of the workers. This sort of freedom was not confined to highly skilled unionised trades like the hatters; in Willenhall in 1843 workers in the subdivided lock and currycomb trades 'came when they had a mind and went when they had a mind: [the] workshops were always open. As they all worked by the piece, it was of no consequence to the employers when they did it: that was entirely their own affair.'[29]

Now it is precisely craft workers in small workshop trades like hatting or locksmithing which observers with such disparate viewpoints as Crossick and Foster unite in saying did *not* form a labour aristocracy in any meaningful sense.[30] Yet I would argue that it was only these workers, whose relative importance in the labour force declined rapidly from the mid-century, who exercised 'craft control' over their work in the full meaning of the term. Groups like the engineers, printers and builders, although they exercised both skill and discretion, did not exercise craft control in this sense; and to that extent Stedman-Jones is correct in arguing that the labour aristocracy had some fundamental experiences in common with the rest of the working class from the mid-century on. This does not invalidate Gray's and Crossick's thesis that there was a clearly identifiable group of labour aristocrats, at least in some areas, after the mid-century. What it does do is reinforce the suggestion advanced earlier that the apparent drawing together of the working class later in the nineteenth century should not be seen primarily as a result of a loss of control by apprenticed craftsmen over their work. The control of work which *was* exercised by old-fashioned craftsmen had already been lost by most skilled workers; and it was lost as a result of that very same development of large-scale production which had created a labour aristocracy, in the sense of large numbers of skilled workers with an identifiable common ethos, in the first place. For in terms of control over aspects of working life such as hours, pace of work and working regulations, the skilled worker under modern systems of production was not significantly better off than his unskilled or semi-skilled brethren.

Notes

1. G. Crossick, *An Artisan Elite in Victorian Society* (1978), p. 127; Royden Harrison, *Before the Socialists* (1965), Ch. 1.
An excellent survey of modern literature on the subject, and a penetrating theoretical discussion, is contained in H.F. Moorhouse, 'The Marxist Theory of the Labour Aristocracy', *Social History*, vol. 3, no. 1 (January 1978).
2. R.Q. Gray, *The Labour Aristocracy in Victorian Edinburgh* (Oxford, 1976); Crossick, *Artisan Elite*.
3. Although Crossick devoted Chapter 4 to 'The Impact of the Workplace', it is mainly concerned with detailing the existence of stratification within the workforce, rather than with the actual formation of the aristocracy within the workplace. One of Crossick's few comments on this is cited in the text below. Gray likewise has little concrete to say: Moorhouse comments that 'while Gray states that he agrees with Foster that authority at work was the key dimension of the labour aristocracy, in fact the analysis of industrial structure is not central to his work'; Moorhouse, 'Marxist Labour Aristocracy', p. 77.
4. J. Foster, 'British Imperialism and the Labour Aristocracy', in J. Skelley (ed.), *The General Strike 1926* (1976); and J. Foster, *Class Struggle and the Industrial Revolution* (1974), esp. pp. 224-38. G. Stedman-Jones, 'Class Struggle and the Industrial Revolution', *New Left Review*, no. 90 (1975), esp. pp. 63-5.
5. As Moorhouse comments, Foster's attitude is slightly ambiguous as he implies that technological developments may have played a part, but 'Foster certainly gives primacy to bourgeois intentions'; Moorhouse, 'Marxist Labour Aristocracy', p. 65.
6. Although Gray explicitly aligns his approach with Foster's (see note 3), his general position seems to me to be much closer to the one I have outlined: thus, 'The upper-artisan outlook was in some respects sharply distinguished from that of the bourgeoisie, and even those modes of thought adopted "from above" could undergo significant transformations, as they were reinterpreted at the social level of the labour aristocracy'; Gray, *Labour Aristocracy in Edinburgh*, p. 144; and, 'one feature of this elite (at least in Edinburgh) was the development of a social identity which cut across the more traditional craft divisions of occupation, and constituted a form, albeit a limited one, of awareness of a common positions as wage-earners'; ibid., p. 4.
7. See S. Pollard, *The Genesis of Modern Management* (1965), pp. 30-48; in engineering, Boulton and Watt used piecemasters in the late eighteenth century (E. Roll, *An Early Experiment in Industrial Organisation* (1930), pp. 200-4). Although Foster presents evidence for widespread piecemastering in Oldham engineering in the late 1860s, there is no question but that this was a highly localised phenomenon (Foster, *Class Struggle*, p. 227). The Jefferys, working from a survey covering over 35,000 adult skilled engineering workers, show that in 1861 only 10.5 per cent were pieceworkers; furthermore, the great

majority of these worked under systems of individual piecework, not under piecemasters. The piecemaster system was, in fact, confined almost exclusively to a few machine-building centres in the North like Oldham, and some locomotive centres. Furthermore, the amount of piecework seems to have fallen still further by 1886 (see Table 9.3). When piecework was revived in the 1890s it was always on an individual basis; M. and J.B. Jefferys, 'The Wages, Hours and Trade Customs of the Skilled Engineer in 1861', *EcHR*, vol. XVII (1947), pp. 39-44. So whatever the validity of Foster's argument *vis-à-vis* Oldham, it is not applicable nationally.

8. See Appendix to Chapter 9, which shows how the tendency towards subdivision of occupations in engineering has existed since the industry began; also A.E. Musson, 'Class Struggle and the Labour Aristocracy', *Social History*, vol. 1, no. 3 (1976), pp. 352-3.

9. Crossick, *Artisan Elite*, p. 157.

10. A conclusion which Hobsbawm would seem to agree with: E. Hobsbawm, 'The Labour Aristocracy' in E. Hobsbawm, *Labouring Men* (1968 edn), p. 275.

11. See Tables 5.1 and 5.2, and the discussion centred around them.

12. Thus FLW respondent no. 229 gave up his apprenticeship because his father had died, and his family needed the extra income.

13. Exactly this point is made by Treble, who points to the neglect by commentators of migration, as a recruiting source for unskilled work; in Glasgow, for instance, Irish and to a lesser extent rural Scots immigrants provided many of the recruits for such work; J.H. Treble, 'The Market for Unskilled Labour in Glasgow 1891-1914' in I. MacDougall (ed.), *Essays in Scottish Labour History* (Edinburgh, 1978). Of course the need of unskilled workers or others living in poverty for an immediate income should not be neglected as a factor perpetuating the 'cycle of poverty', and a survey in 1910 showed that widows' sons, like FLW respondent no. 229, had a lower chance than other boys of following their father's occupation if it was skilled; J.H. Treble, *Urban Poverty in Britain 1830-1914* (1979), pp. 101-2.

It is possible to lend some statistical backing to the assertions made in the text regarding the relative ease or difficulty of entering an apprenticeship. In 1901, the proportion of males aged 10 years and upwards in the main apprentice-taking trades (engineering, ship and boat building, building, printing and lithography, and wood, furniture etc.) was as follows:

Newcastle	31.9%	
Oldham	30.0%	
Reading	18.6%	
Norwich	17.1%	
Hastings	16.5%	Source: printed Census papers, 1901.

Not all the workers in these trades would have been apprenticed, of course.

14. Even where they could acquire skill – as in dressmaking or domestic service – an excessive number of women were forced into these occupations because of lack of opportunity elsewhere, thus keeping wage levels relatively low.

15. Gray, *Labour Aristocracy in Edinburgh*, pp. 111-20.

16. The figure of one given in P. Thompson, 'Meaning and History', *SSRC Newsletter*, no. 6 (1969), p. 18; cited in Moorhouse, 'Marxist Labour Aristocracy', pp. 67-8.

17. H. Pelling, 'The Concept of the Labour Aristocracy' in H. Pelling, *Popular Politics and Society* (1968), p. 54; Crossick, *Artisan Elite*, p. 248.

18. Crossick puts forward a number of other reasons, such as the emergence of a non-manual lower-middle class, and the continuing process of residential

segregation; Crossick, *Artisan Elite*, p. 248.

19. Pelling has drawn attention to this trend, and its implications; Pelling, *Popular Politics*, pp. 44-5.

20. This distinction is particularly emphasised by Stedman-Jones, who would extend the 'specificity' of modern work to apprenticed occupations in, e.g., engineering: 'even the skilled sectors of modern industry bore only a superficial resemblance to those of handicraft. Such skills were precarious and transformable at the will of the capitalist in a way which those of handicraft had not been'; Stedman-Jones, 'Class Struggle', p. 65.

21. T. Matsumura, 'The Flint-Glass Makers in the Classic Age of the Labour Aristocracy, 1850-80', unpublished PhD thesis, University of Warwick, 1976; see particularly pp. 100, 238, 361.

22. See also Pelling, *Popular Politics*, pp. 46-9, who makes some similar points; I think that Pelling underestimates the genuine skill of many such workers, by focusing on the spinners (ibid., p. 46).

23. H.A. Turner, *Trade Union Growth, Structure and Policy* (1962), pp. 141-2, for the spinners' relationship with their piecers. Moorhouse points out that the relationship, apparently so one-sided, must be viewed in the context of the fact that piecers were frequently related to spinners; Moorhouse, 'Marxist Labour Aristocracy', p. 70, note 24.

24. H.A. Clegg *et al.*, *A History of British Trade Unions since 1889* (Oxford, 1964), pp. 205-6 (Steel-Smelters and Ironworkers), pp. 25-6 (NUBSO); P. Bagwell, *The Railwaymen* (1963), pp. 184 and 263 (Railway Servants).

Membership Figures	Railway Servants	ASLEF
1889	20,000	3,600
1895	38,000	8,000
1904	53,000	12,000
1914	273,000	Information not available

Source: Clegg *et al.*, *British Trade Unions*, pp. 234 and 339; Bagwell, *Railwaymen*, pp. 698-9.

25. Similar points are made by Pelling, *Popular Politics*, pp. 46-9 and 43.

26. See Chapter 9.

27. Thomas Wright (journeyman engineer), *Some Habits and Customs of the Working Classes* (1867), pp. 85-92.

28. D.A. Reid, 'The Decline of St. Monday 1766-1876', *Past and Present* (May 1976), esp. pp. 85-6.

29. Frederick Willis, *101 Jubilee Road* (1948), pp. 89-92. Evidence of Jas. Carpenter, the largest employer in Willenhall, to the Royal Commission on Children's Employment, PP 1843, XV, p. 602.

30. Foster, *Class Struggle*, p. 224; Crossick, *Artisan Elite*, p. 247.

BIBLIOGRAPHY

Material in Archive Collections

Public Records Office	Records of Ministry of Munitions (Mun. 5)
	Records of Board of Trade (Lab. 41)
British Library of Political	Beveridge Collection
and Economic Science	Booth MS, 2nd series, A9
Scottish Records Office	Records of Jas. Lovell & Co. (GD. 272/36)

Government Publications and Reports

Select Committee on Artisans and Machinery, PP 1824, V

Royal Commission on the Employment of Children PP 1843, XIV and XV

Royal Commission on Technical Instruction, PP 1884, XXIX and XXXI

Royal Commission on the Depression of Trade and Industry, PP 1886, XXXIII

1886 Wages Census, PP 1893-4, LXXXIII, pt. ii

C. Jackson, *Report on Boy Labour in London and Certain Other Towns*, PP 1909, XLIV

Royal Commission on the Poor Laws, PP 1910, XLVIII

1906 Wages Census, PP 1909, LXXX; PP 1910, LXXXIV; PP 1911, LXXXVIII; PP 1912-13, CVIII

Committe on Women in Industry, PP 1919, XXXI

Board of Trade Handbook on Trades: Printing (HMSO, 1914)

Board of Trade Handbook on Bristol Trades (HMSO, 1914)

Board of Trade Handbook on Yorkshire Trades (HMSO, 1914)

R.B. Smirke, *Report on Birmingham Brass Trade* (HMSO, 1914)

Report of an Enquiry by the Board of Trade into the Condition of Apprenticeship and Industrial Training; printed but not published, 1915

Dilution of Labour Bulletin; Ministry of Munitions, 1918

History of the Ministry of Munitions, 1920-24

Report of an Enquiry into Apprenticeship and Training in 1925-6 (7 vols., HMSO, 1927-8)

Registrar-General's Decennial Supplement, HMSO 1931

Printed census papers, 1891, 1901, 1911, 1921
Reports of Department of Science and Art Education Statistics
    (Various Parliamentary Papers)

Autobiographical Material

Acorn, George, *One of a Multitude* (1911)
Barnes, George, *From Workshop to War Cabinet* (1924)
Bell, Thomas, *Pioneering Days* (1941)
Brearley, Harry, *Steelmakers* (1933)
Burnett, John (ed.), *Useful Toil* (Pelican edn, 1977)
Hannington, Wal, *Never on Our Knees* (1967)
Herbert, Alfred, 'Memories', *Machine-Tool Review*, XLI (Sept.-Oct. 1953)
Jackson, T., *Solo Trumpet* (1953)
MacGeown, Patrick, *Heat the Furnace Seven Times More* (1967)
Mann, Tom, *Memoirs* (1923)
Murphy, J.T., *New Horizons* (1941)
Okey, T., *A Basketful of Memories* (1930)
Pollitt, Harry, *Serving My Time* (1940)
Riddell, W.G., *The Thankless Years* (1948)
Rolt, L.T.C., *Landscape with Machines* (1971)
Watson, W.F., *Machines and Men* (1935)
'Family Life and Work' survey (in the care of Dr. Paul Thompson; see P. Thompson, *The Edwardians* (Paladin edn, 1977), pp. 17-18 for further details)

Books and Articles

Adams, D.R., 'Some Evidence on British and American Wage Rates 1790-1830', *Journal of Economic History*, vol. XXX (1970)
Allen, G.C., *The Economic History of Birmingham and the Black Country* (1929)
Argles, Michael, *South Kensington to Robbins* (1964)
Association for Education in Industry and Commerce, *Report on Training of Manual Workers in the Engineering Industry* (1930)
Austin, E., *The Law Relating to Apprentices* (1890)
Bagwell, P., *The Railwaymen* (1963)
Barnett, Corelli, *The Swordbearers* (1963)

Becker, G.S., *Human Capital* (New York, 1970)

Booth, Charles, *et al.*, *Life and Labour of the People of London*, 2nd series, *Industry* (5 vols., 1903)

Braverman, H., *Labor and Monopoly Capital* (New York, 1974)

Bray, R.A., 'The Apprenticeship Question', *Economic Journal*, vol. 19 (1909)

— *Boy Labour and Apprenticeship* (1911)

Bright, J.R., *Automation and Management* (Boston, 1958)

Burgess, K., *The Origin of British Industrial Relations* (1975)

Campbell, R., *The London Tradesman*, 1st edn 1747 (reprinted Newton Abbott, 1969)

Chapman, S.J. and Abbott, W., 'The Tendency of Children to follow their Father's Trades', *Journal of the Royal Statistical Society*, vol. LXXVI (1912-13)

Charity Organisation Society, *Social Report on Unskilled Labour* (1908)

Child, J., *Industrial Relations in the Printing Industry* (1967)

Clegg, H.A., *et al.*, *A History of British Trade Unions since 1889* (Oxford, 1964)

Cole, G.D.H., *Trades Unions and Munitions* (Oxford, 1923)

Coleman, D.C., *The British Paper Industry 1495-1860* (Oxford 1958)

Cotgrove, S.F., *Technical Education and Social Change* (1958)

Creasey, C.H., *Technical Education in Evening Schools* (1905)

Crossick, G., *An Artisan Elite in Victorian England* (1978)

Davison, J.P., *et al.*, *Productivity and Economic Incentives* (1957)

Dearle, N.B., *Industrial Training* (1914)

— Review of 'Boy and Girl Labour' by Tawney and Adler, *Economic Journal*, vol. 19 (1909)

Denison, E.F., *Why Growth Rates Differ* (Washington, 1967)

Derry, T.K., 'The Repeal of the Apprenticeship Clauses of the Statute of Apprentices', *Economic History Review*, III (1931-2)

Dunlop, J.T., 'Labor Relations and the Development of Labor Organisation' in R.A. Lester and J. Shister (eds.), *Insights into Labor Issues* (New York, 1948)

— Review of Turner's 'Trade Union Growth, Policy and Structure', *British Journal of Industrial Relations* vol. 2 (1964)

Dunlop, O.J., *English Apprenticeship and Child Labour* (1912)

Fairbairn, W., *Treatise on Mills and Millwork* (1861), Part I

Fleming, A.P.M., and Pearce, J.G., *Principles of Apprentice Training* (1916)

Floud, R., 'Technical Education and Economic Performance:

Engineering in the late nineteenth century', unpublished paper

Foster, J., 'British Imperialism and the Labour Aristocracy' in J. Skelley (ed.), *The General Strike 1926* (1976)

— *Class Struggle and the Industrial Revolution* (1974)

Fox, Alan, *Beyond Contract: Work, Power and Trust Relations* (1974)

— *A History of the National Union of Boot and Shoe Workers* (1958)

Fyrth, H.J. and Collins, H.J., *The Foundry Workers* (Manchester, 1959)

Gray, R.Q., *The Labour Aristocracy in Victorian Edinburgh* (Oxford, 1976)

Habakkuk, H.J., *American and British Technology in the Nineteenth Century* (Cambridge, 1967)

Hall, P.G., *The Industries of London since 1861* (1962)

Harris, J.R., 'Skills, Coal and British Industry in the Eighteenth Century', *History*, vol. 61 (1976)

Harrison, Royden, *Before the Socialists* (1965)

Hawkins, C.B., *Norwich, A Social Study* (1910)

Hinton, J., *The First Shop Steward's Movement* (1973)

Hobsbawm, E., 'The Labour Aristocracy' in E. Hobsbawm, *Labouring Men* (1968 edn)

Hobson, J.A., *The Evolution of Modern Capitalism* (1896 edn)

Hopkins, E., 'Were the Webbs Wrong about Apprenticeship in the Black Country?' *West Midland Studies*, vol. 6 (1973)

Howell, George, 'Trade Unions and Apprenticeship', *Contemporary Review*, vol. III (1877)

Hudson, K., *Working to Rule* (1970)

Hunt, E.H., 'Labour Productivity in English Agriculture 1850-1914', *Economic History Review*, 2nd series, vol. XX (1967)

— *Regional Wage Variations in Great Britain 1850-1914* (1973)

Irving, R.J. 'The Profitability and Performance of British Railways 1870-1914', *Economic History Review*, 2nd series, vol. XXXI, (Feb. 1978)

Jaques, E., *Equitable Payment*, 2nd edn (1970)

Jefferys, J.B., *The Story of the Engineers* (1946)

— and Jefferys, M., 'The Wages, Hours and Trade Customs of the Skilled Engineer in 1961', *Economic History Review*, vol. XVII (1947)

Jenks, L.H., 'Early Phases of the Management Movement', *Administrative Science Quarterly*, vol. 5, no. 3 (Dec. 1960)

Jevons, H.S., *The Coal Trade*, 1915 (reprinted Newton Abbott, 1969)

Jones, G.T., *Increasing Return* (1933)

Journal of Careers (1928)

Kerr, Barbara, *Bound to the Soil* (1968)

Kilby, K., *The Cooper and His Trade* (1971)

Kingsford, P.W., *Victorian Railwaymen* (1970)

Kirkcaldy, A.W. (ed.) *Labour, Finance, and the War* (1916)

Lee, D.J. 'Class Differentials in Educational Opportunity', *Sociology*, 2 (1968)

—— 'Craft Unions and the Force of Tradition: the case of Apprenticeship', *British Journal of Industrial Relations*, vol. XVII, no. 1 (March 1979)

—— 'Deskilling, the Labour Market, and Recruitment to Skilled Trades in Britain', unpublished conference paper

Leibenstein, H., 'Allocative Efficiency and X-Efficiency', *American Economic Review*, vol. 56 (June 1966)

Lennard, R., *English Agricultural Wages* (1914)

Levine, A.L., *Industrial Relations in Great Britain* (1967)

Liepmann, K., *Apprenticeship* (1960)

Littler, Craig R., 'Understanding Taylorism', *British Journal of Sociology*, vol. XXIX, no. 2 (June 1978)

Llewellyn-Smith, H. (ed.) *New Survey of London Life and Labour* (1931)

Lowndes, G., *Silent Social Revolution* (1969 edn)

McClaine, W., *New Views on Apprenticeship* (1948)

McCulloch, T.A., 'On the Railway' in J. Commons (ed.), *Seven Shifts* (1938)

McKay, J.M., *Tramways and Trolleys* (Princeton, 1976)

McKenna, Frank, 'Victorian Railway Workers', *History Workshop*, 1 (1976)

Marx, K., *Capital* (Everyman edn)

Mayes, L.J., *The History of Chairmaking in High Wycombe* (1960)

Millis, C.T., Chapter in F.W. Galton (ed.), *Workers on their Industries* (1895)

Milward, A., *War, Economy and Society 1939-45* (Berkeley, California, 1977)

Mincer, J., 'On-the-Job Training: Costs, Returns and Some Implications', *Journal of Political Economy*, vol. 70 (1962 Supplement)

Minchinton, W.E., *The British Tinplate Industry* (1957)

Mitchell, B.R. and Deane, P., *Abstract of British Historical Statistics* (Cambridge, 1962)

Moorhouse, H.F., 'The Marxist Theory of the Labour Aristocracy', *Social History*, vol. 3, no 1 (Jan. 1978)

Mosely Industrial Commission to the United States (1903)

Musson, A.E., 'Class Struggle and the Labour Aristocracy', *Social History*, vol. 1, no. 3 (1976)
— *The Typographical Association* (1954)
Pelling, H., 'The Concept of the Labour Aristocracy' in H. Pelling, *Popular Politics and Society* (1968)
— *A History of British Trade Unionism* (1963)
Phelps-Brown, E.H. and Browne, M., *A Century of Pay* (1968)
Pollard, S., *The Genesis of Modern Management* (1965)
Price, Sylvia, 'Clyde Riveters Earnings 1889-1913', unpublished paper
Pugh, A., *Men of Steel* (1951)
Raimon, R.L. and Stoikov, V., 'The Quality of the Labour Force', *Industrial and Labour Relations Review*, vol. 20 (April 1967)
Rathbone, P.H., 'Account of Shipwrights' Trade Societies' in National Association for the Promotion of Social Science, *Report on Trade Societies and Strikes* (1860)
Reid, D.A., 'The Decline of St. Monday 1766-1876', *Past and Present* (May 1976)
Renold, H., 'The Nature and Present Position of Skill in Industry', *Economic Journal*, vol. 38 (1928)
Reynolds, Michael, *Engine Driving Life* (1881)
Robbins, B.G., 'Engineering as a Profession for Well-Educated Boys', *Journal of Careers* (Sept. 1928)
Roll, E., *An Early Experiment in Industrial Organisation* (1930)
Rosenberg, N., 'Anglo-American Wage Differences in the 1820's', *Journal of Economic History* (1967)
Rosenberg, N., 'Technological Change in the Machine Tool Industry, 1840-1910', *Journal of Economic History* (1963)
Rousiers, P. de, *The Labour Question in Britain* (1896)
Rowe, J.W.F., *Wages in Practice and Theory* (1928)
Sadler, M.E., *Report on Secondary Education in Birkenhead* (1904)
— *Report on Secondary Education in Liverpool* (1904)
— and Beard, M.S. 'English Employers and the Education of their Workpeople' in M.E. Sadler (ed.), *Continuation Schools in England and Elsewhere* (Manchester, 1907)
Sanderson, M., *The Universities and British Industry* (1972)
Saul, S.B., 'The Market and the Development of the Mechanical Engineering Industries in Britain, 1860-1914', *Economic History Review*, 2nd series, vol. XX (1967)
Schloss, D.F., *Methods of Industrial Remuneration*, 3rd edn (1898)
Seymour, W.D., *Industrial Skills* (1967)
Shadwell, A., *Industrial Efficiency* (1906)

Simon, B., *Education and the Labour Movement, 1870-1918* (1965)

Stedman-Jones, G., 'Class Struggle and the Industrial Revolution', *New Left Review*, no. 90 (1975)

Stinchcombe, A., 'Bureaucratic and Craft Administration of Production', *Administrative Science Quarterly*, vol. 4 (1959)

Sturt, George, *The Wheelwright's Shop* (Cambridge, 1934)

Tawney, R.H., 'The Economics of Boy Labour', *Economic Journal*, vol. 19 (Dec. 1909)

Temin, P., 'Labor Scarcity and the Problem of American Industrial Efficiency in the 1850's', *Journal of Economic History*, XXVI (1966)

Thom, D., 'Women at the Woolwich Arsenal, 1915-19', *Oral History*, vol. 6, no. 2 (Autumn 1978)

Thomas, Brinley, *Migration and Economic Growth*, 2nd edn (Cambridge, 1973)

Thompson, E.P., *The Making of the English Working Class* (Pelican edn, 1968)

— and Yeo, E., *The Unknown Mayhew* (1971)

Thompson, F.M.L., 'Victorian England – the Horse Drawn Society', Inaugural Lecture at Bedford College, 1970

Thompson, P., *The Edwardians* (Paladin edn, 1977)

Treble, J.H., 'The Market for Unskilled Labour in Glasgow, 1891-1914' in I. MacDougall (ed.), *Essays in Scottish Labour History* (Edinburgh, 1978)

— *Urban Poverty in Britain, 1830-1914* (London, 1979)

Tucker, R.C., *Philosophy and Myth in Karl Marx* (Cambridge, 1961)

Turner, H.A., *Trade Union Growth, Structure and Policy* (1962)

United States Commissioner of Labor, *11th Special Report* (Washington, 1904)

Wadsworth, A.P., 'The Cotton Operatives' in G.D.H. Cole (ed.), *British Trade Unions Today* (1934)

Weatherill, L., *100 Years of Papermaking* (Guardbridge, 1974)

Webb, S., *The Restoration of Trade Union Conditions* (1916)

— and Webb, B., *The History of Trade Unionism* (1920 edn)

— *Industrial Democracy* (1920 edn)

Whitehead, D., Review of H.J. Habakkuk, 'American and British Technology in the Nineteenth Century' *Business Archives and History*, III (1963)

Williams, C.G. *Labor Economics* (New York, 1970)

Williams, G., *Apprenticeship in Europe* (1963)

Willis, Frederick, *101 Jubilee Road* (1948)

Wolfe, H., *Labour Supply and Regulation* (Oxford, 1923)

Wright, Thomas, *Some Habits and Customs of the Working Classes* (1867)

Yates, M.L., *Wages and Conditions in British Engineering* (1937)

Theses

Blanchet, J., 'Science, Craft and the State', Oxford DPhil, 1953

Clarke, J.F., 'Labour Relations in Engineering and Shipbuilding on the North-East Coast in the Second Half of the Nineteenth Century', MA, Newcastle, 1966

Foden, F.E., 'A History of Technical Examinations in England to 1918', PhD, Reading, 1961

Gintz, H., 'Effect of Technological Change on Labour in Selected Sections of the Iron and Steel Industries of G.B., the U.S., and Germany, 1901-34', PhD, London, 1954

Keane, P., 'Evolution of Technical Education in Nineteenth Century England', PhD, Bath, 1970

Levine, A.L. 'Industrial Change and Its Effects Upon Labour, 1900-1914', PhD, London, 1954

McClaine, W., 'The Engineers Union', PhD, London, 1939

Matsumura, T., 'The Flint-Glass Makers in the Classic Age of the Labour Aristocracy, 1850-80', PhD, Warwick, 1976

Shergold, P.R., 'The Standard of Life of Manual Workers in the First Decade of the Twentieth Century', PhD, London, 1976

Viles, D.B., 'The Building Trade Workers of London', MPhil, London, 1975

Weekes, B.C.M., 'The Amalgamated Society of Engineers, 1880-1914', PhD, Warwick, 1970

INDEX

Acorn, George 71, 109
Addison, Christopher 34
agriculture 54
Allen, J.M. 141, 152
Amalgamated Society of Engineers:
and unapprenticed workers 113;
attitude to piecework 189;
attitude to technical education 212; attitude to women
workers 30, 34; construction
of skill by 35; early history
146; entry regulations 50;
membership by foremen 85;
weakness in mid-century 147
Armstrong Whitworth 67, 85, 202
Asquith, H.H. 34
Associated Society of Locomotive
Engineers and Firemen 233

baking 123
Barnes, George 36, 72, 82, 175, 204
Barr and Stroud 32, 67, 214
basket-making 83, 182, 218
Beard, M.S. *see* Sadler, M.
Bell, Tom 153
Birmingham 112, 149, 171-2, 235
biscuit-making 111
blacksmiths *see* smithing
Boilermakers Union *see* United
Society of Boilermakers and
Iron and Steel Shipbuilders
Boot and shoe making 42, 44;
absence of seniority rules 107;
acquisition of skill 110-11;
adoption of machinofacture
166, 181; boy labour 189;
decline of apprenticeship 148,
156; discretion in 191; learnership 65, 113; migration in 108,
110-11, 156, 181, 231; skill
144, 182-3
Booth, Charles
as source 58-9
Borough Polytechnic 212
brass-founding 112-13
Braverman, Harry: and Scientific
Management 21; and separation
of conception from execu-
tion 23; 'route to skill' 22,
166, 227; theory of

deskilling 25, 192
Bray, R.A. 46, 48
Brearley, Harry 121
bricklaying 64, 128, 138, 153, 173
British Standards 23, 55
British Westinghouse 85, 86, 93
Browne, Sir Benjamin 86-7, 114, 143,
151, 153
Browne, M. *see* Phelps-Brown, E.H.
Brunner Mond 205, 216, 219-20
Bryce Commission on Secondary
Education 199
building: apprenticeship 43, 47-8, 76,
128; craft control 158, 236;
discretion 191; improvership
77; in London 72; method of
training 60; premiums 69;
recruitment 66-7; small firms
in 88; semi-skilled workers
129, 231; technical education
202, 213; technology 154,
157; unions 149; wage differentials 172; *see also* bricklaying, carpenters and joiners,
masons, painting, plastering
Burroughs Wellcome 210
bus-driving 93

cabinet-making 42; apprenticeship
64; improvership 72, 108-9, 138;
migration 108-9, 113; premiums 69; reskilling of 47, 181;
technical education 213
Cadburys 210, 215
candle-making 114
carmen *see* van-driving
carpenters and joiners 89, 155;
acquisition of skill 154; apprenticeship 64, 140, 154, 158;
method of training 84, 140;
skill 139, 154; unionisation
147; wage differentials 173;
woodworking machinists 157
carpet-making 72, 93
carriage building 42, 90
caulking 64, 138
chainmaking 112
chemical manufacture 91, 116, 122,
182, 211, 231-3
City and Guilds 127, 204, 206, 212,

248

and Engineers 146
United Society of Boilermakers and
    Iron and Steel Shipbuilders 50,
    160, 162-3
United States 171-7, 216

van-driving 92, 129
Vickers 67, 205, 214

wall-paper manufacture *see* paper-
    staining
watchmaking 45, 89
Watson, W.F. 81, 85, 86, 108, 113,
    189-90
Webb, Sidney 33
Webb, Sidney and Beatrice: and
    dilution 33, inaccurate view of 34;
    and shipbuilding 68; view of
    apprenticeship 49-50, mislead-
    ing 87
Weber, M. 158
Weir, G. & J. 30
West Midlands 43
wheelwrights 42, 45, 142, 190, 235
'whisky money' 204, 219
Whitney, Eli 174
Willenhall 236
Willis, Frederick 236
Wood, H.T. 209
Wood, Thomas (of Bingley) 73, 81,
    82
woodworking: and engineering
    industry 145-6; apprenticeship
        43, 61, 76, 88, 157; improver-
        ship 72-3, 141; in London 204;
        machinists 84, 157, 183; re-
        cruitment 66-7; skill 139, 155;
        training 166; unions 145, 153;
        and see cabinet-making, car-
        penters and joiners
Woolwich Arsenal 31, 204
Wright, Thomas 81, 236